THROUGH THE
EYES *of the* CHILD
Anthology of the Nigerian Civil War

ScribbleCity
PUBLICATIONS

*This book is dedicated to the children who
lost their lives in Biafra. The unseen, unheard innocents
who paid the price for a cause that was not theirs,
and to the children of Biafra, the survivors who bear the
burden of untold memories.*

The historiography of the Nigerian Civil War has suffered a major gap in the rendering of prominence to first-hand accounts of the 'ordinary people' that witnessed the events of the 30-month conflict. More specifically, the accounts of the children of the war have received even less prominence. This work earns the description, 'ground-breaking' for uniquely giving voice to that demographic. The encapsulations of their experience in a powerful collection of vivid accounts are invaluable not just for Civil War historians, but for any student of the human experience. I cannot commend this work highly enough.

Ed Emeka Keazor BL FRSA
Alto Historical Media

ACKNOWLEDGEMENTS

One of the ardent customs of the Igbos of Eastern Nigeria is the use of the village square. An outside space where the important matters of the day are discussed, the village square is also a place of celebration for the community. Here stories are told and history recalled for the education of those who did not live it, and as a reminder to the elders who were part of the history. Stories always elicited a response in the village square. Pleasant history would be met with smiles and much head-nodding by the elders, while unsavoury stories would have people shaking their heads and snapping their fingers as they prayed that the land must never bear witness to events like that ever again. *Ozo'emena.*

The beginnings of this book are reflective of the village square, and came alive on social media as people relayed their experiences of life in Biafra on the anniversary of the declaration of Biafra, May 30th. We felt that we all owed it to ourselves, our children and generations unborn to pull together the experiences of people who were children in Biafra and capture these memories for posterity. While many stories have been told about Biafra, very few of these stories are by the children who lived in Biafra, were Biafran and survived Biafra. We put out a call for papers and surprisingly, got a significant number of responses back. The responses were from people who believed like we did, that the stories they carried with them needed to be told, and that the history of lives in Biafra was far bigger than the political precepts that often overshadow any purposeful discussions about why Biafra, and what next. Our contributors came from across the spectrum of Eastern Nigeria. They were Biafran children, not Igbo children, and they lived the pain of that war, all of them. They saw privation, pain, untold hardship and scenes of wanton savagery that will stay with them, all of us, for the rest of our lives.

We want to thank our contributors for the heartfelt and often painful stories they dredged up and shared for humanity's sake:

Attracta Okeahialam-Abulu

Okey Ndibe

Nnaemeka Nnoli

Geraldine Akpet-Ekanem

Gloria Ekaette Etekamba Umoren, MNI

Arthur Harris-Eze

Chukwudum Ikeazor

Dr. Godwin Meniru

Dr. Nwakaife Obiageli Nwobi

Fidelis Atuegbu

Onyebuchi Marcus Ukandu

Agu Imo

Uzoma Onyekwere Ogan

Roz Amechi

Meg Amechi

Peter Onwu

Oka Amogu

Chief Nnamdi Ekenna

Chuba Obi

Raymond Obiamalu

Chukwuka Ukadike

Amaka Oguejiofo

Our gratitude to these exceptional people is boundless. Without their contributions, there would be no book.

We would also like to thank those good people who helped us along the way, and in some cases were precluded from submitting stories because they were just outside the cut-off age we had asked for, people like Dr Aloy Chife, and many others.

We are grateful to Chief Nnia Nwodo who took time out of his busy schedule as President of Ohaneze N'digbo to write the foreward for the book, and Professor Okey Ndibe who both contributed a story, and wrote the preface.

We are also grateful to our publishers, Scribblecity and Barbara Ije Ifezue for their help and unwavering commitment to this project, guiding and mentoring us as we worked through and completed all the tasks that led us to publication.

And lastly, we would like to say a big thank you to our families, especially the spouses, Niina Ezewuzie Spiropoulos, Loretta Nnenna Ezeife and Adaora Mozie for putting up with the demands this book made on our time, advising, acting as sounding boards for our ideas and patiently stepping up to fill the gaps we so frequently left. Thank you.

John Mozie
Charles Spiropoulos
Edozie Ezeife

FOREWORD

"The web of our life is of a mingled yarn, good and ill together."
- William Shakespeare - All's Well That Ends Well

It is not often that you find three lawyers collaborating on the publication of a work outside of the law, but that is the case with this book, and with excellent results. John, Charles and Edozie, together with the other contributors to this book, have written of their experiences as children in Biafra (and outside) during the Nigerian civil war of 1967-70. A monumentally tragic period in the history of our country.

Numerous books have been written about this war, but none from the perspective of the children who lived through it, until now. This book is a testament to the resilience of those children. The stories they tell is told with touching sincerity. This book tells the story of life in Biafra as a child and gives an insight into the experiences of war from a child's perspective. It elicits a range of emotions and reflection. There is humour, anguish and innocence, but above all there is hope in these stories. It is an invitation to consider the issues that gave rise to the war in the context of its devastating impact on the civilian population and on a segment of its most vulnerable members. These are stories that have to be told and that deserve to be heard and it is both a pleasure and an honour to be asked to write this foreword.

Chief Nnia Nwodo
President Emeritus
Ohaneze Ndigbo

PREFACE

In my first novel, *Arrows of Rain,* an elderly woman—an embodiment of moral insight—tells her grandson, "A story that must be told never forgives silence." The matriarch's wisdom, for me, is a pithy way of saying that stories and storytelling have a certain ethical purchase. Part of what distinguishes humans from lower animal species is the capacity not only to retain memory but also to voice it— to represent it in some kind of speech: spoken or written, recalled as a "factual" account or alchemized into fiction, drama, poetry, or a combination of categories.

For thirty months, from 1967 to 1970, Nigeria fought a devastating civil war. At the heart of that war was a simple argument: whether or not to abide the desire of the peoples of the southeastern part of British-made Nigeria to secede and order their lives within a separate, autonomous space named Biafra. The rest of Nigeria, with much strategic and military backing from Britain, the US, and the USSR, waged a brutal war on the spurious slogan that "to keep Nigeria one [was] a task that must be done."

At least two million people perished—most of the casualties on the Biafran side, and most of them women and children. Most of the death toll owed to grim starvation and diseases, for Nigeria—in a move that was morally outrageous even in the extraordinary circumstances of a war—blocked the supply of food and medicines to beleaguered Biafrans.

Ultimately, then, two million souls were sacrificed to forestall the dismemberment of Nigeria. This volume is a rich and indispensable harvest of memories by witnesses who were Biafra's children. The accounts amount, I suggest, to an elegiac homage to those who perished, those who were scarred, and those who survived in one of the most horrendous wars ever fought.

Despite the horror of war, these individual witnesses amount to a magnificent achievement. They prove—each in its own way—the point of the Igbo proverbial wisdom: "Speech is the mouth's debt to a story." It is left to us, the readers, to be attentive to these memories, to tune our ears to these stories that must be told.

By Okey Ndibe

CONTENTS

INTRODUCTION

The past is always a rebuke to the present
- Robert Penn Warren

When the declaration of the Biafran Republic was made on 30th May 1967, it changed the course of Nigeria's history forever. In a bid to keep the republic together, the Biafran secession from Nigeria unleashed a response of such unprecedented malevolence that when it was done, some 3 million people were left dead in Eastern Nigeria, and the Igbos of Eastern Nigeria were left near-destitute.

Some may argue that the very foundations of the fission that was the civil war were sown long before the war itself. Perhaps. However, the story of the first republic and her accompanying woes are covered in myriad publications and we are almost certain there will be more. One thing stands out in all the stories told, and that is that no one ever heard from the children who lived this war: the Biafran children.

War does not discriminate. It tramples and destroys, and right at its very core is decimation, destruction, and annihilation of the 'enemy'. In the zest and fervour of war, at the time of perpetration no one ever stops to ask about the children. What about the children? It is also indelibly captured in the very delicate seams of history that no war was ever started by a child. Children end up the fodder of war, but never the propagators. In Biafra, kwashiorkor found the children, and so did the bombs, the machine guns of jets, hunger and countless other diseases. For a lot of those children, even at the end of the conflict, there was no coming back from the damage of the war. That does not include the lost generation air-lifted to Gabon who never came home. This book is a book of memories and experiences of children who lived in Biafra during the civil war, in their own words. It is neither choreographed nor accompanied by any political undertones. It is simply their stories, in their own words: what they saw, what they felt, what they experienced, what they heard, and the very spirit of a child's life in the drama of war. While the stories may have similar themes, no two stories are the same.

As dusk sets on the actors of the Nigerian civil war, there is also another at-risk category: The Biafran children. While this group stretches to children born as late as 1969, for the purposes of this exercise the editors chose to concentrate on people who were born between 1952 and 1964. At the time hostilities started, the oldest of this group would have been in their early teens, and the youngest three years old. As time passes and memories begin to wane and fade, there is an urgency to capture and preserve these memories for future generations. We must never forget our experiences nor should we be forgotten. As pivotal and destroying an experience as this was, there is a need to always remember and bear witness to an event that happened in Nigeria, once upon a time.

The stories you will read will shock you. Some will make you laugh. Some will make you cry. But all these stories should make you stop and think about the true cost of that war, particularly the lives that were lost and those blighted because of practices that continue to devastate children to this day.

John Mozie
Charles Spiropoulos
Edozie Ezeife

Map of Biafra

HOW WE CAME HOME

By Godwin Meniru
From the collection, War Story in Verse

We ran a race for life with no umpire to officiate, chased

By former friends now snapping at our heels, running a

Gauntlet of threats, anger and violence.

There was fear in the air. I smelled it everywhere.
It smelled like blood, our blood that was running freely in the
Streets of the north and the west, worsened by the knowledge
That we were all alone, without a blueprint of an escape route.

We travelled by road and rail, air and sea, day and night,
Crawling through bushes when roads became murder,
Running a marathon with no prior training.

This was not what we planned for when we went to live in Lagos.
This was not in our job description when we went to work for the
Government in Kano, Kaduna and Zaria. We went to work for

"One Nigeria" and the future was bright for all of us.
What could Stop us now that we had self-determination?

The winds of change never blow in one direction. They blow
Forwards for a while, then backwards or sideways, buffeting you
All the time; it was blowing in different directions, all at once,
For the young country of Nigeria.

My people cried out to angels who walked the land in those
days:

> *Lend me your clothes so that I can pass as one of you.*
> *Hide me in your boot and spirit me out of town.*
> *Shovel manure all over me, so that dogs don't sniff me out,*
> *As I hide in your goat shed. Otherwise, I am done for and will not*
> *Even show up in statistics because I will be thrown into*
> *A mass grave or headless, or both.*

The lucky ones made it out alive. Their god was awake.
They were astute. They left on time. They did not go back when
They were asked to do so by the government, that everything
Was fine and back to normal.

For the thirty thousand who did not make it,
I sometimes wonder if

Their Chi, their personal god, was not awake, if it was their destiny, or
If it was preordained.

It could have been their stars, their akaraka clearly marked on their
Palms for all to see. Alas we cannot see them now. They are hidden
In mass graves that we still cannot find.

It rained in the forests of the Midwest, mixing with our tears as we
Ran past, heading for the Niger. We were numb with fear and ached
For the sight of home. We were all alone in the world, in a country
That was meant for all.

That mighty ribbon of water marked the finish line for us, who ran
From the West, in our race for life, and the beginning of safety that
Was denied us elsewhere. Once you crossed that line you were in
Home territory, protected by kith and kin.
At least that was what we used to think then.

Ed Keazor collections

MY BIAFRAN EYES

By Okey Ndibe

My first glimpse into the horror and beauty that lurk uneasily in the human heart came in the late 1960s courtesy of the Biafran War. Biafra was the name assumed by the seceding southern section of Nigeria. The war was preceded—in some ways precipitated—by the massacre of South eastern (mostly Christian) Igbo living in the predominantly northern parts of Nigeria.

Thinking back, I am amazed that war's terrifying images have since taken on a somewhat muted quality. It requires sustained effort to recall the dread, the pangs of hunger, and the crackle of gunfire that once made my heart pound. It all now seems an unthreatening fog. As Nigeria hurtled towards war, my parents faced a difficult decision: to flee, or stay put. We lived in Yola, a sleepy, dusty town whose streets teemed with Muslims in flowing white babariga gowns. My father was then a postal clerk, my mother a teacher. In the end, my father insisted that Mother take us, their four children, and escape to safety in Amawbia, my father's natal town.

Mother pleaded with him to come away as well, but he would not budge. He was a federal civil servant, and the federal government had ordered all its employees to remain at their posts.

My mother did not cope well in Amawbia. In the absence of my father, she was a wispy and wilted figure. She despaired of ever seeing her husband alive again. Our relatives made gallant efforts to shield her, but news about the indiscriminate killings in the north still filtered to her. She lost her appetite. Day and night, she lay in bed in a kind of listless, paralyzing grief. She was given to bouts of impulsive, silent weeping.

Then one blazing afternoon, unheralded, my father materialized in Amawbia, stole back into our lives as if from the land of death itself. "Eliza o! Eliza o!" a relative sang. "Get up! Your husband is back!" At first, my mother feared that the returnee was some ghost come to mock her anguish. But, raising her head, she glimpsed a man who—for all the unaccustomed gauntness of his physique—was unquestionably the man she had married. With a swiftness and energy that belied her enervation, she bolted up and dashed for him.

We would learn that my father's decision to stay in Yola nearly cost him his life. He was at work when one day a mob arrived. Armed with cudgels, machetes and guns, they sang songs that curdled the blood. My father and his colleagues—many of them Igbo Christians— shut themselves inside the office. Huddled in a corner, they shook uncontrollably, reduced to frenzied prayers. One determined push and their assailants would have breached the barricades, poached, and minced them, and made a bonfire of their bodies.

The Lamido of Adamawa, the area's Muslim leader, arrived at the spot just in the nick. A man uninfected by the malignant thirst for blood, he vowed that no innocent person would be dealt death on his watch. He scolded the mob and shooed them away. Then he guided my father and his cowering colleagues into waiting vehicles and spirited them to the safety of his palace. In a couple of weeks, the wave of killings cooled off and the Lamido secured my father and the other quarry on the last ship to leave for the southeast.

Air raids became a terrifying staple of our lives. Nigerian military jets stole into our air space, then strafed with abandon. They flew low and at a furious speed. The ramp of their engines shook buildings and made the very earth quake. "Cover! Everybody take cover!" the adults shouted and we'd scurry towards a huddle of banana trees or the nearest bush and lay face down.

Sometimes the jets dumped their deadly explosives on markets as surprised buyers and sellers dashed higgledy-piggledy. Sometimes the bombs detonated in houses. Sometimes it was cars trapped in traffic that were sprayed. In the aftermath, the cars became mangled metal, singed beyond recognition, the people in them charred to a horrid blackness. From our hiding spots, frozen with fright, we watched as the bombs tumbled from the sky, hideous metallic eggs shat by mammoth mindless birds.

One day, my siblings and I were out fetching firewood when an air strike began. We threw down our bundles of wood and cowered on the ground, gaping up. The jets tipped in the direction of our home and released a load. The awful boom of explosives deafened us. My stomach heaved; I was certain that our home had been hit. I pictured my parents in the rubble of smashed concrete and steel. We lay still until the staccato gunfire of Biafran soldiers startled the air, a futile gesture to repel the jets. Then we walked home in a daze, my legs rubbery, and found that the bombs had missed our home, but only narrowly. They had detonated at a nearby school.

At each temporary place of refuge, my parents tried to secure a small farmland. They sowed yam and cocoyam and grew a variety of vegetables. We, the children, scrounged around for anything that was edible, relishing foods that in less stressful times would have made us retch.

One of my older cousins was good at making catapults, which we used to hunt lizards. We roasted them over fires of wood and dried brush and savored their soft meat. My cousin also set traps for rats. When his traps caught a squirrel or a rabbit, we felt providentially favored. Occasionally he would kill a tiny bird or two, and we would all stake out a claim on a piece of its meat. While my family was constantly beset by hunger, we knew many others who had it worse. Biafra teemed with malnourished kids afflicted with kwashiorkor that gave them the forlorn air of the walking dead. Their hair was thin and discoloured, heads big, eyes sunken, necks thin and scrawny, their skin wrinkly and sallow, stomachs distended, legs spindly.

Like other Biafrans, we depended on food and medicines donated by such international agencies as Catholic Relief and the Red Cross. Sometimes I accompanied my parents on trips to relief centers. The food queues, which snaked for what seemed like miles—a crush of men, women, and children— offered less food than frustration as there was never enough to go round. One day, I saw a man crumple to the ground. Other men surrounded his limp body. As they removed him, my parents blocked my sight, an effete attempt to shield me from a tragedy I had already fully witnessed.

Some unscrupulous officers of the beleaguered Biafra diverted food to their homes. Bags of rice, beans, and other foods, marked with a donor agency's insignia, were not uncommon in markets. The betrayal pained my father. He railed by signing and distributing a petition against the Biafran officials who hoarded relief food or sold it for profit.

The petition drew the ire of the censured officials; the signatories were categorized as saboteurs. To be tagged a saboteur in Biafra was to be branded with a capital crime. A roundup was ordered. One afternoon, some grave-looking men arrived at our home. They snooped all over the house. They turned things over. They pulled out papers and pored over them, brows crinkled half in consternation, half in concentration. As they ransacked the house, they kept my father closely in view. Then they took him away. Father was detained for several weeks. I don't remember that our mother ever explained his absence. It was as if my father had died. And yet, since his disappearance was unspoken, it was as if he had not.

Then one day, as quietly as he had exited, my father returned. For the first—and I believe last—time, I saw my father with a hirsute face. A man of steady habits, he shaved every day of his adult life. His beard both fascinated and frightened me. It was as if my real father had been taken away and a different man had returned to us.

This image of my father so haunted me that, for many years afterwards, I flirted with the idea that I had dreamed it. It was only ten years ago, shortly after my father's death, that I broached the subject with my mother. Yes, she confirmed, my father had been arrested during the war. And, yes, he had come back wearing an unaccustomed beard.

Father owned a small transistor radio. It became the link between our war-torn space and the rest of the world. Every morning, as he shaved, my father tuned the radio to the British Broadcasting Corporation, which gave a more or less objective account of Biafra's dwindling fortunes. It reported Biafra's reverses, lost strongholds, and captured soldiers as well as interviews with gloating Nigerian officials. Sometimes a Biafran official came on to refute accounts of lost ground and vow the Biafrans' resolve to fight to the finish.

Feigning obliviousness, I always planted myself within earshot, then monitored my father's face, hungry to gauge his response, the key to decoding the news. But his countenance remained inscrutable. Because he monitored the BBC while shaving, it was impossible to tell whether winces or tightening were from the scrape of a blade or the turn of the war.

At the end of the BBC broadcasts, my father twisted the knob to Radio Biafra, and then his emotions came on full display. Between interludes of martial music and heady war songs, the official mouthpiece gave exaggerated reports of the exploits of Biafran forces. They spoke about enemy soldiers "flushed out" or "wiped out" by gallant Biafran troops, of Nigerian soldiers surrendering. When an African country granted diplomatic recognition to Biafra, the development was described in superlative terms, sold as the beginning of a welter of such recognitions from powerful nations around the globe. "Yes! Yes!" my father would exclaim, buoyed by the diet of propaganda. How he must have detested it when the BBC disabused him, painted a patina of grey over Radio Biafra's glossy canvas.

In January 1970, after enduring the 30-month siege,

which claimed close to two million lives on both sides, Biafra buckled. We had emerged as part of the lucky, the undead. But though the war was over, I could intuit from my parents' mien that the future was forbidding. It looked every bit as uncertain and ghastly as the past.

Our last refugee camp abutted a makeshift barrack for the victorious Nigerian army. Once each day, Nigerian soldiers distributed relief material—used clothes and blankets, tinned food, powdered milk, flour, oats, beans, rice, such like. There was never enough food or clothing to go around, which meant that brawn and grit decided who got food and who starved. Knuckles and elbows were thrown. Children, the elderly, the feeble did not fare well in the food scuffles. My father was the sole member of our family who stood a chance. On good days, he squeaked out a few supplies; on bad days, he returned empty handed. On foodless nights, we found it impossible to work up enthusiasm about the cessation of war. Then, the cry of "Happy survival!" with which refugees greeted one another sounded hollow, a cruel joke.

Despite the hazards, we, the children, daily thronged the food lines. We operated around the edges hoping that our doleful expressions would invite pity. Too young to grasp the bleakness, we did not know that pity, like sympathy, was a scarce commodity when people were famished.

One day I ventured to the food queue and stood a

safe distance away watching the mayhem, silently praying that somebody might stir with pity and invite me to sneak into the front. As I daydreamed, a woman beckoned to me. I shyly went to her. She was beautiful and her face held a wide, warm smile. "What's your name?" she asked. "Okey," I volunteered, averting my eyes. "Look at me," she said gently. I looked up, shivering. "I like your eyes." She paused, and I looked away again. "Will you be my husband?" Almost ten at the time, I was aware of the woman's beauty, and also of a vague stirring inside me. Seized by a mixture of flattery, shame, and shyness, I used bare toes to scratch patterns on the ground. "Do you want some food?" she asked. I answered with the sheerest of nods. "Wait here."

She went off. My heart pounded as I awaited her return, at once expectant and afraid. Back in a few minutes, she handed me a plastic bag filled with beans and a few canned tomatoes. I wanted to say my thanks, but my voice was choked. "Here," she said. "Open your hand." She dropped ten shillings onto my palm.

I ran to our tent, flush with exhilaration. As I handed the food and coin to my astonished parents, I breathlessly told them about my strange benefactor, though I never said a word about her comments on my eyes or her playful marriage proposal. The woman had given us enough food to last for two or three days. The ten shillings was the first post-war Nigerian coin my family owned. In a way, we had taken a step towards becoming once again "Nigerian." She had also made me aware that my eyes were beautiful, despite their having seen so much ugliness.

Each day, streams of men set out and trekked many miles to their hometowns. They were reconnoiters, eager to assess the state of life to which they and their families would eventually return. They returned with blistered feet and harrowing stories.

Amawbia was less than 40 miles away. By bus, the trip was easy, but there were few buses and my parents couldn't afford the fare anyway. One day a man who had travelled there came to our tent to share what he'd seen. His was a narrative of woes, except in one detail: My parents' home, the man reported, was intact. He believed that an officer of the Nigerian army had used my parents' home as his private lodgings. My parents' joy was checked only by their informer's account of his own misfortunes. He had found his own home destroyed. Eavesdropping on his report, I imagined our home as a mythical island of order and wholesomeness ringed by overgrown copse and shattered houses.

The next day my father trekked home. He wanted to confirm what he had heard and to arrange for our return. But when he got back, my mother let out a shriek then shook her head in quiet sobs. My father arrived in Amawbia to a shocking sight. Our house had been razed; the fire still smoldered, a testament to its recentness. As my father stood and gazed in stupefaction, the truth dawned on him: Some envious returnee, no doubt intent on equalizing misery, had torched it. War had brought out the worst in someone.

My parents had absorbed the shock of other losses. There was the death of a beloved grandaunt to sickness and of a distant cousin to gunshot in the battlefield. There was the impairment of another cousin who lost a hand. There was the loss of irreplaceable photographs, among them the images of my grandparents and of my father as a soldier in Burma during WWII. There was the loss of documents, including copies of my father's letters (a man of compulsive fastidiousness, my father had a life-long habit of keeping copies of every letter he wrote). But this loss of our home cut to the quick because it was inflicted not by the detested Nigerian soldier but by one of our own. By somebody who would remain anonymous but who might come around later to exchange pleasantries with us, even to bemoan with us the scars left by war.

At war's end, the Nigerian government offered 20 pounds to each Biafran adult. We used part of the sum to pay the fare for our trip home. I was shaken at the sight of our house: The concrete walls stood sturdily, covered with soot, but the collapsed roof left a gaping hole. Blackened zinc lay all about the floor. We squatted for a few days at the makeshift abode of my father's cousins. Helped by several relatives, my father nailed back some of the zinc over half of the roof. Then we moved in.

The roof leaked whenever it rained. At night, rain fell on our mats, compelling us to move from one spot to another. In the day, shafts of sunlight pierced through the holes. But it was in that disheveled home that we began to piece our lives together again. We began to put behind us the terrors we had just emerged from. We started learning what it means to repair an inhuman wound, what it takes to go from here to there.

In time, my father was absorbed back into the postal service. My mother returned to teaching. We went back to school. The school building had taken a direct hit, so classes were kept in the open air. Even so, our desire to learn remained strong. At the teacher's prompting, we rent the air, shouted the alphabet, and yelled multiplication tables.

About the Author

Okey Ndibe is the author of the novels *Foreign Gods, Inc.* and *Arrows of Rain,* and a memoir titled, *Never Look an American in the Eye.* He holds an MFA and PhD from the University of Massachusetts at Amherst and has taught at various universities and colleges, including Brown (Providence, RI), St. Lawrence University (Canton, NY), Trinity College (Hartford, CT), and the University of Lagos (as a Fulbright scholar). His latest book is, *The Man Lives: A Conversation with Wole Soyinka on Life, Literature and Politics.*

THE SPIRIT OF BIAFRA

By Chukwuka John Ukadike

It is difficult to write about this traumatic childhood event. Part of the reason being that I really do not have a full grasp and appreciation of all the physical and emotional suffering that adults like my parents endured through it all. I spent the war years in Lomu-Umunze, in present day Orumba South Local Government of Anambra State.

However, I was born in my hometown, Oraifite, which is in Ekwusigo Local Government Area of Anambra State. At my birth, both my parents were stationed at Umunze, as teachers. My father, Late Chief Bernard Chukwuka Ukadike "Chiugo", taught at the All Saints Grammar School, Lomu-Umunze, while my dear mother, Late Mrs. Margaret Chinyere Ukadike "Uno-enu", taught at Saint Peters Primary School, Umunze.

As I think back to my childhood years, I remember the faces and names of some friends and playmates like Edozie Ezeife and Kodichimma Obumneme. There are a few others whose names I cannot now recall. And of course, there was my younger brother, Emmanuel

Ukadike, who would always tag along with us older boys whenever we went out to play. We grew up at a time when the community truly raised a child. We roamed freely to play in those days, after returning from kindergarten classes popularly called "Ota-Akara," and sense of community then mandated that if we did anything wrong outside our home, any adult who noticed would give us a good spanking, and then hand us over to our parents for more of the same.

As children, we were oblivious to the turmoil and the pogroms that preceded the declaration of Biafra as a nation by Chukwuemeka Odumegwu Ojukwu, a Colonel in the Nigerian army. At the time the Nigerian Civil War started in 1967, I had turned 4 years old, and as I mentioned earlier, my mates and I lacked any real appreciation of the danger, suffering, and trauma that was unleashed on Biafrans by the Nigerian forces together with their British and other international helpers. However, as the war progressed through 1968, 1969, and finally into 1970 when hostilities ceased, it dawned on many of us through the utterances and actions of our parents, that danger lurked ever so near us.

All Saints Grammar School, Lomu-Umunze, was converted into a military hospital where the army brought wounded Biafran Soldiers to receive treatment. My clearest recollection of the presence of danger was how quickly our panicked parents would scream and herd us children like sheep into an underground bunker that was constructed by teachers and locals. The bunker was at the back of the school quarters where we lived. Once the sound of fighter planes buzzing in the air signalled imminent air raids and bombing, everyone dashed into the bunkers.

This underground bunker that we crowded into with our mothers and the other children was a cramped space dimly lit with either one kerosine lantern or perhaps a locally made palm oil lantern popularly called "Opanaka." The adults only permitted the least amount of light, and we young ones were hushed, to maintain as much silence as was possible in the circumstances. During these times, we could hear sounds of the buzzing fighter planes with distinct loud sounds of gun fire and the boom, boom, boom sounds of bombs that were being dropped on hapless Biafrans in the distance. In hindsight, I wonder what would have become of us if one such bomb had landed on or close to us. We would all have been buried alive inside that bunker. God's mercy is real.

Once the adult males deemed that all was clear and safe, we climbed out of the bunker and returned to our quarters, and to whatever was normal at the time. I recall an occasion when we experienced one of these air raids. We had one of my young aunties from my mother's side, Ogochukwu Ofiaeli, who lived with us at the time, helping my mother. Mama had sent her to the market popularly called "Nkwo Umunze" to buy some groceries needed for cooking. While she was on that errand, an air raid took place, and as usual we all scampered into the underground bunker for safety. My mother, however, would not stop crying, fearing the worst for Ogochukwu whom she had sent off to go to the market on her behalf. I heard my father conferring with her and contemplating going toward the market in search of her. That was the point when Ogochukwu practically raced into the house with tears still streaming down her cheeks. Her clothes were torn, and there were noticeable blood stains on them, which alarmed my parents and the rest of us even more.

She recounted, sobbing, that shouting and screaming at the impending air raid, people in the market and adjoining roads had run in all directions. She also took off running for her dear life like everyone else, clutching the bag in which her purchases were tied. She ended up jumping into the nearby bush where she hid for protection on one side of a felled tree amid dense shrubs. According to Ogo, once the sounds of the bombing had died down, what remained was shouts, screams, deafening cries from all sides. According to her, she noticed people were beginning to come out from their hiding spots amid the attendant confusion, and it was at that moment that she saw to her utter shock, that the young lady who had crouched on the opposite side of the log from her had been hit by shrapnel, and appeared lifeless. As Ogo told the story, some adults gathered to lift the woman up, and with all the crying, screaming, shouting and the shock of what she had just witnessed, she took off running with her wares until she made it home. This turned out to be my closest traumatic experience of nearly losing a member of my family during the war.

As children, living within the confines of the sprawling compound of All Saints Secondary School, Lomu-Umunze, we often ventured out to play during quieter times. One of the more adventurous things I did in those days was going out with my friends armed with our well-crafted local canes that had tentacles or filament ends. We would invade the sprawling school field, chasing grasshoppers. It was a lot of fun to chase the flying insects and use the tentacle/filament ended sticks to swat and kill them once they perched on the grass. Often, we also ventured into the wooded areas surrounding the school either in search of palm kernels at the base of palm trees, or scouting for other sundry items. On one of these occasions, we stumbled upon the remains of a dead soldier. He had obviously been dumped in the woods for lack of resources for a proper burial. As earlier indicated, All Saints Secondary School was being used as a Biafran Military Hospital. Such a terrible sight prompted us to run back home as fast as our legs could carry us.

Because our parents were teachers at the school before the beginning of hostilities, we often received portions of whatever relief materials were distributed by such agencies as the Red Cross, Caritas etc. It was a joy to get a helping of a powdery substance made from dry egg yolk and other such things from my parents. They tasted so sweet, and these rare occasions were something to look forward to.

Finally, amid all this turmoil, a day came that it appeared that we were doomed to lose everything. The war seemed to have finally arrived at the doorstep of Umunze. With the incursion of the Nigerian invaders and their helpers, it became apparent that Umunze was on the verge of being sacked. Only God knows what must have been going through our parents' minds with all the attendant panic and confusion. All I can recall on this date was that our parents gathered all four of us: Ngozi, Emmanuel, the baby Nneka, and me. You could tell from their demeanor that things had fallen apart. My pregnant mother assisted by our Dad hurriedly scrambled to pack our big aluminum box with whatever belongings that could fit inside, and another smaller box. Everything was done in a panic because of the situation. Our father brought out his bicycle so that we all could take off running as refugees. Our pregnant mother tied Nneka to her back with a wrapper, and carried the smaller box on her head, while our father tied the big aluminum box on the carriage of his bicycle, and slung my younger brother, Emmanuel, on the handle bars of the bicycle, while my sister Ngozi and I trotted along on foot. This was how we set out from the comfort of our quarters at All Saints Secondary School, Lomu-Umunze on a panicked journey to nowhere.

Once out on the road everywhere you looked there were massive crowds of families that were similarly in similar situations, running for dear life due to the ever-present danger of the sack of Umunze by Nigerian forces. Quite honestly, I do not know how far we travelled or what direction we took, neither do I know whither we were headed. Only our parents (bless their souls) both of whom are now late know the answers.

The silver lining is that on 12 January 1970, my mother gave birth to my brother, now Dr. Ikechukwu Oguebie Ukadike, as her third son and fifth child. And to shouts of relief and bittersweet joy, on 15 January 1970, Biafra capitulated as a breakaway republic, and the Nigerian Civil War was officially over. Our parents returned us to All Saints Secondary School, Lomu-Umunze, and we set about piecing together what was left of our lives. It was indeed a new and harrowing beginning as my father later confided that the meager resources he had saved up at the bank at that time was reduced to a hand out of £20 (Twenty Pounds) with which to start over.

I will close by affirming that just as the children of Israel scattered all over the world through suffering and the holocaust re-gathered and excelled, Biafran adults and children came through the eye of the needle, navigated enforced impoverishment, to rise again by dint of hard work, perseverance and entrepreneurship and to excel; and are still excelling to this day. The sun still rises from the East, and the Biafran spirit lives on.

About the Author

Chukwuka John Ukadike is from Oraifite in Ekwusigo Local Government Area of Anambra State. Married with children, he is an Attorney and lives in the state of Texas, USA, where he has a Law practice.

BIAFRAN CHILDHOOD 1966 -1970

By Fidelis Atuegbu

The first few months of 1966 brought an upheaval to Nigeria that was more pronounced in the North. The country had just experienced a coup and a counter coup, which took the lives of prominent politicians and military officers. These crises quickly spilled over to the streets of many northern cities. My first exposure to the fallout was when we visited victims of the Gombe massacre at Jos General Hospital.

On that fateful day, I accompanied my father to visit people of Igbo descent who lived in Gombe and who had been subjected to brutal attacks and massacre. The pogrom was couched as retaliation for the assassinations of prominent Northern politicians, who were killed in the January 1966 coup. On that visit, we heard gut-wrenching stories of brutalities that were meted out to Igbos. There were reports of people being hacked to death with machetes, pregnant women disgorged of fetuses and left to die in a pool of their own blood. It was a harrowing visit, to say the least.

The situation worsened after that, with the bloodletting spreading like wildfire to other cities in the far north. When the crisis started to make its way to Jos, Igbo parents began to repatriate women and children to the east, our ancestral home. I was among the first group to be sent home. I can still remember how rushed that evacuation was. We had only a couple of hours to pack up everything in our house in Jos, and load our belongings into a chartered truck, and then proceed to Adazi-Nnukwu. We left Jos on that momentous day in the wee hours of the morning. The trip itself was uneventful. We were not harassed as we made our way through the middle belt of the country, which eventually became a hotbed of massacre.

We arrived in Adazi-Nnukwu very late at night. The driver made his way all over town to drop off other families in the truck first before heading to our family house, and so we were among the last to reach home. When we arrived at the gate of our ancestral homestead, we met a hostile reception. A relative, wielding a machete, accosted us and vociferously insisted that we were to return to whence we came. That was an unexpected reception, and it quickly degenerated into a spectacle as the rukus awoke neighbors and they all congregated in front of my grandfather's compound. People were pleading with this relative to let us come into the compound, but all to no avail.

Here we were, having been chased out of our place

of abode in the north, and now this imbroglio? We had headed to the east with the hope of getting respite in our village, only to see that hope eviscerated in the blink of an eye. It was a surreal experience. However, our faith in the goodness of people was soon restored. Keep in mind, that this relative in question, our cousin, was a grown man, who was basically harassing women and children. So, entered one of our clansmen, my father's confidant cum age mate. He happened to be visiting home from his base in Lagos at the time. He pleaded with this cousin to give us access to the compound and to make his grievance known to the Umunna at a later date. Unfortunately, his appeal was met with deaf ears and of course my cousin had the full support of his mother, my aunt.

It was a rude awakening and foreshadowed many ugly events to come. Meanwhile, the situation left us in a quandary in terms of accommodation. Where should we go? Our family home's construction had just begun when the crisis erupted, so the structures were still at a rudimentary level and not ready for us to move in. We needed a plan B, and we needed it fast. That was when my clansman stepped in. He cleared two bedrooms in his house, and gave them to us, one to my mother and the other to my aunt, who was widowed. Both families shared the space with his own family, who were later chased out of Lagos.

It did not take us much time to assimilate into the day-to-day life of the village. As a primary school age boy,

I was registered to continue my education at St Andrew's school, Adazi-Nnukwu. A number of my cousins from Atuegbu and Ogbukagu sides of the family joined me in the school. Given our antecedents as Altar Boys in Jos, my cousins and I were quickly integrated into the cadre of Mass Servers. Furthermore, our football prowess earned us spots on the junior team at St Andrews.

We quickly settled in, and our lives in the village acquired a routine. On a typical day, we woke up early in the morning to fetch water from the stream which was a mile and a half away. Depending on the water available in the house, we might make two or three trips to the stream. We also bathed there. When we made it back from getting water and bathing, we prepared for morning Mass. As Mass Servers, we were required to be in church thirty minutes before Mass. The church/school was about three miles away, and we trekked the distance. On the days that we were behind time, we ran, and sometimes were lucky enough to get a lift from one of the vehicles that plied the Adazi-Nnukwu - Onitsha route.

First up on any weekday morning was Mass at 6:30 am. Thereafter, football practice from 7:15 to 7:45 am. The school bell rang at 8:00 am and you had better already be standing in your assigned spot for the assembly by the time the second bell rang, or you would get punished. Punishments for lateness were instantaneous and they came in the form of caning, or if you were lucky, push-ups or after-school detention.

When assembly was over, classes commenced. We broke off for recess at midday and resumed at 1:00 pm, closing for the day at 2:00 pm and 3:00 pm for lower and upper classes, respectively. It was customary for pupils in lower classes to wait for their older siblings, relatives, or neighbors before heading home.

For those of us on the football team, the day did not end at 3:00 pm. We hung out at the school until practice at 4:00 pm. The football practices lasted one and a half hours. After the session, we headed home. When we got home, we quickly changed out of our school uniform and went to the stream to bathe and swim. If we were lucky, we might make one trip to the stream, but in most cases, it was two. By the time we got home, we were exhausted, and we would have dinner, and it was time to sleep. The adage "early to sleep early to rise," rang true for us at the time.

A couple of months or so, after our arrival at Adazi Nnukwu, our older siblings (who were in secondary schools) joined us. They had been evacuated from their boarding schools in Vom, near Jos. The massacre of Igbo people had made its way to Jos and the surrounding area. So, our dad pulled my siblings, Nicholas and Andy, out of school and sent them home to join us. Papa stayed back in Jos, due to the dictates of his job, and was lucky to escape unharmed after we had given up hope that he was still alive.

According to him, the story of his escape was as follows:

His driver, a Hausa man, was at a Friday mosque service. As was the practice at the time, names of the infidels who were marked for execution were announced after the service. On this particular day, my dad's name and that of his close friend, Mr. Mbanefo, from Ogbunike, came up as next in line to die. Mallam Sule, on hearing his master's name, was perturbed. He quickly went to my dad, and relayed the information to him. My dad, in his typical fashion, dismissed the man's dire warning. Mallam Sule was undeterred. He escalated his concerns to my dad's General Manager (GM), who was British. The GM, fortunately, took the matter seriously and sprang into action.

The first thing he did was transfer my dad from Jos to Onitsha with immediate effect. Keep in mind that at that time, there was no longer any news of people making it back from the north to the east alive. To place things in context, this happened after a train from the north arrived Enugu with badly hacked remains of people who had been fleeing the pogrom, only to be butchered enroute. The GM knew that my dad's life was in peril if he went by road. The only way he could escape was by air. As luck would have it, the GM was connected to a religious organization that owned a plane, and this plane made daily flights to Lagos from Jos. He approached the organization and talked them into adding my dad to their flight list that Saturday, which was the next day. Papa got on that flight and reached Lagos safely. From there, he made his way to Onitsha. Between Lagos and Onitsha, he donned Yoruba garb to hide his identity. His command of the Hausa language also helped him navigate his way to the Niger River Head Bridge. My father made it to Onitsha just in the nick of time. He was among the last people to cross the bridge before it was shut down.

That day, he arrived at Adazi-Nnukwu around mid-afternoon. By the time he got home, construction on our family home had already been completed, and we had moved in. At that point, all hope was lost that he was still alive. As a matter of fact, my uncle and aunts were planning his last rites. It was like a dream when the shadowy silhouette of somebody who resembled my dad walked toward our house that day. My late baby sister, Patricia, was the first to see him moving toward us with nothing but the clothes on his back. Her scream of "*Papa a na ta go,*" figuratively and literally sent a shockwave through the household and the entire neighborhood. It was one of the few good days we had throughout that period.

My late older brother, Mathew, was also caught up outside the East when the crisis was brewing. Mathew had gone to Lagos with the Plateau Highlanders Football Club for the Challenge Cup Match. The team also had other notable Igbo sons, such as Tony Igwe and Sam Garuba Okoye. In light of the precarious state of things in the north for Igbos at the time, going back to Jos was out of the question. He and his other Igbo teammates therefore remained in Lagos, and from there, Mathew made his way back to the East. His journey was precarious at best, and he was saved only by the grace of God. He successfully navigated his way to Onitsha by speaking Hausa most of the way, and made it back home just a few days before our dad.

With the arrival of all my family members, we started to find our respective strides. My brother, Andy, was posted to St Mary's Ifite Dunu, Nicholas to Holy Cross, Umuawulu and Mathew to Bubbenduff Memorial Grammar School. Life for us was getting back to normal, but the incessant unrest between Nigeria and the nascent Republic of Biafra was ever present in the background. No matter how people tried to live their lives in the moment, the ever-present shadow of war clouded our sense of well-being. We could hear our parents speak in hushed tones about the various conversations between the Federal Government and Biafra as they negotiated for an amicable resolution to the issues at hand. The Aburi Accord was well received, at least in Biafra, and with that, we thought there would be a cessation of hostilities. To our surprise, Lieutenant Colonel Yakubu Gowon, reneged on the Aburi Accord, which to all intents and purposes marked the end to the possibility of a negotiated settlement. This left war as the only option on the table.

We did not have to wait long for the conflict to start.

Shortly after the Aburi Accord failed, Lieutenant Colonel Odumegwu Ojukwu, following due consultations with stakeholders, declared the secession of the Eastern Region from Nigeria and the establishment of the Republic of Biafra. The declaration of the Republic of Biafra was quickly followed by what was dubbed a "police action," by Lieutenant Colonel Yakubu Gowon. The purported "police action" quickly spiralled out of control, and soon led to an all-out fratricidal war. The "police action" that was planned to end in forty eight hours lasted thirty months.

As the negotiations for peaceful resolution were going on, the eastern region used that opportunity to build up military infrastructure. Talented, able-bodied, and inspired men were enticed into defending the fatherland. The new government provided accelerated military training, and young men were recruited from high schools and universities. Those in universities were diverted to the officer training course, and after they completed the training, they became part of the officer cadre.

One of my older brothers, Nicholas, was among the first group of recruits to be lured into military service. He surreptitiously left school and headed to Enugu, where he joined the Biafran army. We were not aware of this development until he completed his training. Among all of us children, Nicholas was the only person with the gumption to take such a step without the approval of parents. He was well aware that our parents would object to it, hence his decision to join and ask for forgiveness later.

My parents had the premonition that something was amiss, because for a span of three weeks, there was no word from Nicholas. He was attending Holy Cross Secondary School Umuawulu at the time. That was where he was enticed into joining the fight to defend Biafra against the invading Nigerian troops. Like other able-blooded young easterners, he bought the Biafran propaganda, hook line and sinker. My parents sent me to Umuawulu to check on him. When I arrived and asked after him, I was told that he had not been around for three weeks and nobody knew where he was.

I went home and gave the information to my parents. It goes without saying that this development was disconcerting and worrisome. The puzzle was answered a few days later. One mid-afternoon in late September of 1966, a military Land Rover pulled up in our compound. Two men in military uniform stepped out from the vehicle. One of them was Nicholas, and the other one was introduced to us as Triggerman from Uga. It was at that point that my parents knew that their second oldest son had enlisted in the Biafran military.

Shortly after this episode, the Federal Government of Nigeria initiated the infamous Police Action against Biafra. Nicholas was attached to the 7th Battalion of the Biafran Army, and his battalion was deployed to the Nsukka sector, which was the first sector that saw action.

He was wounded a few days into the fight, and was sent home to recuperate after getting much needed treatment at the hospital.

By the end of 1966, all school activities had shut down. Schools in the enclave that Biafra was able to hold unto were converted into makeshift military barracks. My primary school, St Andrews Primary School, was no exception. The 87th division of the Biafran army took over the school grounds and turned it into their barracks. This lasted for the duration of the war. My oldest brother, Mathew, ended up in that battalion as a staff member of the Quarter Master. He served in that role until the end of the war.

In the absence of school, we occupied ourselves with childish things whenever we had the opportunity. However, as Mass Servers, we still had daily obligations. Our days started with attending morning Mass and serving Mass on the days that we were designated to do so. Additionally, the Mass Servers had their own dance troupe, the Etilogwu group. We practiced on Mondays, Wednesdays, and Fridays. Attendance to these practice sessions was compulsory and lateness was not tolerated. Our Sacristan, who doubled as the dance troupe leader, was a teacher first and foremost, and he used all the tools available to teachers to keep us kids in line and engaged.

In late 1966, before things got completely out of hand, we represented Adazi-Nnukwu in a cultural dance competition in Awka. The competition was organized for villages in the defunct Njikoka Province. The competition on that day was fierce. My Etilogwu dance group ended up in second place, just behind the Nkpokiti group from Umunze. We outperformed them with our dance choreography and presentation, but their acrobatic displays flabbergasted the audience and earned them the top spot. The Nkpokiti group ended up representing the Province at Enugu, and the members of the group got numerous recognitions, including academic scholarships.

As the war dragged on, life in Biafra became unbearable. Food, fuel, salt, and other basic items were in short supply. The only way to survive was to grow your own food, and to do this, you needed to have seeds and land to cultivate. A large contingent of returnees, had serious contentions with their relatives over land ownership. It was common for those in the village to monopolize lands that were owned in common, and to use them for their sole benefit. We were no exception to this experience, and my father had to lodge a complaint against his own brother, who claimed that he solely owned a 4-plot area of land that was procured for the quartet of brothers. At this time, my father had already lost two of those brothers, so my father had to lodge the complaint against his surviving oldest brother, who was the only one among the four who never left the village. He claimed that he bought the land from the proceeds of the dowry he got from marrying off his first daughter.

This issue dragged on for a long time, but thanks to the goodwill of our extended family members, my father was offered the use of lands in nearby Neni. My family farmed these lands for the duration of the war, and it helped us to survive the war. I was also fortunate to have been selected at the onset of the kwashiorkor scourge to run errands and to control crowds when food was prepared and ultimately distributed to malnourished children. The food items were supplied by Caritas, headquartered at Ichida. We typically accompanied the adult women, who ran the food distribution to Ichida on a weekly basis, to pick up our consignments. The consignments consisted of corn meal, stockfish, dry milk, salt, etc. We got vegetables and other items needed to prepare soup from around us. People either donated them or we bought such produce. At the end of these biweekly food distributions, we were fed, and we went home with leftovers of cooked and uncooked food items. These food items helped in bridging the gap of meals available to us for the duration of the war.

In the later part of 1968, the Nigerian Army advanced all the way to my village. They made landfall in the middle of the afternoon. I had gone to Nnewi on foot to run an errand for my father. On the way back, I saw people running in the opposite direction. When I got to my village, the place was deserted. I dashed to our compound, and it was completely deserted. For the life of me, I had no idea where my family had fled to. We had no prearranged plan as to where we were supposed to converge, should we need to leave abruptly, so I was in a quandary. I could not stay in the house by myself. What should I do? I decided to head to Nnobi, to see my cousin, late Professor Ogbukagu, who was stationed there at the time. He was the one who took me to my parents in Oraukwu, where they had fled, and I was reunited with my family.

As luck would have it, my village's refugee status was short-lived. A few days after the fall of Agulu and Adazi-Nnukwu, the Biafran solders mounted an offensive and drove the Nigerian soldiers back to Nise. So, after three days in exile, we went back home. When we got back, there were dead bodies littered all over the place. People were so hungry that they hacked off human body parts for consumption. As the war progressed, life got tougher and tougher. The Biafran solders were not getting enough to eat, nor were they getting the supplies they needed to fight the war. The food shortage gradually became even more pronounced and desperate. At some point, the solders resorted to invading people's farms and absconding with foodstuff and livestock.

On our part, we held things together, but only barely. My older sister and I had to grow up quickly, the reason being that for the duration of this period, my dad and Aloysius were responsible for the 87th Division's motor pool, so they were not around much of the time. My mom on the other hand, was incapacitated for the duration by some strange malady. So my sister and I had to take care of ourselves and our two baby sisters for the most part. Things got so bad that on the invitation of my cousin, we trekked to Maamu to gather as much foodstuff as we could carry - a distance of approximately forty to fifty miles each way. It was torture of immense proportions, and this was the lowest point of the war years for us.

The following year (circa 1969) was no different. It was more of the same. We started school after two years of shutdown. We were all promoted one class above our grade levels. The classes were conducted in different locations and also in people's homes. They were done undercover to prevent detection by aircraft that were on the lookout for air raid targets. Classes therefore held under very difficult circumstances and of course learning was hampered. By the later part of the year, things had degenerated even more, and all hope was waning that the Biafran experience would survive. The territory held by the republic had shrunk substantially at this stage. It was no surprise when on January 15, 1970, Biafra surrendered, and the war ended.

The experiences of that period were simply terrible, and I cannot wish it on anyone. "*Ozoemena*" is the refrain that fits the bill in this instance. It was only by the grace of God that we survived.

About the Author

Fidelis Atuegbu was born in Jos. He attended St Theresa Boys' School, Jos, until the 1966 crisis erupted, when the family moved back to Adazi-Nnukwu where they stayed for the duration of the civil war. He is a Finance Executive, and lives in the San Francisco Bay Area with his wife and three children.

WE SURVIVED THE WAR

By Nwakaife Obiageli Nwobi

I was a Primary 6 pupil in 1967, taking the common entrance examinations to transit to Secondary school in 1968, when the Nigerian-Biafra Civil War started. I am the second child and first daughter in a family of eight (2 boys and 4 girls). My father was the Principal of All Saints Grammar School, Umunze, formerly in Aguata Local Government Area and now Orumba North Local Government Area. The school was one of the many schools the Anglican Church owned and supervised. Papa had been Principal and Vice Principal of many other schools, including his renowned alma mater, Dennis Memorial Grammar School. (DMGS).

My father was barely eighteen months in this school which was sited in the middle of "nowhere" when the war started. I can recall the day in 1966 when our father stopped his car in front of a small house with three rooms, surrounded by bushes and shrubs, and said we should alight, that we had reached his new posting. You can imagine our sense of disappointment, having come from Onitsha, where as Vice Principal, my father's accommodation was a palatial six-bedroom house with two living rooms, pipe-borne water and electricity, located in an area with tarred roads and other beautiful homes. It was from this urban area that we were taken to the middle of a "forest". We made feeble complaints and disembarked, as he reassured us that everything would be well. Throughout that period, I was always scared, but God Almighty saw us through as we did not experience any robbery attack or insect/snake bites.

The school's infrastructural development was supported by an entrepreneur from Umunze, the Late Chief M. N. Ugochukwu. With my father's experience in school start-ups, the premises which comprised a three-room Principal's house, a single-storey building which doubled as the classroom/administrative building, two dormitories, and a small teachers' house when he assumed the role of the principal in the institution's second year of existence, was transformed within just eighteen months. Thus at the start of the war in late 1967, the school had a new seven-room Principal's house, a science block comprising biology, chemistry and physics laboratories, an extended staff quarters, three additional dormitories, a five-room Peace Corps house and two giant football fields surrounded by Gmelina trees. Other facilities of the school included good road networks around the whole compound that were paved but not tarred, the principal's house surrounded by trees such as mangoes, guava, orange, and other cash crops. With the support of my mother, the late Lady Jessie Ezeife, we planted yams, cassava, corn, vegetables, and reared goats and chicken which thrived very well because the community was endowed with very rich soil and vegetation. The school also had farms which the students cultivated, and the teachers were allocated pieces of land and were encouraged to engage in subsistence farming. Our mother's poultry farm provided plenty of meat and eggs for our nutrition.

We attended the local school which was in the immediate vicinity of the secondary school and did very well academically, largely because of our background, and the fact that we had little or no distractions from our studies. Our leisure periods were used for doing our homework and reading books, or helping to feed goats and chicken. We competed on the number of novels we read, as we were mostly indoors reading and studying current affairs.

Whenever there was the need for hospital visits, either for antenatal or immunization, my immediate younger sister Ifeoma, of blessed memory, and I, used to take turns carrying our baby sister, Nwamaka. Cars in those days did not have seat belts; while our mother drove the car to Iyi-Enu Hospital, Ogidi, a distance of about 23 miles, (58 kilometers). Most of us were born there. Whenever my mother drove, people would surround the car and admire her because they had never seen a woman driving, something my mother had been doing since 1960.

There was a woman with a mental disability called Akum who wandered around the town, and each time she saw Mama driving, she would ask for a lift. Though Akum was never violent toward us, we were scared of her, but not our mother. Mum would from time to time oblige her and take her for rides in the car. She enjoyed these rides tremendously and always told my mum, *"Nwokem, moto gi nke a nato"* (literal interpretation is "my friend this your car is so sweet.") At times she would ask my mum to take her back to where she picked her up, and she would oblige, because you couldn't argue with somebody who beat up men when in a bad mood.

This is what life was like for us in 1967 when the war started. We had been hearing of and anticipating the war, based on the news from the radio and the discussions between our parents and other members of the staff and community. The situation eventually dawned on us when the school was forced to close, and the students evacuated and returned to their homes. We stayed in the school compound and did not return to our hometown, Igbo-Ukwu, partly because Umunze was considered safer economically as we had our farms and could still farm. The bungalow my father erected in our village which had six bedrooms and two living rooms could not accommodate us and his three brothers and their families. The duplex he was erecting for his immediate family, in line with our tradition, was still under construction.

One evening, some weeks after the closure of the school, two truckloads of people arrived in the school compound. They were members of some families from Awka, the current capital of Anambra State, who fled the town as Nigerian soldiers approached, and subsequently took on the toga of refugees, as explained to us by my father. They were housed in the main block of the school. That day, we the children, as well as some relations staying with us, helped our mother to prepare huge meals which we sent to them along with other provisions. By the next day, more refugees had arrived in the school compound and the dormitories were opened for them to be housed and we also cooked for them. My mother then took it upon herself to mobilize the villagers who were our closest neighbors and associates to donate yams which was their staple food, palm oil, vegetables, and anything they could afford for the refugees. She became a one-woman advocate moving from one house to the other with us in tow explaining the predicament of the refugees and the extent of losses they had suffered. With time, more women joined in the advocacy and in no distant time contributions started flowing from the villagers and the school kitchen served as a general kitchen for the refugees. We cooked and served food to them from there. Within a few days almost all the dormitories were taken over by more refugees, while my father ensured he kept the school records, books and laboratory equipment safely stored in one room of the Science Block since the other rooms of the block were occupied by yet other refugees. He also kept the school records and documents of his alma mater, DMGS, as war approached Onitsha.

The school soon became a certified Refugee Camp with a Camp Director who managed affairs in line with the current government's protocol. He ensured the refugees' welfare was taken care of through distribution of relief materials donated by the government and individuals, allocation of accommodation, effective sanitization and cleanliness of the area as well as provision of health services. Initially the refugees were fed with food cooked in the school kitchen, but with time, raw food items were distributed, so that each family could use them as they wished. Some of the refugees engaged in small business operations to supplement supplies from the government. Not unexpectedly where there was a large congregation of families, there was always quarrel and rancor among the refugees.

By 1968 the main block of the school was converted to a Military Hospital, and the former occupants who were family members of some technocrats of Awka origin were relocated to the house of an indigene of the town, while the Medical Director of the hospital was housed in the Science Block and the former occupants also relocated. The hospital was used for treating wounded soldiers brought from the war fronts, and the refugees in the adjoining refugee center. The Medical Director posted to the hospital was coincidentally the younger brother of my father's student in DMGS. My parents warmly received and entertained him, helping him as he settled down in his new duty post. He got married a few months later, and my parents supported the new couple as best they could.

By mid-1968, war had been ravaging the region with deaths, the maiming of soldiers and civilians, all of which was accompanied by hunger for about two years. There was so much hunger, since many towns and villages had been overrun by the Nigerian soldiers, and more refugees fled to the communities that were not close to the fast moving war fronts. As a result, fewer people were able to farm and could not produce enough food for everybody. There was therefore hyperinflation and starvation which led many people - children, youths and even the aged, to suffer from severe malnutrition. Kwashiorkor which is an ailment mainly caused by lack of sufficient protein became the prevalent health challenge. The children suffering from this ailment had distended stomachs, spindly legs, and scanty hair. People resorted to eating all forms of foods and even leaves like cassava that were hitherto never eaten, just for better nutrition. On some occasions, people had to come to our house to beg for food, and my parents would give whatever they could. A particular case was when one man entered our house through the side gate of the kitchen, and my aunty was dishing out food for everybody - yam porridge. He begged my aunty to please give him a piece of yam to put in his mouth, (translated in the local language), and it was so touching. My aunty had to reduce everybody's portion to give him some food.

Our mother forced us to eat what was going to be a major source of protein for us as the war progressed. One day around the onset of the war she prepared a species of beans we were not used to, and we refused to eat it because it had a horrible taste and smell. She locked us inside the dining room and would not let us go until we finished our portions. We managed to eat it by putting the food in our mouths and chewing while using the other hand to cover our noses so we could not smell the food. Thus, we could swallow the food and quickly gulp drinking water without perceiving either the smell or the taste. She eventually planted this specie of beans and it thrived. She continued cooking it for us, and we got so used to it that with time we could harvest the pod when not matured, boil it with salt and eat it as a snack in the evenings, or use it to garnish our rice while the mature seeds were dried and cooked as bean porridge. This bean specie known in the local parlance as Odudu, is still relished in Old Aguata Local Government area because it has a high nutritional value, being very high in protein and low in fat.

At Umunze there was a central refugee kitchen where food was prepared in bulk and sent to various centers for distribution to refugees, hospitals and officials who were providing one form of service or another for the government. My father eventually became the Camp Director of a refugee camp situated in St. Augustine Church, Umunze. My mother had training in catering, sewing and homemaking which was the practice then for new brides, and so possessed great culinary skills: baking, frying and cooking all varieties of food. Our house became a center for producing "Dry Packs" of pastries, rolls, chips, which were packaged and sent to the soldiers at the war front. Our dining room served as the preparation/storage room while the frying was done in the kitchen. Some female teachers and young girls from certain high net worth families that were either from Umunze or who were refugees were assigned to work with my mother who supervised the entire business. The raw materials were wheat, dried egg yolk, vegetable oil, flour, barley, corn meal, corned beef, powdered milk, which the World Council of Churches, Caritas International, the International Committee of Red Cross and other humanitarian agencies donated to Biafra to help minimize hunger, starvation and kwashiorkor which was ravaging the entire Eastern Region at that time. They had periodic deliveries of the stock. Their terms of engagement were daily supply of cooked meals from the central kitchen for lunch, and weekly supply of rations such as rice, wheat, barley, beans, powdered milk, corned beef, corn meal, stockfish which of course served as their salary. My late Sister, Ifeoma, and I took turns to trek to the central refugee kitchen located near St Augustine Anglican Church, Umunze, with basins on our head to carry their daily allocation covering Monday to Friday, a round trip of about 12 kilometers. The cooked food was always shared to the ladies and thereafter there would be enough for us, the children, as lunch. With our farm produce and the weekly provisions my mother and father earned as a result of the services they rendered to the Biafran government, we were able to maintain healthy living standards and to give to other needy neighbours, friends and relatives.

My mother's immediate older sister who was a midwife and whose husband's town, Awlaw in current Enugu State, had fallen to the Nigerian soldiers, brought her three children to live with us in 1968 while she travelled to the war front periodically to discharge her duties. They were aged between eighteen months and five years, and the baby at that time suffered from kwashiorkor. We became saddled with the responsibility of taking care of the children especially the youngest in view of his health condition. We fed him with a lot of eggs and vegetables which we would shred and put in his food, but he would refuse to eat it, preferring plain food. Within months, however, he showed signs of recovery and started growing well.

The Medical Director was interested in occupying the Principal's house and annexing it to the hospital premises and he did everything possible to get us to move to a house at the other end of the school compound. When my father received a letter to the effect that he should vacate the house for the Medical Director, he pleaded that he be allowed some months so he could at least harvest his crops on the farm within the principal's compound which was fenced. They refused, and we were made to pack out to a house at another end of the school compound formerly occupied by an American Peace Corp volunteer who by now had left Nigeria to his country because of the war. We subsequently obtained a gate pass from the soldiers at the check point erected within the compound to harvest our fruits and farm produce for that year only. At the time, the Medical Doctor was reportedly heard boasting and jeering at my father, that he had taken over his house and all the choice fruits in the garden. That was how my father's kind gestures were reciprocated. There were similar stories of such acts of callousness amongst people throughout the war. My father also suffered forceful confiscation of his Peugeot 403 at the instance of the very people he helped because they were now soldiers and felt they could do anything they liked. After that, the only way he could move about was by trekking.

People could trek for more than fifty kilometres as there was no public transport since the soldiers had commandeered people's vehicles for the war effort. Some people, however, were able to demobilize and hide their vehicles inside their compounds to prevent confiscation. My immediate senior brother, Okechuku, now late, would trek to our village, Igbo-Ukwu, to visit our uncles and aunties and some of them also visited by trekking that distance. Whenever people wished to travel or go to the market, they took off very early in order to get to their destinations before the sun rose when there was more likelihood of air raids. Most of the markets were sited under groves of thick forests, with the ground underneath cleared so that people could trade without attracting air raids.

By 1969, we had settled down at the new house and started cultivating vegetables and some food/cash crops to prevent starvation, while my parents continued with their assigned roles within the Biafran government. By this time, we had started to experience increased air raids, and we would go inside a bunker which we constructed at the back of the house each time there was an air raid by the Nigerian Air Force. In our former house, we would run to a thick forest at that end of the school compound whenever there was an air raid. A particular incident happened on a market day when the aircraft launched rockets into the main market located in the centre of the town, then flew toward the direction of the school to reverse. For more than thirty minutes, we were in the forest, terrified for our lives, and we only went home when the back and forth stopped. We were told that many people died, and many others were wounded in that attack. From the balcony of our house, we could see explosions from anti-aircraft guns and other ammunitions used by the soldiers in a war front about 50 kilometres from the school compound, due to the topography of the area. The practice at this time was that holes were dug in the school fields and any open spaces, and palm fronds were used to cover them, so that during air raids such places would appear like bushes to the pilots. Palm fronds were also placed on the roofs of houses to mask them from air raids.

In 1969, schools re-opened in Umunze and other towns and villages that were not severely affected by the ravaging war, and my siblings and I enrolled. I started at a Secondary School that was allocated some classrooms out of the existing primary school building and enrolled in class one having lost almost two years. Many students were happy to resume schooling and we made do with the few available notebooks while borrowing textbooks from some of our senior friends who were in secondary school before the outbreak of the war. I made many new friends among the refugees and the natives who were forced to come back from cities such as Lagos, Benin, Kano, Onitsha, etc. where they resided before the war. We continued to attend the church which was in our school, and were involved in religious activities. With the mix of young boys and girls in the school, there were a few social/academic activities such as science clubs, and parties even amid the war that was raging around us. Everybody had to trek a distance of more than five kilometres to fetch water from some streams at the outskirts of the town for domestic use, especially during the dry season when the water reservoir in our house was depleted. I could not recall any of us having serious health challenges apart from the occasional malaria which we self-medicated, and my aunt was always there to treat us when necessary.

We continued living our lives as best as we could, avoiding places that were potential targets for air raids from the Nigerian Air Force. Even on Christmas Day, life was as normal as possible with the usual attendant lack of provisions, upsetting news from the Biafran radio about the war, and sad news about relations and friends who had died at the warfront or because of sicknesses. In my village, families were made to volunteer their grown-up sons to join the army, and this continued till the end of the war. A major problem people faced at that time was insufficient accommodation. Some families that were very well to do, on relocating to their villages, had to share accommodation with their siblings' families because prior to the war they did not own homes in the village. That generated a lot of skirmishes among siblings and their families. This is why since the end of the war and up until now, people in South Eastern Nigeria have made it their priority to build comfortable houses in their hometowns as soon as they can afford it.

When on that 15th day of January 1970, Biafra announced that the war had ended, we were very happy and thanked God Almighty for sparing our lives as no member of my immediate family was lost during the war. Many people and even some soldiers did not know that the war was over. People, especially the refugees, remained where they were, and waited to be sure of their safety before planning to go back to their own towns. Before they travelled back, they had to ensure availability of houses where they came from, as many towns were totally levelled and required rebuilding. Another fear was the risk of exposure to land mines which killed/maimed many refugees who went back to their towns after the war. There were also uncertainties about people's safety because there were stories of how the Nigerian soldiers were capturing young girls with a view to marrying them off and also commandeering cars from people who were returning from Biafra. My father started life penniless after the war, because he was given only twenty pounds after depositing his personal cash and that of those of his relations who did not have bank accounts into his pre-war bank account for exchange in the bank. He had to distribute the meagre amount to all of them and had nothing left.

Before the end of the first quarter of 1970, schools started to re-open. My parents arranged that I should accompany one of the young ladies who produced dry packs for the war effort, and who prior to the war was a teacher in Anglican Girls Secondary School, Alor, in present day Idemilli Local Government to re-enrol in the school. My mother travelled with me together with this lady. A truck travelling to Onitsha conveyed us to Nnobi, about 40 kilometres from our home, and we disembarked there with our luggage. From Afor Nnobi junction, we trekked about twelve kilometres, carrying our heavy load of clothes and food items, and arrived the school compound around 8pm. I enrolled as a class one student, lodged in the school dormitory along with two other girls who were in the care of the Mistress. She re-engaged her former house help who cooked and fed us, and this continued till January 1971 when the school started to operate a formal boarding school. We were grateful for her kindness and the excellent care we got from her, even as difficult as things must have been for her at that time.

The practice then was for students who were not day students to lodge in the school dormitories, attend classes, buy food items, and prepare their own meals. My father managed to buy some notebooks and could not afford textbooks. He occasionally visited to bring cash and food items for my upkeep and after some months he was able to purchase a motorcycle for mobility. We were given one Nigerian pound a couple of times during the year and this was money donated by the World Council of Churches to help in rehabilitation efforts of the then East Central State. This was our reintegration back into Nigeria. We had survived the war.

About the Author

Nwakaife Obiageli Nwobi is a Management Consultant based in Lagos, Nigeria. She holds a Doctorate in Management and is from Igbo-Ukwu in Aguata Local Government of Anambra State. Dr. Nwobi is married with four children and a grandchild.

36 MONTHS OF TERROR

By Attracta Okeahialam Abulu

My memories of the Nigeria-Biafran Civil War between 1967 and 1970 run the gamut of vivid and vague all at the same time. The events that had the most impact on my life then, are the most vivid, and those are the stories I intend to tell. On a general note, everyone suffered horrible deprivation, hunger, disease and loss, but the intensity of the deprivation was often more brutal depending on a family's socio-economic status and connections. This became more apparent with regards to issues of nutrition and resultant health problems. My stories are not political. Some of them may even seem flippant. That may be so, but at the heart of it, they are the memories of a little girl, between the ages of six and eight years during the civil war, who witnessed events that no child should have ever experienced.

Leaving the Familiar (Enugu circa 1967)

By the time I became aware that there was a war, the civil war which started in 1967 had been raging for a few months already. I was suddenly aware that something unusual was happening, but my childish mind could not appreciate the concept of war. All that changed soon enough, as my family's idyllic life at our home on Constitution Road in GRA (Government Reservation Area), Enugu, was shattered by unusual comings and goings involving friends of my parents. I began to feel a certain unease. I remember hearing my dad and his friends arguing loudly in our living room on those evenings when they came over. The adults would be hunched over the radio listening to something I heard them call Radio Biafra, or watching the news on the black and white television set in the centre of the room. There were incomprehensible conversations about someone named "Ojukwu". He seemed to be a very important man, the way his name was mentioned so often. Eventually I would become familiar with that name. Every now and again during those gatherings at our home, the room would erupt in shouts of "Ore has fallen!" "Agbor has fallen!" "Asaba has fallen!" Or whatever other place had fallen on any particular day. I did not know where those places were, or fully understand what it all meant, but I knew something was happening, and it was something bad. When my siblings and I would enquire, we were told to be quiet because we were kids. There was tension in the air, and everyone was uneasy especially my mom, and any time he unwittingly let his guard down, my dad as well. Friends we used to play with suddenly stopped coming out. Apparently, their parents had moved away due to the impending war. We never saw most of them again.

Life continued, although in my childish eyes, things looked somewhat strange. A couple of months before the end of 1967, I must have been about six years old or so at the time, my father then a senior civil servant, came home from work one evening and told us we were moving away from Enugu. I still did not connect our move with "the war." All I could remember feeling was sadness at being torn away from my home on Constitution Road, and my beloved Enugu. All our friends were there, our toys, our big house with lots of space where my six siblings and I could run around and play, climb the huge mango trees around the compound, pretend to catch fish in the small stream at the back of the house, and enjoy our childish pastimes.

Leaving Enugu and moving to our hometown, Umuelegwa Onicha, in Ezinihitte Local Government Area of Mbaise, in the South Eastern part of Nigeria, was traumatic. We did not go to our hometown often, and were not excited to be going there to live. That fact did not hold any weight with my parents no matter how much we complained. We were running for our lives. I later heard the term, *"osondu"* which in Igbo language literally meant running for your life. I recall that we were not allowed to take our toys or anything that was not crucial as we hurriedly gathered our belongings. How do you explain to children that all the things they knew and loved were not important, and they had to leave them? We had no say in the matter. We had to leave, and we had to travel light. My mom, a teacher by profession, who also owned a catering business at the time, insisted on bringing her teaching bag and a large box filled with all her baking equipment and supplies. She would brook no argument about those particular items from my dad. That, in fact, turned out to be a good decision later on when we began our new lives in Mbaise. It provided another income stream for our family.

The night we left our life in Enugu and all things familiar, I remember my parents bundling me, my six brothers and sisters and as many of our belongings as they could stuff into the family car, an Opel Rekord station wagon. That was not a comfortable trip. I remember my dad avoided the busy major roads and instead, used alternative, unfamiliar routes, driving all night until we arrived at our village in Onicha, Mbaise. That became our home until 1969 when we suddenly had to pack up and leave again.

Lost and Found

We settled somewhat comfortably into our village after we left Enugu. Even as a child I knew life was different there. I felt it. All the silly little things that made life good for a child were no longer available. There was no butter for our bread. We could not have ice cream anymore. We could not have sausages. People talked about "the war" all the time. The very fabric of our lives was infused daily with all kinds of talk about "the war," and how "Ojukwu" did this and "Ojukwu" said that. I came to understand that Ojukwu was the leader of our new country, Biafra. I noticed people in my village seemed fearful and more irritable. Everyone walked very fast. No one lingered to chat or anything like that. To the child I was, the entire situation was very scary and strange. Then the air raids began. Every now and then we would hear this persistent and unfamiliar whirring sound, quite unlike anything I had ever heard before. I later learned it was the sound of sirens warning us of impending air attacks from the enemy; the Nigerian Air Force. That sound is burned into my memory to this day. It represented terror, chaos, and destruction. Whenever the air raid sirens sounded, we would be shepherded into the nearby bushes and told to "Take cover, take cover!" We became accustomed to those terrible words "take cover." Flyovers by "enemy" planes happened fairly often. I was later told they were looking for where "rebel" Biafran soldiers were hiding. That did not make me feel any better. Sometimes the planes dropped bombs in the distance at targets we could not see, but we could hear the explosions from wherever we were. In fact, once, the planes dropped bombs in an open market not far from my village. I recall hearing the adults talk about traders and buyers in the market being hurt, and their stalls destroyed.

Sometimes, the air raid warnings turned out to be a false alarm, because it would be Biafran military planes flying by. The watchers knew them. How they could tell the difference, I did not know. This happened quite often. All I remember is that as soon as the sound of sirens signalling an impending air raid went off, we would scamper into the bushes and lie down flat on the ground with our hands covering our ears as hard as we could. I later understood this was to protect our ear drums from being blown out.

In spite of all the fear and uncertainty, we still had to go to school. In Enugu I remember that I had just started elementary school before we left. Shortly after we arrived at my hometown, my mother and the other teachers in my village went back to teaching at the elementary school that served the village. The local school was Saint Dominic's Elementary School, fondly referred to by the villagers as "Saint Dom." It served as school for everyone from elementary through high school. We started the day everyday as usual, with a prayer and the singing of the Biafran National Anthem, "Land of the rising sun we love and cherish..." Life went on as well as it could, until the day it happened.

That was the day the air raid sirens went off suddenly, and our elementary school erupted into utter chaos, with terrified little bodies dressed in their white school uniforms hurtling helter skelter, screaming in sheer terror and scattering in every direction. Our school was the target of an air raid! We all ran into the bushes near Saint Dom for safety. We were supposed to go in groups should such an event occur, but that was not the case that day. I cannot tell exactly how long we were in the bushes. It seemed like we took cover forever. Eventually when we emerged from hiding, shaken, dirty and dishevelled, our school compound was a mess. The walls of the school were pockmarked with bullet holes. The teachers quickly dismissed and sent us home after that traumatic event. In all of the ensuing chaos, we got separated from Angie, my five-year-old younger sister, who was in kindergarten at the time.

We searched for Angie everywhere for hours and hours to no avail. We could not find her. Where could she be? We dared not let our minds venture to the unthinkable: that she may have been killed in the air raid. At that point, no one was sure if anyone else was hurt or not. We enlisted the help of others to try and find her. We had this sense of deep foreboding, but we continued the search. I can remember we prayed like we had never prayed before. By evening, my entire family had dissolved into full-fledged mourning. Our hearts were broken. We felt helpless. We all cried for hours, and could not be consoled, but later that evening, out of the blue, a uniformed Biafran soldier walked into our house with a terrified five-year-old girl in tow. She was red eyed from crying, had tear streaks down her face, and was wearing a very dirty white school uniform. It was Angie. We were shocked and ecstatic at the same time. She was alive. Our compound erupted in shouts of joy. God had answered our prayers. I still remember the feeling of pure joy knowing that my sister was not hurt or worse. Apparently, she had bolted in the wrong direction from the rest of us during the air raid at school earlier that day and had gotten lost. The Biafran soldier saw her wandering around, terribly scared, and covered her with his camouflage uniform shirt to prevent her from being spotted due to her white school uniform and hid her for hours until it was safe to come out. The kind soldier was able to question her, figured out who her family was, and brought her home to us. Our school had to change the colour of our uniform from white to dark green after that attack. Apparently this was due to the fact that white is visible from the air, and the colour green, like camouflage, blends with the trees and is not easily visible from the air. That, though, is a story for another day. The events of that day are deeply engraved in my memory.

Caritas

What do dry salted cod fish, chicken of the sea or Tuna, powdered eggs, dry enriched milk, canned corned beef, rice, wheat, and dried vegetables have in common? You guessed it. Those are the contents of a protein enriched survival food care package distributed to

Biafran families during the Nigerian Civil War years by Caritas International, a Christian humanitarian organization, which provides hunger relief to countries in the world where there is a need. My family benefited from their generosity.

On the days Caritas was scheduled to distribute food in our village, there was always an air of excitement. We would all get up very early in the morning, head to the distribution centres, and line up family by family. Every child and every adult received a food package. One of the best food items in that care package was salted cod. Salt was a rare commodity during the civil war. Most people did without, but when we received the cod, my mother would soak it in water, and extract and save the salty water for cooking. She did not use her regular salt until the salted cod was gone. I later learned that the salt in the cod was iodized to prevent the disease, goitre. I remember seeing people with large goitres on their necks due to a lack of iodine. Those packages were precious lifesavers. They really helped, but they were still not enough. As a result, during those years, hunger was a constant companion. Unlike most people, my family managed to eat three meals everyday due to my mother's ingenuity. Her efforts to keep hunger at bay for my siblings and I were nothing short of heroic. We were active, growing children, and always hungry. Before the war, we were accustomed to going to the refrigerator between meals and eating whatever our hearts desired;

but now, in this strange new world, we were only allowed to eat at mealtimes to make the food last longer. Being a child who was wise beyond her years, I felt the change intensely. Those were difficult times.

With seven adolescent children varying between the ages of five and thirteen, the stress, pain, fear and worry my mom had to endure to keep us alive and free from the devastating protein deficiency disease, Kwashiorkor, was constant. The disease resulted in children who had it developing strange, distended stomachs. They appeared like little pregnant women. Death usually came swiftly. We lost many classmates, friends and neighbours to that awful disease. One day, they would just not show up to school or in church. There were funerals almost every day and the wailing of parents who had lost their children to Kwashiorkor is a memory I will never forget.

My dad, who worked for the Biafran Government, was not around much in those years. He was wherever the headquarters of the government was. He would visit us, bringing extra food and money and then leave again.

Mum had the job of raising us singlehandedly during those awful war years. She had a farm close to our family home which we all helped to tend. We grew vegetables and staples such as cassava, yam, and cocoyam. Anything we could grow, we did. She sewed, she baked, and she fried all kinds of snacks for sale from a mixture of cassava flour and wheat flour which she processed herself. She had a mud oven made for her at the back of our house for this purpose. How she maintained her sanity through those times, is a mystery to me up to this day.

Saved by Benson and Hedges

The year was 1969. The war seemed endless, although it only lasted for 30 months, ie 2 years and 6 months. One night in December, my dad came home and told us that Nigerian soldiers were about to enter our hometown and so, we had to get out fast. I remember it was December, because we were all looking forward to Christmas. The chilly Harmattan winds that blow in from the Northern parts of Nigeria between November and January had already begun. Not again, we complained, but his demeanor was serious and worried. So, as usual, my mother started marshalling the troops like an army sergeant and got us packed and ready to leave in a short time. In addition to our Opel Rekord, my dad had hired a lorry, the kind with the wooden sides used for transporting goods locally, referred to as Gwongworo in Eastern Nigeria. It was sitting in the middle of our family compound. We had several gallons of petrol stored at the back of our house, and the cars were filled up. My dad, during his visits would bring some gallons of petrol back each time, and he would ask my mom to keep it for emergencies. I was never quite sure what the emergency could be, but now it seemed it had finally arrived.

My dad split our family into two. I was not sure what the reasoning was at the time. My older sister and two older brothers had to ride in the lorry with the hired driver, while my mother, my two younger sisters, my brother and I, had to ride in the Opel Rekord station wagon with my dad. We waited until early evening to head out. Our family car was in the lead and the lorry was in the rear. This time I did not know our destination.

We had been driving for about two hours and had arrived at a town called Ubulu-Ihejiofor, in Oru Local Government, in Imo State, when we began to sense an eerie silence. We realized that we could not see the lorry carrying my older sister and brothers anymore, and we became worried. There were no other people on the road. No cars, and no pedestrians anywhere. We were all alone. All of a sudden, an army utility transport, the kind that is open at the back with several seats for carrying troops, covered in leaves and netting, literally jumped out in front of our car from the bushes. We were not expecting this at all. Several Nigerian enemy soldiers jumped out with guns pointed at us shouting, "Stop! Stop!" My dad slammed on the breaks, and our car came to a screeching halt. The car was immediately surrounded on all sides by screaming soldiers. I remember them shouting "Hands up! Hands up or we shoot!" We had just run into an ambush!

Absolutely terrified, we climbed out of the car, and as soon as my dad got out, one of the soldiers hit him hard on the right shoulder with the butt of his rifle. My dad screamed in pain and collapsed to the ground. The soldier was about to hit him again, when my mother jumped between him and the man. My siblings and I started to cry very loudly. I thought the soldier was going to shoot both of them. Instead he grabbed my mom, all five feet one inch of her like a rag doll, and flung her to one side. She was there on the ground, bruised, and would not stop screaming. We ran to her, huddled together and continued sobbing. It was total chaos. The soldiers threatened to shoot us if we did not stop crying. We could barely comply. We were so scared. They pushed us into the army jeep, but my dad could barely stand up. They had broken his collarbone. The soldiers did not help him; they just scooped him up and threw him in the car, then took the car keys and commandeered our family car. That was the last we ever saw of that car. We were driven to a school where we saw a lot of women and children huddled in different groups by the sides of various cars. Until this day I do not know the name of that school.

As soon as we arrived at the camp, we were told to wait beside one of the cars, close to a long wall. A soldier grabbed my dad and lined him up against a wall with several other men. We did not know why. While he was standing there in line against the wall, we saw my dad fidgeting and motioning with his head to the soldier who had taken him to the line. That man went over to my dad, looked around as if to check, put his hand inside my dad's shirt, and brought out a long package wrapped in shiny cellophane. What he removed was a carton of Benson and Hedges cigarettes that my dad carried inside his shirt every time he came home. He has never smoked, so it was odd. When we asked, he would not tell us why he carried it on his person. After a while, we stopped inquiring. The soldier left briefly, and came back to take my dad out of that line and help him back to us. The minute he removed my dad from the line, some other soldiers came up, and as if in a movie, we heard the staccato sounds of gunshots. We watched all the men lined up on the wall slump to the ground, lifeless. We had just witnessed a firing squad. It was such a horrific and macabre sight that I had nightmares about it for a long time. To this day, violent movies terrify me.

We were held at that camp for almost two weeks, surviving on very little food, hungry, and with my dad's shoulder getting progressively worse. Mom tore the outer layer of a piece of cloth she had tied around her waist, and made him a strap to stabilize it. One early morning, the soldier who had saved my dad's life came to us and asked us to follow him. He led us to a gate and told us to leave the compound. He did not explain why. We had no car. It had been taken away from us. My mom, propping up my dad who was in a lot of pain, asked us to move quickly. We left, walking as fast as we could without looking back. Dad could not walk fast because of the pain, and my mom and I took turns piggybacking my two younger siblings when their feet hurt from walking.

I was worried about my older siblings, and when we took a rest from walking, I asked my parents what had happened to them. That is when I learned that my parents had made a contingency plan when they had us travel in two different cars. If anything happened to us, the driver of the lorry was instructed to take my siblings back to our family home in Mbaise. He must have done that when they saw our car ambushed. I found some comfort in that.

Walking for miles and miles trying to find our way home, hungry, exhausted, dirty, providence smiled at my family once more. We stopped at a house in one of the villages whose name I cannot recall. We cautiously went into the compound to ask for some water and to rest before we continued on our way home. A man came out, saw my dad, and started shouting, calling him by his nickname which only his good friends addressed him by. He kept saying "Happy survival!" "Happy survival!" As it turned out, he and my dad knew each other from Enugu. Just as suddenly as it had begun, our ordeal now seemed to be over. He welcomed us into his home, and his wife fed us and helped my mom clean my dad's wounds. We were able to get a shower, and they offered us a place to sleep, allowing us to rest for a couple of days. After we were refreshed, in talking with our host, we realized that we had spent Christmas at the detention camp, and we did not even know it!

Happy Survival

Our kind host offered to drive us back to my hometown, and he did; into the loving arms of my older siblings who had been taken home after our capture.

By the time we got home, it was January 1970, and the war was officially over. The Nigerian/Biafran War had taken a savage toll on all of us. I saw things no child should ever have to see. I experienced grief and deprivation, but I also saw amazing acts of bravery and kindness. I saw my mother accomplish near miraculous feats to keep her family together and healthy. I learned resilience, strength and endurance at that young age. All of my immediate family survived the war. My parents worked hard to make sure that we healed together and slowly recovered everything we had lost. So many people and families did not fare so well. We were the lucky ones. Happy survival indeed.

About the Author
Attracta Okeahialam Abulu is from Mbaise in Imo State. She is an Attorney based in Minneapolis, United States and is married with children.

The Okeahialam Family, 1970

I LIVED TO TELL THE STORY

By Marcus Onyebuchi Ukandu

I was about six years old at the outbreak of the War in 1967. We were living in Enugu in the Eastern Region of Nigeria at the time. I remember my father bringing me home from school one day, and I could see he was not his usual boisterous self. At home, I met a pensive mother. I was later to find out why. They had just heard that Gen. J. T. U Aguiyi-Ironsi, the Head of State, and also my mother's relative by marriage, had been assassinated. My mother had lived with Nwanyiocha, Mrs. Victoria Aguiyi-Ironsi, and Ironsi himself and my father were also kinsmen.

My father always boasted of the General's prowess and his exploits during our country's peacekeeping operations during the Congo crisis of 1962. My mother's older brother, Sergeant Jonah Ogbuapu Ogueri of Obuohia, Okwu Olokoro Umuahia, participated in the same peacekeeping operations with J.T.U Aguiyi-Ironsi, and told captivating stories of the crisis, and of General Ironsi's exploits. My father, therefore, held the General in high esteem.

Papa operated a welding/blacksmithing workshop in front of our house where he retired to work at the close of his paid employment daily. He loved listening to the news, and always had his transistor radio by his table at the workshop. For current news, his workshop became a rendezvous of sorts, where various people gathered to listen and discuss the unfolding events. Usually during lunch, he would give us updates on the news, before hurrying back to his workshop.

When Gen. Ironsi's death was confirmed, people in the East were very unhappy. My father was among those who trooped to the airport at Emene, Enugu, the day his body arrived. They were also offended at the rumour that it was not Ironsi's body that was in the coffin that had landed. As if that was not enough, there was pandemonium when lorry loads of easterners with injuries and gory tales about the pogrom of the Igbos in the north were offloaded at Enugu.

The gathering at my dad's shop was becoming alarming, and my mother was afraid at how quickly tempers rose at each news update, fearing that it could degenerate to a mob action one day, from where attacks might be launched against the northerners in our neighbourhood.

Events occurred quickly and kept on affecting my father's moods. There was always news about Biafra.

One day, there was an uproar which made us come out to see the usual crowd gathered at his workshop. Shouts of "We are free, we are Biafrans now," rent the air. This was followed by news the next day that Nigeria had declared war against Biafra. There was confusion. "What is happening? What is all this?" I thought to myself.

I heard my mother ask my father, "Yesterday, just yesterday, was the declaration of Biafra and today, Nigeria has already declared war against Biafra that is yet to come into being." "Never mind them," my dad responded. "Is it a joke or a real war?" The wry smile on my father's face as he left the room for the shop did not help matters for my confused thoughts. My mother did not want war and preferred our not being part of Biafra if there was a possibility that Nigeria would wage war against us. I demanded to know what war meant because of the concern in my mother's voice and on her face, but nobody paid any attention to me.

Dad and his friends wanted it and looked forward to some action. He later informed us that he would be taking us to the village so that he would be free to fight for his fatherland. In no distant time, we were in the village. The place brimmed with returnees from the cities. The civilian population had vacated the big cities to ease the refugee situation on Col. Chukwuemeka Odumegwu Ojukwu's hands. The propaganda had started.

Village life was fun, people rejoiced at the reunions. Many of us children were meeting our uncles, aunties, and cousins for the first time, and vice versa. We fed from the same pots, and shared many things in common, although some mothers got involved and took sides in the never-ending scuffles between the children. Before long we started feeling the effects of the war. Not long after, we were taught some civil defence measures. For instance, we were taught not to run out into the open at the sound of air planes as we used to do, but to scamper for safety under the trees and bushes because they had, of late, become harbingers of death. By this time there were few volunteers for enlistment in the Biafran Army.

With the fall of Enugu, the number of the students at University of Nigeria, Nsukka, who had excitedly responded to Col. Chukwuemeka Odumegwu Ojukwu's oratory/emotions and had enrolled in the Biafran Army, had depleted tremendously. They had become convinced that no magic could restrain the rampaging onslaught of the better-trained Nigerian soldiers and thus became dispirited. The propaganda that "No power in black Africa could stop Biafra" no longer held water. There was now a dearth of recruits into the Biafran armed forces, so enlistment changed to forced conscriptions which were extended to include teenagers and even child soldiers.

Many of those who went to war, never returned. Able-bodied men began to consent, conspire, and connive with their parents, especially their mothers, to evade military service. They took abode in evil forests of their communities, far away from their homes. Their younger sisters and brothers brought them food day and night.

The Biafran soldiers knew about this conspiracy, collusion, and connivance of kinsmen and village heads with families of the service evaders to prevent them from going into the army. They would therefore lay ambush around the village and swoop on homes in the wee hours of the morning, erupting from different directions. They would kick and force open doors of houses and take away any males they saw. It always paid off, for more often than not, they emerged dragging along well fed and rested men who had hitherto stayed hidden at home while children were conscripted to fight for their fatherland.

Loud noise always rent the air at any such discoveries by neighbours, who knew that the men had escaped conscription for too long. Trailed by their loved ones, the new conscripts were beaten as they were taken to depots by soldiers who didn't listen to anybody's pleas. Shouts of surprise greeted their every step as they approached the depots where other military service evaders from different locations were quartered.

At the Camp, they were manhandled for not voluntarily answering the call of duty. They were given little or no training and could be driven off to the war front just like that. Those who took abode in the bush would only enjoy that luxury for as long as families whose sons and wards had been taken, did not give them away. These bushes were reputed to be so evil that no stranger could find their way through unaided, and no arrows, bullets, or missiles could "penetrate" them.

At a point, the commanders were informed secretly that such forests teeming with a youthful population existed. Consequently, they adopted the measure of lying in wait for those who brought food to those in hiding. The soldiers held these food couriers captive, and using them as escorts, raided the bushes. What a haul came out of those forests. There was much noise and consternation as the Biafran soldiers marched the latest conscripts along to the depots. The numbers were so many that the depots which were not fenced, could not contain them, and they were taken to other places. That was how some of them went to the war fronts without as much as a goodbye to their loved ones.

Dad decided not to be a victim of this sort of humiliation. From what she had seen of the treatment meted out to service evaders, my mother agreed with him amidst sobs, that it was time to go. It soon became clear to all that it was better to be recruited than conscripted. It was not an easy decision. Convincing my mother and the older members of our family was not easy either. He decided to make his way to the NDD Depot, Apumiri, Ubakala, Umuahia. He had heard that artisans and tradesmen were highly sought after, treated better, and not hurried to the war front with little training.

The next issue was how to get there without being

detected or caught along the way. They decided that on the set day, my mother and a child should go ahead of him to keep a lookout, while he trailed them, meandering through short cuts and bush paths. On that day, Mama and I went ahead of him as planned. He emerged at the back of the depot, and sneaked around it until he saw an opening and dashed in.

The ready-made answer he gave the man who accosted him, "that he only went to receive something from his wife across the bamboo fence," still amuses us whenever we remember it. The man fell for it, and demanded a share of what my dad had in his nylon bag. Stepping aside, away from the prying eyes of others, dad quickly obliged him with some of the dry cassava chips and palm kernels mum had parcelled for him. As he did so, dad whispered to the man that he was actually new to the depot but was a seasoned welder. After intoning, "I said it that you are new, for I know that my instinct cannot fail me," the man took dad to his superior officer. He informed my father that he was lucky to have escaped the notice of those at the gate. The next day, he was taken to where he was tested, and according to dad, the foreman excitedly reported, "this is one of the masters."

Dad was there for quite some time, and mum regularly brought him supplies which his superior officers also benefited from. My mother's visits were interrupted by the camp's move to Umudike, Umuahia, from where he occasionally accompanied his superior officers to Uzuakoli. Mother recounts that she did not know which time was worse for her, the time dad went to the depot to enrol, or the movement outside Umuahia to the front.

Dad observed the regularity with which the infantry was stuffed into open lorries and driven away. The soldiers wore mournful looks because they could not even return the goodbyes from family members who crowded the bamboo fence to catch a glimpse of them. This was quite unlike the usual bonhomie, laughter, noise, songs, dances of the everyday atmosphere at the depot and parade ground. The joyous mood disappeared once they become aware of their movement. Complaints of inadequate training, and short notice flew around. Family members and friends who thronged the depot were usually mostly elderly parents, uncles, and aunties.

After my dad went off to war, I became the field commander in the village, re-enacting what I had seen them do at their depot. With my improvised rifle made out of sticks, I would sing, march, and lead parades round our compound with the other children till I lost my voice, wore myself out, and went home to eat and sleep. Mother maintained a careful watch over me, lest I be kidnapped and conscripted as a child soldier "for possessing too much energy that could be channelled to a better and more gainful employment"

My father was always in the good books of his

commanders. He secured passes and usually visited, dressed in his uniform. He was not molested by other soldiers who respected the Ogbunigwe boys. He brought us food supplies including milk, corn flour, salty stockfish and drugs, more than what families who queued up with their sick children for hours at Relief Camps got. There was too much suffering and starvation in the land. He would warn us not to waste food as we were fortunate to have anything to eat.

He admonished us not to be too selective of food or meals. Kwashiorkor was taking its toll on malnourished children. The number of the many cousins we played with on our return from Enugu was continuously depleted by death. They became sickly, lost tremendous weight, with lean limbs and legs, developed swollen faces, protruding bellies and big heads so much so that you could hardly recognize them, and died. The wails of their mothers would attract the mothers of other children to the victim's house to commiserate with the mother. Afterwards, they left to trust God that similar fate would not befall their own children. We therefore made it a point to eat everything we were given, and would also hunt for other creatures to eat, for instance, insects – grasshoppers, termites, crickets, grasscutters and other rodents etc. Some sick children were taken by the Red Cross and other humanitarian organizations to Gabon and other countries that sympathized with Biafra, for treatment. There is a huge possibility that many of them never returned or ever got reunited with their families. My cousins, Nwobilo and Pius Onwukanjo, never came back. That is why I believe that Igbo communities must exist in the countries they were taken to, like Gabon, and the Government of Nigeria should have located and re-integrated them as an integral part of its policy of reconciliation and rehabilitation after the war.

Dad on these visits, would inform us that they had moved up and were using pawpaw, cassava, and yam tuber leaves to cook soup aside from cooking and eating unripe pawpaw and snakes. He informed us that it was dangerous to leave your post without a "pass." If other units saw you, you would be conscripted and could be taken straight to the war front. If your unit got wind of it, you would be punished for being away without leave (A.W.O.L) – a straggler. His presence always lifted our spirits and his stories about the war sustained our interest.

With a "pass," he visited us for some time and told us wonderful stories. He sent messages thereafter of their encampment at Umu-Alumakum, Owerri etc. His last visit was when the fall of Umuahia into the hands of Nigeria became imminent. He had just been moved from Ama-Imo, in present day Ikeduru L.G.A, to Afor Ogbe, Mbaise. By now we were used to sounds of heavy artillery, gun fire, shelling and bombings so that up till now, I am yet to overcome my phobia for lights in the sky, whether of lightning during rains or whatever. My father took us to Afor Ogbe, Mbaise, where we stayed till the end of the war.

All along, we had been living in the village, but this time, he was taking us out of it. It was a long and tortuous journey on foot. There was chaos, with sporadic gun fire, shelling and tracers at night. There were random air raids and bombings. We ran into some berserk soldiers as they made their way to heaven knows where. We travelled through bush paths through Ubi (the thick forest) behind our backyard, and emerged around Umuokpara, after the Amachara General Hospital. From there, we were facing the present Imo State, and it was as if there was a spillover of people unto the tarred main road. Both sides of the road were taken up by people fleeing for their dear lives, loads on their heads and children strapped to their backs or led along by hand. Carrying me on his back, and holding my elder sister, Ihuoma's hand, my father led the way, briskly trailed by my mother who carried my kid sister, Ngozi.

There was also the pathetic sight of wailing children, sick with kwashiorkor, crying mothers facing the dilemma of abandoning their sick children, the elderly with swollen legs, faces, and protruding bellies who could not continue, and were left to die outside their homes. It was horrible. Many did not have any destinations in mind or any idea where they were headed. The elderly were simply left to die, abandoned on the roadsides when their loved ones could no longer cope with carrying them.

Our luggage was not much. Mother regretted the

journey, blaming herself for not taking us to her father's house at Okwu Olokoro. She was convinced her clan would never fall into the hands of the enemy. She had told us about the ancient paintings of Nwachi Nwangbala and Igwu Okwu River that responded to calls like humans, and boasted that no enemy gun pointed toward her birthplace, Olokoro would go off.

We were lodged in a private residence near dad's depot at Afor Ogbe, Mbaise, when we heard that the war had ended. There was jubilation, but my father was apprehensive. We did not embark on the return journey immediately. Dad was afraid the soldiers on the other side might go on a killing spree, so he hid for a while. He had his doubts about the "No Victor, No Vanquished" declaration by Gowon at the end of the war.

It was a long, horrible trek home, with the roads full of people; children, men, and women with luggage on their heads, children strapped to their backs, while other children who could walk were pulled along by their hands. Getting to the boundary, we saw that the Imo River Bridge had overflowed. It was not as it was when we crossed it on our way to Mbaise.

I had not seen a corpse before, was terrified of coffins, and would not dare go near a dead person or to the cemetery, but dead bodies – corpses lying in various positions and at various stages of decomposition, littered the roads, bloated and full of squirming maggots. Flies and vultures jumped up from the corpses they were feeding on at the approach of the returnees. There were shrivelled remains of the skeletons of deceased people under dark, stained clothes, with their legs looking like hockey sticks still trapped inside their boots. The skulls and faces of others were contorted in various degrees of agony. I would scream at the sights, but managed to hold unto my father's hand firmly. The atmosphere was polluted through and through with the pungent odour of decomposition. Getting to the bridge, we had to be carried on people's backs across for a fee. Our own carriers had no problem with the light weights of us children, but with the heavier adults and those who had luggage it was a different story. Some sadly abandoned their valuables on the river bank or threw them into the river if no one agreed to ferry them across with them. Maggot infested, bloated dead bodies floated in the river, and some got lodged in between parts of the bridge that were in the river. If the bearers' feet slipped while walking on the bridge, people fell into the river with their cargoes. Their plunge into the river threw up the corpses into their faces. They took in water as they opened their mouths to shout, swallowing liquid from the contaminated river, and swimming with the floating corpses before being rescued. There was a lot of noise and confusion. People were desperate to return to their homes and compounds. It was a horrible and dangerous journey. Not until we were ferried across to the Umuahia side of the bridge and checked our numbers to be sure that no one was missing, did we heave sighs of relief. I vomited most of the way.

Home at last, it was almost incredible. Our parents battled for us to regain our lost appetite for food. My father started crying when we entered the family compound. He had seen a grave. He did not know whose grave it was, but the soil was so fresh that the person had obviously almost survived the war. It turned out to be the grave of his immediate older brother, Gabriel Ukandu, and he wept. A little while later he became aware that such fresh graves also dotted the compounds of other families in our kindred. He had to pick himself up and find the will to keep going.

This was how I discovered the meaning of war that my parents could not tell me. I am grateful to God that I lived to tell the story.

About the Author

Marcus Onyebuchi Ukandu is from Umuahia in Abia State of Nigeria. He is a Lawyer and the Principal Partner in a Lagos-based Law firm specialising in Real Estate. He is married with children.

BIAFRAN BABY

*By John Mozie (**2020 Collection**)*

Head's small, belly's swollen,
Caught in a strife that I did not cause.
How can hunger bloat an empty stomach?
Just shoot me and end my pain.

Dead children with the few that lived
Hunting for game that's also starved
Day in day out waiting on relief rare
Oh shoot me and end this pain.

The rains are here, made of lead
Lead and rain, raining lead
Screeching planes, targeting crowds
Women and crowds, crowds of children
Oh just shoot me and end this torment.

A land of promise, framed by the sun
Named for a river, source of life
Lady Luck smile, an upside-down smile

Where is the promise, oh cruel luck?
And still I ask, will you end my pain?

Now it's all done, this strife of brothers
No vanquished he said, victors all
Those who starved, and the fatted many,
All under one flag, still a nation denied?

The yellow sun is full again, where's the promise so
longed for?
The shooting's on again, can I live this peace?
Tarry now, says Lady Luck; because the best, is yet to
come;
When and how I am still to see
Still unsure my growing heart can live this peace.

THE UNFORGETTABLE PAIN

By Peter Onwu

My Umuahia Days

L ife as a student at Government College Umuahia had become a frenzied affair in the early months of 1967. I was a student in class three and had just started to enjoy the privileges of being a "semi-senior" student at the prestigious secondary school. The political situation in Nigeria was engulfed with great uncertainty. There had been mass killings of Igbos in the northern and western parts of Nigeria. A pogrom, forcing the mass return of Igbos from other parts of Nigeria to their homeland in the eastern part of the country. This also meant that students fleeing with their parents from the troubled parts of the country needed to be found new schools for admission in the east to continue with their education. Government College Umuahia had a quota of these "white shirts" as we called them, some of whom had been students at King's College Lagos, St Gregory's, Lagos, to mention just the two. Fortunately, they had no difficulty in settling in, as the "Umuahians" made them very welcome.

I had joined the school cadet unit, which made my parents proud. We went on a 5-mile march from Government College, Umuahia to Umuahia town centre dressed in full battle gear with our rucksacks, to show support and solidarity to the administration of Col. Chukwuemeka Odumegwu Ojukwu, Governor of Eastern Nigeria. A few days later, on a crispy morning in the first week of May 1967, the school bell tolled loudly in the grounds of Government College Umuahia. This meant only one thing, and that was that all the students were being summoned to the assembly hall. As we all sat huddled in the assembly hall, bustling with excitement and chatting among ourselves, there was sudden silence as the principal, Mr. S. B.Ogujawa, (popularly known as antimony because of what his initials denoted on the periodic table) emerged on the dais with some members of his staff. He told us that the school would be closing for a brief period because of the uncertain political climate, and that we would be sent home to our parents. I was not at that time aware of the gravity of the situation, and felt inwardly pleased at the thought of going back to Enugu to stay with my family. I then trotted to the administration block where I could use the phone to call home, so that my parents could send the driver to pick me up.

Enugu

I had been home now for nearly three weeks and had begun to comprehend the magnitude and gravity of what was unfolding in the history of Nigeria. H. E. Governor Emeka Ojukwu had appointed my father and four others as special members of the Eastern Nigeria Consultative Assembly. On the 30 May 1967 Col. Ojukwu, after due consultations, proclaimed that Eastern Nigeria was now to be known as the Republic of Biafra. There was pride and jubilation, as we felt we had a right to "self-determination." "People rejected by others can't reject themselves."

Peter (first from left) as a cadet

There was a flurry of activity at Eagle Lodge, my family home. Col. Emeka Ojukwu came to our home on at least three occasions at night, to consult with my father. On the last occasion, a small crowd gathered outside our gates to catch a glimpse of the great man as he left. Between the months of May and July 1967, I remember meeting a few people at Eagle Lodge. They were Madam Ojukwu, Col. Ojukwu's mother, Tom Bigger, (Ojukwu's half-brother), and Brigadier Banjo who was the Commander of the Biafran Liberation Forces.

On the 6th July 1967, we all sat in front of the television listening to Governor Ojukwu's broadcast informing the nation that Nigeria had launched its war of aggression against Biafra. This was a game changer. Everyone had to do their bit for the motherland. My elder sister, Stella, volunteered as a relief worker to cook and deliver food to our soldiers at the front. My mother, along with Lady Ibiam and some members of their Women Ecumenical Council, gave moral support by visiting soldiers at the war front. My eldest brother, Ken, was personally commissioned by H. E. Ojukwu as a captain in the Special Task Force (STF), and he went on missions abroad for Biafra. My eldest sister, Christine, was a dietician working at the Specialist Hospital, Enugu. Being nearly 14 years of age, the harsh reality hit me that with all the bravado and gusto I had as a cadet at Umuahia, I was not eligible to serve as a soldier in the Biafran Army. My father assured me that one day there might still be a part for me to play in our effort towards the execution of the war.

The sad reality of war began to trickle home to me, when news got back to us that Christopher Okigbo, Tom Bigger and Chude Soke had all been killed at the Nsukka sector of the war. To drive things closer to home, Nigerian B26 bombers had begun sorties into Enugu's air space. The air raids were dastardly and unnerving experiences. We would take shelter under the staircase, but later, my father had a bunker built at the bottom of the garden, shielded by an apple tree. All sorts of rumours abounded; some said that Nigeria was planning to drop chemical bombs on us. An old wives' tale was that if this happened, we should wear a mask coated with ash.

Fortunately, there was some good news from the battlefront in the western sector. Biafran liberation forces under Col. Banjo had liberated the Mid-West. Biafran forces were now in Ore, Western Nigeria, and were making gains. Just before the good news had time to settle, disaster struck. Sabotage and treason were unearthed. The Mid-West, which had declared itself the Republic of Benin after its liberation, had been recaptured by Federal troops due to alleged sabotage. Banjo, Ifeajuna and Alale were publicly executed. A Captain Shadrack, Head of the Biafran Military Police, took me to see the camps where they had kept some of the saboteurs in Abakpa-Nike. I recognised one of the inmates as a driver to the family of a friend of mine.

He gestured at me, and I felt traumatised that there was nothing I could do to assist him.

In September we started seeing strange faces in Enugu. Some infiltrators were arrested. Mortar shells started falling on the outskirts of the city. The old colonial town was being sacked. I saw my father repeatedly using the phone. We could not head back to my village at Affa, as it was under federal control. Fortunately the telephone rang at around 8 pm that late September evening, it was one in-law, Mr. Josephat Okoli, ASP in charge of the divisional police force in Orlu asking my father to come to Orlu with the family; that he had arranged accommodation for us. We piled what suitcases we could into the boots of three cars the next morning and were off to Orlu.

Orlu

We arrived in Orlu at about 12 noon on the 27th September 1967. Our new home was a modest three bedroom bungalow, a far cry from Eagle Lodge which comprised 3 sitting rooms, 2 bathrooms, 3 toilets, 7 bedrooms, and an office for my father, a kitchen, pantry, dining room, as well as my father's study. The cramped space frayed a few nerves. My father assembled us the next morning and spelt out to us that our "history had changed." How prophetic those words were, I came to realise years later, both on a personal level as well as for ndigbo. The Holy Rosary sisters learned that my father and his family were in town and kindly offered us the use of two spacious bungalows. My parents, my grandmother, Nne, my sister, Nana, myself, and my two younger brothers, Richard and Edward, took up residence in the bigger bungalow. My sister, Christine, and her husband, Charles, with their two children, Simone and Charles, went to live in the smaller bungalow. It was bliss as there were still a few old perks that we could savour. There was electricity, running water and fridges in our new homes.

My father sadly suffered a stroke on 15th February 1968. Dr. Ekpechi, a good, kind doctor based at Amaigbo Hospital looked after him, and my mother put her nursing skills to use by lovingly nursing him back to health. I was taught to use the sphygmomanometer to take my father's blood pressure periodically. This was the time I truly bonded with my father. I was by his side as he made a steady and rapid recovery. There were, however, incidents that reminded us that we were still at war. Air raids, the distant shelling explosions, scarcity of once common commodities were among the factors. Fortunately, the bungalows the nuns made available to us, had some bookshelves stocked with novels and other reading literature. The whole family were avid readers, including my aged grandmother, Nne, who would at times suggest some novels to me to read which she found interesting.

One sunny morning in September 1968, I was in

my parents' bedroom with my youngest brother, Edward. My mother had just finished giving my father a bed bath when suddenly we heard the thunderous sound of a Nigerian jet bomber strafing. Everyone in the room reacted instinctively and dove under the bed. I looked at my father lying on the bed and quickly put myself on top of him, spread-eagled, using my hands to cover his ears. Moments later, we heard the explosion of bombs being dropped. Sadly, we later learnt that Orlu market which was about 500 metres from where we were as the crow flies, had been bombed and that there had been some casualties. My father asked me why I threw myself over him when the plane was flying by. I simply told him my thoughts, which was that I wanted to protect him. If a bullet had come through the roof of the building, I wanted it to hit me rather than him as my mother and other siblings were depending on him and his life was more important than mine. He gazed into my eyes, smiled, and said nothing.

As my father recovered from his stroke and his balance and mobility improved, I would accompany him on his morning and evening walks so he could build up strength and stamina. Secretly I asked our driver to teach me how to drive and practiced while going with him from Umuna to Amaigbo hospital to collect my father's medication. On one occasion as I pulled into Amaigbo hospital, a family friend, Dr. Sam Egwuatu, saw me behind the wheel. He was shocked that I could drive. A couple of weeks later, I went back to the hospital, this time with my father and the driver, and we met with Dr. Sam Egwuatu, who told my father that he was pleasantly surprised to see me driving the Mercedes to the hospital a couple of weeks prior. My father said nothing until we got into the car to go back home, when he asked me whether what Dr. Sam Egwuatu had said was true. I told him it was, and that I got the driver to teach me to drive in case there was urgency for us to leave Umuna and there would be no one else to drive the other car, a Pontiac Parisienne. Thankfully, he understood the logic behind my action and asked me whether I felt confident enough to drive. I said I did, and we went straight to the Orlu police station to secure a learner's permit for me. I felt a great sense of relief that the "cat was now out of the bag."

Three other refugee families also came to live in quarters on the grounds of the Holy Rosary compound. In the month of December, my father gifted a goat to them for their Christmas celebrations. I had become friends with some of the children and discovered that they were from Asaba. The months rolled by, and my sister, Nana, got married to an army officer, a Major Azubuogu, 2nd-in-Command of the Biafran artillery unit. A white wedding which took place, brought a rare glimpse of normalcy during those trying times. Not long after that, our driver who had gone to Orlu town without carrying his papers was conscripted. He was away for four weeks and was only released after he was able to establish that he had a pass. Meanwhile, while he was away, I was able to drive my father from Umuna to Umuahia, to attend a Consultative Assembly meeting. My driving skills were now paying dividends.

My father and sister, Nana,
at her wedding to Major Azubuogu

By March 1969, my father's health had begun to play up again. Five years earlier he had been treated for lymphoma, a form of cancer and had since been in remission. Sadly, the dreaded disease had resurfaced. Dr Akanu Ibiam paid us a visit at Orlu and insisted that my father travel abroad for medical treatment. H. E. Col Odumegwu Ojukwu approved the trip. My father was reluctant to go, as he did not want to leave his beloved wife and children behind in war torn Biafra. My mother insisted that he must travel as that offered some hope of him being able to beat the illness. My father then decided that I would accompany him. I on my part was bustling with excitement and mixed emotions. I dreaded leaving my mother and the rest of my family behind. We were all in this together, so one can understand my predicament. So many uncertainties. Nonetheless I took my passport photograph and had it sent to Umuahia. A few days later, I was issued with a Biafra travel document. I was scheduled to leave Biafra with my father from Uli airstrip on the night of 30th April.

30th April came, and there were emotional scenes at the bungalow as my father and I said our goodbyes to my mum, and the rest of the family and friends before being driven to Uli airstrip. On arrival, Major Akabogu who oversaw the airstrip welcomed us. We were told that federal planes had earlier during the day bombed the tarmac, but airport authorities had made repairs. Archbishop Patterson had just flown into Biafra and we would be leaving with the same plane he had arrived on. My father and I were the only two passengers in the aircraft. It was a Caritas plane. There were only about 12 seats in the aircraft. The rest of the seats had been removed, I presumed to create space for relief materials it carried. As the plane taxied off, the pilot said over the blower that the lights in the aircraft would be switched off until we were out of Nigerian airspace. This precautionary step was to avoid being shot at by Nigerian anti-aircraft guns. The time of the flight to Sao Tome, our destination, would be approximately 50 minutes. My father and I each took our Rosary and he led us both in prayers.

We touched down safely in Sao Tome and were met by Biafra government officials and taken to our hotel. It was as if I was in a new world. Elated but with a nagging feeling of guilt because of the family I had left behind in Biafra. The next day we were joined by Mr C. C. Mojekwu, the Biafran foreign minister, and two other officials. This time we boarded a turbo propeller plane for a flight to Faro, Portugal. On arrival we were met by more Biafran government officials and driven to Lisbon where we lodged in a hotel. The next day my father and I flew to London, our destination. It was the 4th of May 1969. Amazingly that day marked the 45th anniversary of his very first visit, with his guardian and brother-in-law, Chief Onyeama of Eke, in 1924.

London

On arrival at Heathrow Airport, I was faced with a degree of uncertainty. My father had a Nigerian diplomatic Passport which had been issued by the Nigerian Authorities prior to the secession of Biafra, and I had a

Biafran Travel document. Fortunately, my father had a few good friends in London, and after a series of phone calls and having spent about two hours at the airport, I was granted entry into the United Kingdom. The first thing that struck me was that racially I now appeared to be in the minority. Though it was spring, the weather was considerably colder than it was in Biafra. My father and I took a Taxi and headed for a hotel at Lancaster Gate, West London.

My older brother, Gilbert, who was studying in London at the time, came with his friend, Mike Obioha, to meet my father and I at the hotel. It was a joyous reunion. After spending a couple of days at the hotel, they decided that my father and I move into Gilbert's cosy apartment in Porchester Terrace, Bayswater, and stay as a family unit while an appointment was made for my father to commence his medical treatment. After a series of tests, my father was admitted into St Bartholomew's Hospital on the 13th May, under the care of Sir Ronald Bodley-Scott, a specialist oncologist.

I paid daily visits to my father in hospital and he appeared to be in good spirits and bearing up with the treatment. He dictated letters for me to write on his behalf to my mother and H. E. Col Odumegwu Ojukwu. These letters, I would put inside their respective addressed envelopes, then put them inside a bigger envelope, and mail to an address in Libreville Gabon. On reaching Gabon, the contents of the bigger envelope would be couriered to their destinations in Biafra. This was how I communicated with my mother throughout the duration of the war.

I went as usual to visit my father at the hospital on the 28th May 1969. He told me that he had dreamt that he was on this raft drifting in the sea, and that his good friend, Francis (Dr. Ibiam), stretched out a hand to him. I interrupted and asked, "Did he pull you out?" He merely smiled and said, "Does it really matter?" I felt bothered by this, and after I left him, I made my way to the Catholic Church at Queensway, Bayswater. I prayed fervently, and a little voice in my head told me that "no amount of prayer will save your father".

My eldest brother, Ken, was at that time on a mission to Spain on behalf of Biafra. My father asked Gilbert to contact Ken and ask him to come to London immediately. On the 30th May, my father had a sudden relapse. Ken thankfully flew into London the next day. There were now three of us keeping vigil at his bedside.

My father died on the 4th June 1969. I was still fifteen years of age and just shy of my sixteenth birthday. I felt devastated and inconsolable. It was the first time I felt the pain of losing someone so close. The news spread rapidly within the Biafran community in London. St Bartholomew's Hospital Authorities were exceedingly kind and supportive. My father's body was laid out in their crypt for a few days for Biafrans to come and pay their last respects. I remember the scene distinctly as I filed around his body with my brothers, I bent over and kissed him on his forehead. It was ice cold, but he had this gentle, peaceful smile on his face.

Dr Nnamdi Azikiwe flew in from Germany to visit with my brothers and I, to offer his condolences. Dr K. O. Mbadiwe delivered the eulogy during the Requiem Mass held for my father at Westminster Cathedral, London. Mr. Kobara, Biafran Representative in the UK, saw to the arrangement for my father's remains to be flown back to Biafra for temporary interment at Ihioma Cathedral near Orlu. This was undoubtedly the biggest impact the Biafran war had on my family.

In London, there were fund raising events such as dances, cultural events and jumble sales organised by Biafrans in support of the Biafran cause. There were also protest marches, placard displays against the Harold Wilson UK Government because of her support for Nigeria in the ungodly war being waged against Biafra. My brothers and I participated in some of these events.

I had by now not been to school since the early months of 1967. My eldest brother, Ken, arranged for me to have private tuition with a tutor on a one to one basis in Notting Hill Gate, London. He tutored me for two months during the months of July and August. I had my lessons three times a week, and plenty of homework. After two months, he felt that I could sit for my "O" levels within a year.

My brother Ken, arranged for me to resume my

education at a prestigious boarding school, Rockwell College, Cashel, Co. Tipperary, in the Republic of Ireland. I arrived there in September to find to my surprise, that I had a classmate in form 5 who was also from Biafra. We introduced ourselves, and I discovered that his name was Lotanna Ojukwu, a younger brother to H. E. Col. Odumegwu Ojukwu. He was previously at a British Public School, Millfields, but had now switched to Rockwell. We became great friends and shared study desks.

While on a term holiday break in Dublin, I learnt that there was another Biafran boy in town. When we met, I was pleasantly surprised to find out that he was my first cousin, Seretse Njemanze, who had been evacuated from Biafra. It was comforting to know that I had close family ties around, thousands of miles away from Biafra.

The war ended abruptly in January 1970. I was glad to learn that my dear mother had returned all the family safely back to Enugu. Sadly, the harrowing events had changed our lives and history forever.

About the Author

Peter Onwu is a Businessman and lives in London. He is from Affa in Enugu State. Peter is the 3rd son of the late Dr Simon Onwu, the first Igbo doctor.

YES! I LIVED THE BIAFRA – NIGERIA CIVIL WAR

By Nwabueze Chukwuedozie Ikemefuna Ezeife

My family spent the war years in Umunze, in present day Orumba South Local Government Area of Anambra State. My father, Ide (Sir) J. N. C. Ezeife, was the foundation Principal of the local Secondary School in Lomu Village, Umunze. Lomu, Umunze, was an idyllic, quaint place with all the trappings of a typical Igbo village. Although my family was middle-class and the locals looked up to us as part of the elite, I quickly assimilated and frolicked with newly minted local friends. We enjoyed playing football, and I loved going out to watch local masquerades like the scary Mgbadike and the dance-a-holic Icheoku which irked my father to no end, and for which I received a fair amount of floggings. I recall, with nostalgia, visiting my local friends and spending time with them in their mud huts which I recall felt very much like being inside an air-conditioned room. I also remember that water from their earthenware pots was as cold and soothing as water from the fridge.

I enjoyed church. Ours was located just about half a mile from my father's School. St. Peter's Anglican Church, I believe it was called - I may be wrong about the name. The primary school was also located in the same area. I enjoyed the hymns and the Children's Sunday School. I loved the Bible stories and relished listening to our teachers regale us with them, especially about Jesus and his miraculous exploits.

My father's school, All Saints Grammar School, was located on the outskirts of the village. Mission secondary schools, dating back to the colonial times, were named "Grammar Schools" because they were set up principally to teach reading and writing to the locals who would eventually work as clerks and interpreters for the missionaries and the colonial government. The only thing south of us was the jungle, the local streams, and the local cemetery. And beyond that was Owerri Ezukala, I believe. East of the school were more forest and a dirt road leading to Unyo River. Unyo River forms the boundary between Umunze and Isuochi in modern day Abia State. We had a wide range of forests and grasslands to forage. The school was located on a humongous plot of land. Because it was on the outskirts of the town, the villagers were generous in their allocation of land. I remember that it had one of the largest sports fields I had ever seen. The sports grounds could conveniently accommodate eight soccer fields. It was that immense.

Some of the members of the academic staff at my father's school included the Ukadike family from Oraifite, the Obumneme family from Oba, the Ezeagu family from Achina. And then there was young Herbert Chuma Illoh, now a Professor at the Obafemi Awolowo University, Ile-Ife. He is my townsman. I was close friends with Chukwuka and Emma Ukadika, as well as young Kodi Obumneme. The local families that eventually became family friends included the Ukaejiofor family, the Anyagafu family and the Sibudu family. There were several other families, but memory fails me presently.

I was about 5 years at the onset of the Nigerian Civil War. I do not have a clear recollection of how it started since there was no spectacular event that commemorated the start of war for us. As a child, I do remember the ominous atmosphere that pervaded that period. I recall that my parents, and everyone around, were glued to the radio (we had no television at the time) and talk of war was everywhere we went. People around, including our parents, were talking about it. The radio was almost always all about it. People were making frantic efforts to gather and store essential supplies and necessities. The fear, dread, and excitement all around was palpable. I did not really know what the fuss was about. I somehow gathered that we Igbos were fighting for our freedom from "*Ndi Awusa* (Hausas)". The concept of nationhood was not something I grasped as a child. I was unaware of the fact that there were other tribes involved besides us and Ndi Hausa. Biafran Igbos referred to the other side collectively as *"Ndi Hausa."* It is interesting that I only actually met people from the North and some Yorubas in 1972 when my father was transferred to Corpus Christi College, Achi in present day Oji River Local Government of Enugu State. Half the school compound at CCC Achi and swathes of the surrounding bushes were taken over by a Nigerian Army Battalion under the command of a dashing young Lieutenant, Peter Cigari. This young officer was eventually executed in 1976 for taking part in the Dimka Coupe d'état. But I digress.

The world did not grind to a halt at the inception of the war. Life continued, as far as I can recall. We still went to school, played after school and went to church on Sundays. You know, the usual activities continued to grind. Initially there was no noticeable change to our routine. The war at the time was far away from us. Life was somewhat normal. At some point the students in my father's school were dismissed and they left for their respective homes. The school was empty and with the students and their usual hustle and bustle gone, the silence was deafening.

After several months, things began to change dramatically. The Biafran Army sent a Medical battalion to occupy my father's school and set up a hospital for injured soldiers. The battalion commander was a

Captain Okonkwo, a medical doctor from Nnewi. Soon after arriving, Captain Okonkwo requisitioned the Principal's official residence for his use. We were forced to move in with the other academic staff in their already cramped quarters. He also commandeered my father's Peugeot 403 and we became car-less. The entire two-story school block, library, and laboratories was transformed into the hospital. The troops took over most of the student dormitories. Weeks later, the war refugees from present-day Ebonyi and Enugu States started arriving in droves. The remaining students' dormitories and the surrounding grounds became home for our new neighbours. In the distance, we could hear constant bombardment. The war had finally reached us.

Nkwo Umunze like most markets in Igboland, was located smack-dab on the main road that runs through Umunze to Ibinta and on to Okigwe in present day Imo State. The sprawling market is the main commercial hub for Umunze and the surrounding towns and villages commonly referred to as Oru Mba. One day, the Nigerian side staged an aerial attack on the market. Several people were seriously injured. I do not recall if there were fatalities, but I do recall vividly that the fighter plane flew so low that we could see the "white man" flying it. In those days Biafrans widely believed that the Nigerian Airforce did not have officers qualified to fly the sorties since the elite of the Nigerian Military had been people from Eastern Nigeria and they had all left the Nigerian Armed Forces for Biafra. True as that may be, the larger truth was that Biafra had white mercenaries flying its own military jets as well. I guess in those days, there was no sophisticated technology in the planes, and the pilots flew their sorties by manual sighting, hence they flew so close to the ground. That singular incident more than any other event brought home the fact that things were not normal anymore and that we were not safe from "Ndi Hausa," even in remote Umunze. After that incident, things began to change. Nkwo Umunze and other local markets, including Nkwo Igbo-Ukwu, were relocated from the major roads to wooded areas of town. Several of the markets changed their hours of operation from day to night, because apparently the planes could not carry out night sorties.

After the aerial attack on Nkwo Umunze, the Biafran soldiers who were camped at my father's school, with the help of the refugees, the staff of the school and the local villagers, embarked on the task of cutting, splitting and piling bamboo stems into the massive sports field in the school grounds. The bamboo sticks were sharpened at the top. The belief was that at some point, the Nigerian troops might decide to parachute into the enclave using open fields such as the one in my father's school. The strategy was to impale any such paratrooper who attempted to jump into that field from the air. As fate would have it, no such attempt was ever made by the invading Nigerian troops.

Parents in the school's staff quarters, with the assistance of their house helps, dug an elaborate bunker behind the staff quarters. It was about eight feet deep. The dimensions were about ten feet long and five feet in width, with a step running down into it. The top was covered with several dozen palm tree trunks thick enough in circumference to protect us from a possible bomb drop. We, the children, spent our days inside the soothingly cool bunker, while our parents went about their daily activities.

As the war ground on, Biafra began to lose territory to the advancing Nigerian Army. Most of the lost territories were the food baskets of the enclave, including areas in present-day Enugu, Ebonyi and Abia states, as federal troops pushed from the north and south. Besides territories, including fertile lands and farms, healthy adult males and teenagers that used to do the farming were taken into the Biafran army to defend the territory. The dual loss of farmlands and farm hands was a debilitating blow to Biafra. Because of this double-whammy, the territory faced acute shortage of food. In addition, the siege by the federal troops around Biafra made it impossible to import food either from Nigeria or neighbouring countries. At this time, with the loss of present day Rivers, Cross River, Akwa Ibom and parts of Delta States, Biafra lost access to the sea. The two airports at Uli and Uga respectively, were used principally for staging aerial sorties against the invaders, and for bringing in military supplies and medicines. There was widespread lack of food, leading to malnutrition. The Old, the sick, the infirm, infants and young children bore the brunt of the malnutrition. Millions of Biafrans were lost to hunger and disease, although NGOs such as Caritas, Red Cross, UNICEF, the Catholic and Anglican Missionaries made efforts to help fight the scourge. I remember the massive importation of powdered egg-yolk, cornmeal, codfish, and cod liver oil. I am still haunted to this day by images of young Biafrans, particularly infants and toddlers, with their discoloured, bulging stomachs perched on their skeleton-like frames, wailing in pain, hunger, and discomfort; oftentimes too weak and hungry to even cry. It was a terrible sight to behold. They were in the throes of "Kwashiorkor."

The Biafran enclave as a whole was in the throes of acute shortage of everything ranging from food, medicine, salt, fuel, building materials and vehicle parts to every conceivable household good and necessity. Soon there was severe shortage of staples like rice, beans, wheat, etc. Biafrans relied heavily on Cassava which they consumed in a variety of ways. The roots were made into garri or just local foo-foo (akpu) and the root peels were dried and crushed into flour for baking. The leaves became substitutes for regular vegetables. Faunas and floras such as cassava leaves that were traditionally fed to goats and sheep soon became vegetables on dinner tables. For protein, practically anything that walked, waddled, flew, crawled, or slithered was fair game. Lizards, insects, worms, snakes, rats and almost every bird, except vultures, were on the menu. I recall the first time I ate an alligator was during the war. I ate it again a couple of years ago in New Orleans, United States.

On the heels of the suffocating scarcity of necessities, including food, medicine, and basic household items, the ingenuity, and the entrepreneurial spirit of the Biafrans kicked into high gear. Courageous and daring Biafrans, especially women, embarked on a perilous and dangerous pursuit called Afia Attack. It entailed sneaking past enemy positions and venturing into Nigeria and parts of the conquered Biafran enclave to procure goods such as salt, medicine and even currencies. To navigate around scarcity, Biafrans innovated. I remember that my father had to dip batteries into a salty liquid solution to power his radio. I also remember that people had winders to crank their vehicles since there were no batteries and no parts to fix kick starters. Old tire threads were cut and used as shoe soles.

My older brother, Afam Okechukwu, used to accompany the local teens to the forest to set traps for birds and game. They fished the local river and streams as well. This one time, he went to check his trap. When he got there, lo and behold, the trap had caught a huge snake. The darn thing was thrashing the bushes around the trap. My brother took one look at the serpent and fled for dear life, abandoning his costly iron-cast trap in the forest. That was the end of his hunting career. Looking back, millions of people survived the threat of hunger and starvation simply because, unlike today that everything including toothpicks is imported, a majority of what was used and consumed by Nigerians then was sourced locally and not imported. Between farming and foraging, people managed to survive. Help also came from Caritas, Red Cross, UNICEF, the Catholic and Anglican Charities.

We were often glued to the radio listening to the great Biafran broadcaster, Okoko Ndem. In the annals of war propaganda, this man made the likes of Tariq Aziz of Iraq and the Nazi's Goebbels look like rank amateurs. With the initial Biafran incursion into Western Nigeria up to Ore, on the way to Lagos, the then capital city of Nigeria, Okoko Ndem made us feel like the war had been won. We would be hearing the distant rumbling sounds of bombardment and mortar rounds from the advancing Nigerian troops, and the man would be on the radio telling us that our enemies had been chased back to the north. That man was unbelievably clever. He would often begin his broadcast with the admonition *onye nd'iro gbara gburugburu naeche nduya nche mgbenile, umu Biafra, unu araruna ura,* meaning "a besieged people must maintain vigilance at all times; Biafrans don't get indolent".

I still remember some of the motivational and inspirational songs that were commonplace in the

Biafran enclave during the war. They often touted the prowess of the Biafran troops and recounted our illusory military successes while denigrating Gowon and the Nigerian Army. While they still ring in my ears, I cannot quite remember the entire lyrics, just dribs and drabs. In any case, most of them would be objectionable to our brothers in the north. I will not attempt to recreate the songs here. There were also wonderful musical records and tracks produced during the war. Celestine Ukwu had the beautiful rendition of the track, "Hail Biafra, the land of Freedom." There was one by the Onitsha minstrel maestro, Afam Ogbotobo. I still remember bits and pieces of the lyrics but not the name of the track.

At the beginning of the war, the Biafran Army had a pick of enthusiastic volunteers eager to join the struggle in defence of the enclave. As the war progressed, the pool of volunteers dried up, forcing the Army to resort to forced conscriptions. Eventually the enclave ran out of adult candidates and started recruiting teenagers and even precocious pre-teens. As more and more adult males and teenagers were lost in the battlefield, children and early teens became targets of forcible recruitment. My parents often had to hide my older brother, Afam Okechukwu Ezeife, in the ceiling during the day for fear of being conscripted as a child soldier. My brother was about 13 years old at the time.

Conscription into the Biafran Army during the war presented opportunities of sorts for corrupt individual conscription officers. Some of the soldiers who were tasked with the responsibility of scouring the enclave for eligible recruits into the Biafran Army, saw it as an opportunity to have their palms greased. They would take money from eligible recruits and look the other way. They would also round up men who were too old to be eligible and boys too young and use the threat of taking them away to the training camps as a ruse to shake them down for bribes. It happened to my uncle. Uncle Alexander "Dogo" Ezeife, was my father's immediate older brother. He must have been in his late fifties then, and thus ineligible for the draft. That did not stop the recruitment officers from snagging him. My uncle was stubborn; a typical Ezeife trait. They took him, knowing fully well that they could not possibly justify bringing him to camp. Their intention was to use the threat of recruitment to finagle some money off him. To cut a long story short, they took him round Igbo-Ukwu and some other neighbouring villages, apparently on their way to the training camp. Every few miles, they would turn to him and tell him "*nwoke megharia ahu*" meaning "dude drop something so you can go." Each time they tried, my uncle's retort was "*okwa army, kanyi jebenu,*" meaning "I am ready to join, let us go." After a while it dawned on them that he was not going to budge, and they asked him to go home.

One day, the distant sounds of bombardment and mortar sounds ceased, as the news of cessation of hostilities filtered in. We all heaved a collective sigh of relief and there was widespread jubilation from those of us who had survived the war. Soon the reverse migration began, much like the wildebeest migration of the Serengeti, as the refugees from present day Enugu and Ebonyi States, who had sought refuge in and around the school and had been our neighbours for the past several months, embarked on the arduous task of returning to an uncertain future; to homes they had abandoned months before as they fled from the rampaging Nigerian federal troops. So too, did the Biafran Medical battalion that was stationed at the school. Captain Dr. Okonkwo left unceremoniously, taking with him my father's Peugeot 403. We were suddenly enveloped in an eerie quiet, after months of noisy dread.

Only a few of my relatives fought in the war, as far as I can recall. They include my maternal uncle, Sunday "Ajondu" Onyekwelu, who after the war attended the Institute of Management and Technology, Enugu, where he majored in Civil Engineering. There were also my late mother's two cousins, Ernest and Onuorah Umeweni. They both left after the war for the US for further studies. Ernest died several years ago in Dallas, Texas. Onuorah is a medical doctor in Pennsylvania.

I do not have any recollection of our family losing anyone to the war either in battle or to hunger and disease. We were lucky on that score. But we lost all the savings we had in the Nigerian banks before the onset of the war. We also lost monies we made during the war since the Biafran currency became worthless at the cessation of hostilities. Of course, we lost our Peugeot 403 to Captain Dr. Okonkwo. Yes indeed, I lived the Biafra-Nigeria Civil War.

Papa just after the war

About the Author

Dr Nwabueze Chukwuedozie Ikemefuna Ezeife is a lawyer from Igbo-Ukwu in Aguata Local Government Area of Anambra State. Married with four children, he lives and works in the San Francisco Bay Area, California.

WE RAN TO SAVE OURSELVES

By Agu Imo

Many people have written about their experiences of the Nigeria-Biafra War and since I was there, I feel I owe a duty to myself and all the others who lived through this war, to write. The war left an indelible mark on all of us and we simply should not forget what we went through.

We were regular children on the eve of war. I recall I had just started school at Corona School - must be the Yaba or Gbagada branch as most people lived on the Mainland. I vaguely remember that there was some tension around, which informed our seeing a lot more of our big uncle, Professor O. K. Ogan, who now virtually seemed to be staying with us away from his Ikoyi home. Apparently, he was on some wanted list of Igbos to be killed.

One day, we all had to speedily clamber into my dad's Peugeot 404 and take off from Lagos. All Igbos did, and my dad, who was the President of Item Union in Lagos, endeared himself to older Item people as he arranged with his in-law, Chief Ugorji Eke, to send lorries to Lagos to evacuate all Item people of limited means to the East. Our journey to Umuahia, where our big uncle, Professor Ogan, had a house, in late 1966, felt like an adventure. It took over one day as the roads were full of returning Easterners. Biafra had not yet been declared. Several families congregated in that house, and the so many cousins to play with. Within a few weeks, we had to relocate to Port Harcourt, where my mother, who was a British-trained educationist, was in hot demand. She was employed in Girl's High School, Elelenwo, and my dad who was also a hot pharmacist worked in the government hospital. We lived in a beautiful cottage in the school grounds and I loved playing around and drawing comic characters in the sand. I started off in a private convent school - I think it was called Santa Maria - but after a while, I had to join my brother, Ike, in the public school known as Township School. I was immediately traumatised at the sight of the floggings perpetrated against the students. Nobody flogged me, but I hated it. I must mention that I had never liked the idea of going to school to start with. Very soon however, we all had to leave Port Harcourt. I think the war had started at this stage and schools had closed.

We went back to Umuahia and then on to Item, where we were greeted with the sight of a beautiful house that my parents had built. Apparently, when we fled from Lagos, my parents had given Uncle Kalu Ogwo, my dad's best man, friend, and confidante, instructions to sell their undeveloped property on Calabar Street in Surulere (New Lagos) for cash. Uncle Kalu was the last man out of Lagos, and had returned to the East through the creeks bearing the proceeds of the sale of the property in cash. This money was invested into building the Item house in the months that we sojourned between Umuahia and Port Harcourt courtesy once again of my dad's in-law, the Item merchant, Chief Ugorji Eke. So, we arrived Item in 1967 and remained there in our beautiful home. About five families, the Chukus, the Akwaris, the Ogans, the Ugorji Ekes plus we, the Imos, gathered and started a school named Emergency School with a full complement of staff. I remember my teacher, H. U. K. Kalu and the Headmaster, whose name I don't recall. Life was fun. My dad worked in Umuahia and joined us at the weekends. My mum was at the head of the voluntary food distribution effort since everyone knew she would never abuse the process. We however had to stop going to school as it became too dangerous with the daily air raids. We knew as children, the difference between the sounds of the approaching enemy planes. The bombers dropped bombs, and the fighters strewed bullets.

Every day, more and more refugees returned to Item as Biafra valiantly fought almost with bare hands. Food became non-existent. Basic necessities disappeared. But my parents fought to give us a semblance of a childhood. My mother would dress us up every day in socks and shoes, and we would walk around in the midst of our naked neighbours - up until 30th March 1969. I remember that day, because the day before, the 29th, was Ike's Birthday, and despite the severe hardships, my mother had insisted on celebrating the day with a party for him. She even made a cake. And then, the next day, we started to hear the unmistakable sounds of war. The sounds of the Ferrets, the staccato of the machine guns, the shelling of the armoured cars. The roads were filled now with fleeing refugees. And then the news came, the Nigerian troops had entered Okoko Item, a mile or two away from us. We had to run. We too, had become refugees. We fled into the forest. My dad's trusty 404 could go some way but had to be abandoned. That was the last we saw of it. The enemy soldiers seized it. We remained in one forest settlement after another from then. At some stage, the Biafran Organisation of Freedom Fighters (BOFF) had to ferry my dad across enemy lines into Biafra as his life was in clear danger. We ended up with my mother, all five of us, (Ugonma was born in 1967, a month before the declaration of Biafra) in Amaepu Item where there was no running water. There was nowhere else to run. We lived in a hut with no doors or windows. Our neighbour at this time was a woman who was said to have leprosy and whose son was mentally deranged. Every day, enemy soldiers would come to raid the community. All five of us would cower around my mother as they arrived to pillage and take away young girls for forcible marriages. I remember the day they caught my Auntie Jane. I remember her screams as they took her away. I watched as my mother, day after day, stood up to these men. She showed no fear.

One day in January of 1970, they came and burnt down the whole village, shooting and killing. We ran again into the thick forest. My mother had Ugonma strapped on her back and held unto Chima and Nnenna (Oriaku). Ike and I ran by her side. She had given me Ugonma's baby bag to carry. We ran all day and all night. I did not drop the bag. We remained in the forest for about a week. Absolutely no shelter. No shoes. Only the clothes on our backs. Then one day, a rescue party arrived from Amokwe, our home. They came to fetch us. The war was over. Biafra had surrendered. We returned that day to our home. The vandals had made a sport of shooting at the building. All the louvered windows were shot off. Gaping holes everywhere. I remember when foreign journalists came and took photographs of us malnourished children. I resented it. We remained in Amokwe Item for two months until March, when once again, our uncle, Professor Ogan, courtesy of his friend, Gen. T.Y. Danjuma sent a military lorry to convey us to Enugu. In Enugu, we went to school at the W.T.C Practicing School in Uwani, Enugu. I was going on nine, so they put me in Class Three. I had never learnt how to read. I had never spent a full year in any class. My parents returned to Lagos.

The Langleys were instrumental to our rehabilitation. My mother got her job back in Methodist Girls High School. The expatriate principal, Mrs Walker, had been searching for her and was overjoyed to see that she had survived the war. My father got his job back in Lagos University Teaching Hospital (LUTH) where he had been a foundation staff. The only thing was that he had to resume in the same position that he held in 1966, so the people he employed were now his seniors, but then, it did not matter. He was just grateful to be alive, and to be able to cater for his family. In June, we went back to Lagos. Of course, there was nothing like Corona School anymore. We went to Ladi Lak Institute which was a public school. I hated it. I was moved to Class Four. However, I coped. We all did.

About the Author
Agu Imo is from Item in Abia State. He is a Lawyer and runs a practice in Lagos. Agu is married with children

SURVIVING THE CIVIL WAR

By Arthur Harris-Eze

LAGOS 1966

My first contact with Nigeria at the age of 5 was a trip down the ramp of a British Overseas Airways Corporation aircraft. Of course, I have no recollection of the date or month of the trip from London. Why this event remains with me, I can only ascribe to Psychology. I say this because I am unable to remember something as basic as the time of day. All that remains is the image of my mother frantically trying and failing to keep her only child in check. We came home to be with my dad who had returned months earlier by sea and enrolled at the Nigerian Law School. I believe we headed back to the Law School hostels - the present Air Force Barracks on Ahmadu Bello Way, Victoria Island, Lagos - opposite the Federal Palace Hotel.

I was enrolled in a school somewhere in Ikoyi. My paternal aunt and her family lived in Ikoyi, within a short bicycle ride to the school. It was therefore convenient for me to live with them during the week. This suited me perfectly because there were other kids to play with as my cousins were young, and I preferred being ferried to school on a bicycle to making the same trip in the comfort of a car. My aunt, a perfect cook, doted on me, so there was no end to the flow of cakes and pastries. Weekends were lovely as then, I had the full attention of my parents and we could be seen zipping around Lagos from one relation to the other. Sometimes we were on the beach or in one shop or the other. For a while we lived there without any issue until things started getting funny. Some of our neighbours had their flats broken into at night and the men were taken away. I do remember that day because I was at home with my mother. She kept moving the curtains aside and peeping out. My recollection of that day is that our houseboy, who was not Igbo was never around when my dad left for school. But surprisingly, she saw him in the midst of some soldiers pointing at our flat. When my dad got back, she insisted we stop sleeping in the flat. From then on, every night, we had to go to Surulere to pass the night. It continued that way until the day when in the company of several other families, we left Lagos by road to Awka, in the wee hours of the morning.

Awka

At Awka my life revolved around my numerous cousins, some older and others younger, my mum and my two grandmothers. Both grandfathers were already late. My cousins comprised those who were resident in Awka and the cousins I had been staying with in Lagos. My aunt continued to bake and cook for "my pleasure." I was the cynosure of all eyes and the recipient of love from every side. It was a very large house with all the modern facilities. In addition, there was an outside kitchen which was always smoky because firewood was used to cook. At the time, my main abode was my family house at Umudioka which holds magical and beautiful memories for me, and which is a place I call home to this day. Occasionally, I stayed with my cousins where the culinary availabilities were second to none.

Day to day life consisted of waking up, getting bathed, eating, and playing till the next meal. The compound was spacious and there was always something going on. There were numerous trees, and snakes were prevalent. Other "wild" animals were of the grasscutter family (eyi in Igbo). Some of my cousins were ardent "hunters" and knowledgeable in setting traps. Some of these animals had several burrows in the earth. As a matter of practice each of the occupants of these holes ensured that they had a minimum of two holes to ensure a quick getaway when threatened, with a number of tunnels connecting the holes. On one occasion, my older cousin, Ben Ndigwe, and I happened upon a newly dug burrow. We proceeded to locate the escape burrow and blocked it with stones and leaves. Thereafter, we set up a trap in front of the other hole. We got a metal cylindrical can, pierced several holes in the bottom and filled it with lumps of charcoal. We then lit a fire in the can. Thereafter, we proceeded to the other hole, removed the stones, and leaves and placed the can in the hole, with the bottom in the hole. The idea was to smoke out the eyi through the other hole and into the trap. When nothing happened, my cousin blew into the fire so that more smoke could go into the burrow. Surprisingly, there was a "return fire." Something within the burrow was also blowing smoke at us. My cousin said from his experience, only snakes reacted this way. This was happening late in the evening and with daylight fading, we left the scene.

The next morning at first light of day, we proceeded to check our trap. Lo and behold there was a big snake caught in the trap and struggling violently. At the sight of this our bravado left us. We ran and got my grandmother. She came and killed the snake. That was my last attempt at 'hunting'.

For some reason, I was prone to nose bleeds most times I was at play with my friends. For this reason, my grandmother was always watching out. She would call out to me when things started to get rough. If I hesitated or refused to end the play, she would seize me and throw me between her laps and cross her legs, using them as a vise. This vise-like position is known as *ipa* in Igbo. It is akin to being placed in a cell. Worse still, you occupy a ringside position and watch your mates at play. I avoided my grandma for this and our relationship was never good. The reverse was the case with my maternal grandmother. She was totally enthralled with me. She said she was an only child and considered me her "younger brother." With her it was play time all day long!

On the day we had to leave Awka, I remember it was late in the afternoon. My mum was cooking, and so my maternal grand mum strapped him on her back to go for a walk. Our compound has its gate on the major road, and an approach through a twenty-meter drive down a 45-degree incline. The compound opens up at the end of the drive to the left and to the right. This meant that the road was hardly visible from the compound. As my grand mum and my brother were walking up the driveway, she saw that there was some commotion. Half of the town was streaming to her left while the other half were moving in the other direction. She ran back, shouting that my mum should abandon what she was doing and pack up to leave the town. Apparently, the Nigerian soldiers were almost in Awka.

My mother's Volkswagen car was in the compound, but she was still learning to drive. Her brother, my uncle and driving instructor Okey, lived away from us. While my mum pondered what to do, Uncle Okey arrived. We all got into the car, dropped my grandma at her house, and proceeded to my aunt's house at Umuokpu Awka. My paternal grandma was on hospital admission somewhere outside Awka. My dad was trying to set up at Port Harcourt and was yet to get a place for us. He was living with his younger brother, uncle Agwuna. At my aunt's place, the only car available was my mother's Volkswagen which could not take everyone. My cousins lifted baskets, packed clothes, and other personal items they were able to take, put the baskets on their heads, and headed out in the direction of Onitsha by foot. In the confusion, I forgot my mother and went with my cousins on the long trek to Onitsha!

It was late evening. We trudged in the company of thousands of people on foot, passing Nawfia Town, and stopping for the night before Oba Nwandu's house at Enugwu Ukwu. There were no mats or blankets to spread on the floor, so we used some cloths from the baskets to cover ourselves as no one was willing to share theirs. It was a dry but chilly night. While we were on the trek, my mother was frantically searching for me amongst the crowd – a near impossible feat considering the number of persons trekking. She was not successful. The next morning, before daylight, a car stopped to ask about the situation at Awka, and behold, it was my dad. People told him that everyone had left, so he took me and we headed over to pick his mother from the hospital. Through word of mouth we were later able to trace my mum to Ogidi.

I have no recollection of our stay at Ogidi as it was a very short stay. This is understandable as Ogidi is just about 20 Kilometres from Awka. Having occupied Awka, it would have been only a matter of hours/days for the Nigerian army to get to Ogidi.

Port Harcourt

I have very fond memories of our time in Port Harcourt. It was here on 8th of March 1967 that my immediate younger brother, Benedict Onyeka Harris-Eze, Mbalaugulu Awka, was born. Second, I was able to go back to school. Here at Port Harcourt, there were a number of kids my age living in the other flats above and below us. Their parents shared the duty of dropping us off at school. The couple living below us also took part in taking us to school. They had this habit of bathing together, and while bathing, they left the bathroom door open and we kids were allowed to go in and talk to them fully unclothed! This was quite appealing to us and we always got ready earlier than usual whenever it was the couple's turn to take us to school. It was a wonder our parents never found out the reason we were so eager to finish breakfast and rush down.

At some point, we moved into an estate at Borokiri. The estate consisted of only bungalows. Life was fun as there were many more houses, therefore more neighbours than in our former block of flats which was situated somewhere in the centre of town. Borokiri was at one end of Port Harcourt, after which was the sea!

We woke up every morning to the chimes of the BBC. Then the voice of a man we later came to know as Mr. Okokon Ndem would come on. Listening to the man brought joy to the hearts of the adults, as he relayed the gallantry and triumphs of the Biafran soldiers at the war front from the comfort of his office. My mother who trained as a Secretary in the United Kingdom arranged to teach anyone willing to learn, how to type. This was to keep people occupied. Much as she tried, I never showed any interest. This lost opportunity irks me to this day.

Very often, we would hear a long siren, and this would send everyone scurrying from their houses to the back where a number of pits had been dug as bunkers to hide inside to be "safe" from bombs. The siren sounded whenever enemy planes were in the area. These bunkers were covered with palm fronds and other vegetation as camouflage. The idea was to confuse the pilots into thinking that they were flying over an uninhabited forest. It worked, and there were relatively very few incidents of bombing in the area. As the bunkers were only a few metres away from houses, people would run to them every time the sirens sounded. Often, people jumped in without looking, only to be met with the presence of one animal or the other taking refuge in the pit – snakes, lizards and rats were quite common co-occupants. At this stage, one had to choose the risk of shrapnel or a snake bite. Whether or not people were bitten was perhaps either down to pure luck, or maybe a function of the animals' attitude to the intruders on the day.

It was also here in Borokiri that I witnessed first-hand the sheer cruelty of which people are capable. In the estate, there was a family who had a young girl, not much older than us, as a househelp. Their kids were always perfectly turned out and were never given any chores to do. They were privileged, spoilt and untouchable. The house girl was a totally different matter. Each day the mother of the house meted out the most inhuman punishments to her. Whenever she offended the lady, she was stripped naked and red pepper was introduced into her eyes and private parts. The girl would scream and run out of the house into any available neighbour's house. This almost blinded the child as a permanent redness developed in both her eyes.

One pastime we engaged in while in Port Harcourt was boiling sea water dry to get salt. Salt was a scarce commodity at the time. Even then one could hardly get much salt from boiling buckets and buckets of Port Harcourt sea water. Whatever little was achieved went a long way to improve the taste of meals. So also, was the quest for body oils for women. Traditionally the Palm kernel oil was very dark – near black – in colour. It also had a strong smell, which was not very pleasant. In place of this, women used coconut oil. A number of coconuts would be cracked open and the fruit extracted from the hard shell. The fruit was grated into pulp and the milk extracted. The milk was then used to prepare coconut rice or some baked pastry, while the remaining chaff was boiled with water for a while. At a certain temperature, a light brown film of oil would rise to the surface. This would be scooped by spoon until it stopped appearing. This was either added to a lotion or used as it was as a body cream.

Umuobasi (near Aba)

How we got here I do not remember. Here at Umuobasi, I was with my maternal aunt and her family. My Dad had joined the Biafran Army. My major recollection of life here was that I was so sickly that many doubted I would recover. I was rake thin since everything I ate, I threw right back up. Occasionally I would be able to get something down, but excessive play still played on my weight. One thing I do remember was the fear we had of the community. Word had gone round that children had to mind how they moved about as kidnappings and killing of people for food were not unheard of in the area.

Once a man with a cutlass chased us while we were plucking ripened palm fruits from a tree on his farm. From Umuobasi, we moved to Alor to join my maternal grandma.

Alor

Prior to the war, my maternal grandpa owned commercial property along the popular Williams and Bright Streets in Onitsha. My Grandma was also successful in business, dealing mostly in the women's wrapper fabric called abada. It was one of their tenants, Mr. Willy Oyeka, that granted us accommodation. His compound was large and comprised a number of bungalows. Our host was polygamous and had built bungalows for each of his wives and their children. But for the fact that a war was raging, a visitor would have been fooled into believing that life was normal. Day to day activities carried on oblivious of what was going on in most eastern towns. Commercial activities were also in full swing. Markets were in session. I remember the market as a place we young ones hardly went because there were a number of very tall Breadfruit (Ukwa) trees at the approach. The Ukwa tree produces a very large round spiky fruit the size of two basketballs. These hung menacingly from great heights. As they reached their maturity, on windy days, they just dropped to the ground. Each of these fruits weighed about 30 kilograms or more. Within the short period we resided at Alor someone was unfortunate to have been standing under a dropping fruit. It killed the person instantly. It was therefore, a no-go area for us. The fear was such that no amount of truancy or rascality or stubbornness would take us to the area. Apart from that, we were privileged and carried on life as if we were natives. The Oyeka family were the most hospitable hosts. Our relationship has remained as strong as ever to this day, and I ended up attending the same university with one of the children.

I remember Pa Oyeka vividly. He was of a big frame and had quite a girth, a jollier fellow you could not find. He was a kid at heart, nice to a fault, and a father to everyone. His business in Onitsha could not go on as Onitsha was at the centre of the conflict. He quickly adjusted from his daily trips to his shops to a new life that revolved around farming. He could constantly be seen in his large shorts, shirtless, going to his farm, checking the large concrete water reservoir in the compound, or sitting in the shade of a tree drinking palm wine.

Three incidents are indelibly etched in my memory of our stay there. One morning there was some commotion in the compound around our bungalow. As I came out, I saw a crowd cowering in a corner and pointing to the front of the house. There, fully coiled, was a large and very colourful snake. On hearing the commotion Pa Oyeka came out. Seeing the snake, he started talking to it. He even called out to people to come and stroke it. He then casually, with the assistance of some other men, lifted it out of the compound and into the surrounding vegetation.

We were later told that the snake was a Royal Python. Generally harmless to humans. Its food consisted mainly of poultry and eggs. Folklore had it that it visited whenever there was a new baby in a family. This I never witnessed. For this reason, Alor Community were forbidden from harming, killing or eating the python. This is the case for most Communities in Idemilli and environs. It should be noted that the observance of this custom cuts across the entire community irrespective of the Faith professed. Unfortunately, once in a while a python is killed as most refugee elements whose communities did not have this restriction killed the python for food or out of fear that the python would harm them. This was sacrilegious and huge penalties were exerted. The killer was expected to fully mourn and bury the python as if it were human! This practice exists in all these communities till today.

The second incident involved my mum's youngest sibling, Aunty Theresa, called Aunty Tee by everyone. We had all retired to bed, and it must have been around midnight. Aunty Tee had suffered a bout of measles and was losing her sight. We were all in the room sleeping. My grandma and Aunty Tee were on the bed, while I was on a mattress on the floor. Suddenly, Aunty Tee let out a terrifying scream. We scurried up to find out what the problem was. There was no electricity, so we lit the mpanaka, a palm oil lamp, which was made from a little can with a hole in the top, through which a woollen thread protruded. The fuel for this lantern was palm oil, and it produced a lot of black smoke.

Back to Aunty Theresa. While sleeping, she had felt something crawling on her night dress in the tummy area. When she touched it, it stung her, hence the screaming. By this time, our neighbours had arrived at our house. Aunty Tee's finger had started to swell up. One of the men said it was a scorpion that stung her. He got a thread, tied it at the base of the finger, got a sharp knife and inserted it in the flame of the lamp. Then he cut open the swelling part of the finger and sucked up the blood, which he spat out. All attempts to locate the culprit which she flung away were unsuccessful, as the lamp was hardly able to illuminate the room. Days later, as my mum was trying to sew on her Singer sewing machine, there was Mr. Scorpion, tail erect, and waiting for his next victim. He was inside the needle box attached to the machine.

The third incident had to do with me. On a bright sunny day, I was out and about around the water reservoir. There were a couple of coconut trees around and some were fruiting. As I was contemplating how to harvest one or two, I felt a very painful sharp sting on my ear. I never saw what it was that caused the pain. I ran all the way to the house shouting, crying, and holding my ear. Within minutes the ear was swollen and extremely painful. The same "doctor" who attended to my aunt's finger procured some leaves and rubbing them together, applied the sap to the sting area. In time the pain subsided. I was never found around the coconut trees again till we moved on from Alor.

One special day, a truckload of Biafran officers and soldiers pulled up to our compound. There was some apprehension from the occupants of the compound as to the soldiers' mission that morning. When the door of the truck opened and the soldiers alighted, we were delighted to see my maternal uncle, Lawrence Adigwe, who enroute to an officers meeting decided to make a detour and visit his mum. They were very well turned-out, smart in their crisp army uniforms. Although the war never got to Alor and the community was never routed, we had to move to Ihioma in Orlu province as my mum had secured an appointment as Secretary to His Lordship, Bishop Godfrey Mary Paul Okoye, the Catholic Bishop of Port Harcourt.

Ihioma, Orlu

CARITAS *(Latin for 'Love for All')* is the worldwide Catholic organisation that works to assist the poor and vulnerable through the Catholic Relief Services. They offer their services especially in war-torn areas. They were in Biafra to help. The official head for the Biafran effort was Bishop Okoye. Caritas was based at Ihioma where they had a large church and ample space for the tons of aid they received from abroad. As the Secretary to the Bishop and head of CARITAS, my mum had to live at Ihioma, which explained our move away from the comfort of Alor and the kindness of Mr. Willy Oyeka's family and the Alor Community.

Our stay at Ihioma was short but eventful. Each morning, my mum walked the short distance to the Cathedral where she had her office. In keeping with tradition, the Cathedral grounds were very large with sufficient parking for over a hundred lorries. These lorries were beautifully adorned with all sorts of art works. They had names like "I believe In God," "Ave Maria" etc. Over time we started making songs out of their names.

The Biafran Airport was at Uli Town, a distance of about 50 kilometres from Ihioma. Supplies from abroad consisted mostly of food items - dry food in sacks like egg yolk, corn meal and powdered milk. There were also tinned foods – sardines and corned beef as well as stock fish. Their distribution was handled by the Catholic Relief Services. Lorry loads of food were sent to various communities throughout the enclave to stem the hunger, death, and disease.

Staff of Caritas were given allocations. By virtue of my mum's position we received a sizeable allocation which we were able to share with our neighbours and relations. My favourites were the egg yolk and powdered milk. The sardines came in golden oval cans and apart from being a great source of protein, when the cans were empty, we made toy cars out of them as well.

Children were able to get some education, as the church utilised the empty schools. Students' desks consisted of four sandcrete blocks for each student. The table was made out of two blocks horizontally placed apart from each other and a third laid out flat on top of the two blocks. The fourth block was placed flat on the floor behind the 'desk'.

From time to time, two of my cousins who were in the Biafran Air Force, Ken Chinweze and Patrick Uyanwune, visited from where they were posted as signal officers. Often, they tried to tutor me too.

There was neither electricity nor running water. We fetched water from the stream which was a tributary of the great Orashi River. Access to the stream was via a steep 45-degree incline composed of clay soil. Over the years, little dimples - foot holds - formed in the soil. It was a common sight to see girls and boys slip, lose their balance, and topple with their earthenware pots. There were a lot of trees hanging over the path to and over the river. Once, a large branch broke off and landed on a young girl shattering her skull, she died on the spot. It was a very sad day in the town.

Children climbed up trees and jumped into the river from great heights. My dear cousin, Ogechukwu, was a champion at this. She was fearless. She swam like a fish, defying the strong currents of the Orashi River. My cousin, Dilibe (Dee) and yours truly were "chicken." We could not swim and were not ready to learn or even dip our feet in water!

While at Ihioma, my sight started deteriorating. I was unable to see in the dark. It was the same for my Aunty Theresa who was now almost blind from the measles she had suffered earlier. My British Nanny and her husband, Mr. & Mrs. Stace of Kent, United Kingdom, who I lived with almost from birth till the day I left the UK for Nigeria were calling for my return to London. Apparently, they were reading about and watching the humanitarian disaster going on in the country. Through her office, my mum sought to fly my aunt and I to London on one of the Caritas planes. Her boss and head of Caritas Mission asked that medical reports certifying the state of our eye sights be obtained before he could approve.

Unfortunately, we were unable to get the reports, and so unable to undertake the journey. In due course, my aunt became totally blind. In my case, my night vision was totally extinguished.

On my way from school one day, as I was passing a charcoal depot, I noticed some stray lumps of charcoal on the path. I bent and picked a few pieces of charcoal which had rolled out of the compound onto the path. I thought they would be useful for my cousin who sold cigarettes by the stick. The practice was that the cigarette seller would also have a ready source of light for customers who could light up immediately after their purchase. This was usually a can, whose sides and bottom would be pierced for ventilation. Lumps of charcoal were then thrown into the can, and a sling handle added to the can. The sling handle was used to swing the can in circles to ignite the coal and keep the fire lit most of the day.

As I was picking the charcoal and tossing them into my bag someone from inside the compound started shouting "thief, thief!" They beckoned on me, and I went inside the compound which was more of a material dumping yard. When I got in they accused me of stealing charcoal. I tried to explain why I needed the coal, but they would not listen. They demanded that my parents had to come and bail me out. At this stage, my friends who were with me from school ran home to call my grandma. Moments later I heard my grandma's voice asking, "Where is the thief?" She met the workers who were detaining me and they told her what happened. My grandma gently chastised them, explaining that the lumps of coal I took were a negligible quantity and had been picked outside their compound. I had not gone into the compound to take from the mounds of coal that stood in heaps over there. The workers apologised and released me.

Another notable experience at Ihioma was a funeral we attended. At the time, unlike today, the death of anyone was a very solemn and scary event for the young. Several customs and practices were observed. The person's photographs were put face down or rearranged to face the wall. Children were not allowed to see the dead body, etc. This funeral, which was held in an open field was open to all. They brought the coffin into the arena and placed on two benches. There were speeches etc. The highlight of the event was when the pall bearers lifted the coffin and started dancing with it. They were tossing it in the air and catching it. It was a new experience for most adults who were used to treating the dead with a lot of reverence in their own communities.

It was not all sadness. Once in a while, we had some joyful moments. The high point of these was my Uncle Ifeanyi's wedding at Umuchima in the same Orlu area. Umuchima was just 10 kilometres away. Most of the Adigwes - my mum's family, were within a ten kilometre radius of Ihioma. Umuchima also had quite a number of Awka families residing there – the Chinwezes, Uyanwunes, Ndigwes were all resident there. The wedding was therefore a huge event. There was a big church wedding followed by a massive reception that spilled out of the church hall unto the surrounding field. People defied the air raids and menacing heat. There were no canopies, and the sun was merciless. At the time, of all my maternal aunts and uncles, only the first, Mrs. Kambili Chinweze, and my Mum, were married and had children. There was Kenneth, a Biafran Airforce Officer, Ogechukwu, and Dilibe Chinweze. On my mum's side were Onyeka, two years old, and my good self eight years at the time. My main buddy was Dilibe who was a whopping 365 days my junior in age. Dee and I were assigned the duty of ferrying the food in a Peugeot 404 pick-up, from where the food was being prepared to the reception venue. There were all sorts of foods and in great quantities. We ferried fried beef, puff puff, a local fried delicacy made out of batter, garri, and different types of soup, rice and chicken that were hardly to be found on most family menus during the war. It was a harvest of unquantifiable proportions, fit only for a king. Dee and I ate so much that it was a wonder the food was able to go round. To this day, we still reminisce about this particularly happy time for us.

The turnout was good, and people brought out their best clothes and were only happy to have the opportunity to display them. My three maternal uncles, Ifeanyi (the groom, Lawrence (a Biafran Officer) and Charles were resplendent in suits. The groom and Charles were financially very comfortable and owned cars – a Zephyr 4. The wedding is talked about to this day.

One afternoon, while most people were at work or on the farm, news started filtering into the compound that the capture of the town was imminent. Within hours, people had started packing up and headed out of town toward Owerri Town, a distance of about forty eight kilometers. My mum was at work, and at home were my grandma, my aunt, my cousin, the cigarette seller, and myself. There was no way to communicate with my mum. Someone had to physically go to her office. Seeing the commotion going on and remembering how I got "missing" for twelve hours at Awka, my grandma chose to wait. She said my mum must have heard and may be planning for transportation. As there was no one able to drive it, the Volkswagen that took us out of Awka had been given out to one of my uncles, who lived quite a distance away.

In due course, mum appeared with a car from Caritas, and loaded our already packed items. We headed for Owerri where the new Caritas Head office would be located.

Owerri

The office was moved to Assumpta Cathedral, (Control) Owerri. Two reasons would have justified this choice of location. First, it was the official residence of the Bishop of Owerri Diocese, and appropriate for the head of mission who was a Bishop. Second, like the Church at Ihioma, the Cathedral had ample parking space for the lorries used to collect and ferry relief materials from Uli airport to the various delivery towns.

At Owerri we were only able to secure sleeping space on the upper landing at the back of the church in the choir stand. There were about ten families sprawled out on the floor. Apart from the discomfort of accommodation I remember nothing of note about our stay.

We were here for a few days before Owerri had to be evacuated too as the Nigerian soldiers had stormed Owerri's environs. We headed for Okija, forty two kilometres away. I do not recall how these destinations were chosen. However, one can hazard a few guesses.

Ogidi was not really a destination. It was merely a stop to catch our breath and plan as the departure was sudden. Other areas had to do with relations and friends going in those directions.

Okija

Our stay here was short and memorable. Our chief memory of Okija was the birth of my cousin, the indefatigable Augustine Nkemakonam Udoka (Peace is greatest – named by my maternal grandma) Adigwe, Mgbologwu Awka, on 15th February 1970. A few weeks afterward, we headed back with the new addition to the family.

Back Home To Awka

Early in the year after the birth of my cousin, the family headed back to our hometown, Awka. At this time, all Biafran soldiers, rank and file as well as officers had disposed of their accoutrement of war– uniforms and armaments. Most buried theirs, while others tossed them into rivers. History was therefore obliterated in this wave of fear.

The first shock that we met was a town empty of houses. Most homes had been razed – some by fire, others by demolition on account of the heavy bombardment from shelling and mortars. Having been with my maternal grandma and aunts throughout the war period, I went home with them. Their house was also razed by fire. My grandma went straight to a corner of the compound and started digging. Minutes later, she dug up a small sack of money in coins. Before the war she had been Treasurer to the church. This cache of money belonged to the church and had been in her possession by virtue of her being the Treasurer. The money was intact, and at the earliest opportunity she handed it back. Unfortunately, her personal cache of coins though she found it, had been burnt by the shelling which also razed the family house. We spent several days brushing and scraping with sand to bring them to an exchangeable state. At my own home at Umudioka, we found no house standing. When my dad got back from the war, he initially had to stay with relatives before leaving for Lagos in search of employment.

In the early days immediately after the war, there were no schools. Our days as kids were spent at the Government Trade Centre (GTC) in Awka, now the Federal Science and Technical College, playing with soldiers. Various ranking Nigerian Soldiers were camped out on the field in shanties made out of aluminium zinc roofing materials. The soldiers were mostly Northerners and Muslims. They were friendly however, and courteous to the community, elders, and children. This must have rubbed off from their Boss, Major Muhammadu Buhari, who displayed exceptional humanity and respect for both Municipal and International Law with regards to his prosecution of the war as it related to his Command.

We were told that when most Awka families fled Awka in 1967, a number of people remained, either because they refused to leave, or were unable to leave. These were mostly elderly people - the very old and frail who did not want to be obstacles to their families' quest for safety. There were also young people too, who had stayed back to take care of them. There was another group who stayed back, and these were the stubborn and egoistic older but strong men who saw no reason to run from their homesteads. Finally, there were those who were ill and physically challenged.

These people all remained in their homes within the town. When the Nigerian Army captured Awka, under the command of Major Muhammadu Buhari, they set up camps on the grounds of St. Paul's School, and across the road at GTC. Major Buhari brought out all persons found to have remained behind and camped all of them at St. Paul's. He fed, clothed, and took care of them. As time went on, he started paying them stipends. He finally encouraged those with skills or occupations to carry on with their trade – hunters, palm wine tappers, carpenters etc. resumed their businesses under the supervision of the Nigerian Army. While in the camp, some invariably died either of natural causes, or from complications of pre-existing conditions.

Many, however, survived and were reunited with their families. Amongst the survivors were Mbiko Okoye (Ozo Dugbo) of Umumbele Village, Molokwu (Otochalu Umumbele), the oldest man in Umumbele Village, Nne Nwambiko and her daughter also of Umumbele Village, Awka, and Okeke Nwaoma, Otochalu Awka (oldest Awka man before the war).

About the Author

Arthur Harris-Eze is from Umudioka, Awka, Anambra State. He is a Lawyer, and a Curator of Awka history.

Having retired after a career in Corporate Law and Arbitration with Agip, he now spends his time on his fish farm in Awka and at The Awka Museum, which he helped found. He is married with children.

WE FOUND A COMMON CAUSE

By Geraldine Akpet-Ekanem

By 1967, my parents having returned from studying in the United Kingdom, worked at the University of Nigeria, Nsukka. While my father, an Engineer, Samuel Missang Obaji Akpet, was a Lecturer in the Department of Engineering, Faculty of Environmental Design, my mother, Mrs. Mary Anne Akpet, was the Housekeeper, Continuing Education Centre (CEC), Nsukka.

One day in 1966 my father got a call from Kaduna to pick the family of his elder brother, Captain Akpet Obaji Akpet of the Nigerian Army, from the train station at Enugu. The caller told him that his brother was involved in the 1966 coup, and had been called out and shot at the Army Officer's Mess, Kaduna. My dad changed overnight, and became moody and sad; all his thoughts were focused on avenging his brother's death. So, in 1967 when the war was beginning, he enlisted as a volunteer in his thirst to avenge his brother's death. Papa was made a Colonel of II Division, Nnewi. (I think he was placed in charge of II Division at a point). All around us, there was so much talk of the war. My mother and our neighbour, Mrs. Okonjo-Iweala, used to discuss, imagine and laugh about when, how, and if Ndi Hausa (as the Federal troops were called) would invade Nsukka. Would there be captives? Who would be killed?

Then came news that the Nigerian army was advancing toward Nsukka. There was a hurried evacuation immediately. No one knew what to take. In the panic, people picked up the wrong things and stuffed into boxes. For instance, instead of originals, some took photocopies of documents. In the panic, people hardly remembered where anything was. Throughout my school years, my baptismal certificate was my proof of age; we left the actual certificate in Nsukka. For my parents, their employment after the war was effected with photocopies of credentials and on self-recognizance. So it was also for several UNN employees after the war.

While people were leaving Nsukka, they saw the "darling boys" of UNN, like Chris Okigbo, at Opi Junction. My dad said everyone who passed the junction on their way out stopped and pleaded with them to leave with the rest of the evacuees. Their response was always that Nsukka would fall only over their dead bodies. That they would rather die defending this territory and sadly, so it happened. They were among the first casualties of the war. My father, Colonel Akpet, or "Colonel Akpati" as he was fondly called by the Igbos, played an active role in the civil war. He was a combatant. I remember once when he returned to one of the places we were staying with wounds on his back. He told us how he was seriously pursued by an armoured tank and kept rolling on the ground and almost got killed, but managed to escape.

For some reason best known to him, we did not live with him in the barracks with the children of the other officers nor did we get airlifted out of Biafra. Rather, we travelled the circuit of Biafra, although we were always under discreet cover, protected by a few soldiers, his "boys." As the war progressed, so did we, moving from place to place ahead of his regiment but usually accommodated in nearby villages. We went the whole circuit – Umuahia, Owerri, Ukana Iba, Ikot Ekpene, Abak, Awka Etiti and finally Ezinifite where we were when the war ended. Movements were always sudden, sometimes within hours or minutes. I remember that on one occasion, my late younger brother, Sam Akpet Jnr, who was two or three years old at the time, dressed in his miniature Colonel's uniform with his wooden rifle, and went out in the open to shoot at the sky during an air raid when everyone was running for cover. My mom almost went berserk - her only son that she almost died giving birth to in July 1966! Provision though, was always made for us to hide out during raids as everyone had to leave the house and take cover. Air raids mostly targeted buildings for strafing and bombing.

We used to visit the barracks when we could, and enrolled in any school that was on at the time wherever we found ourselves. We were constantly changing schools and learning funny songs like "Gowon, Gowon *oji ngwele esi ofe.*" I recall my older sister, Cornelia Akpet, and Cousin, Ifumi Akpet, (now Njor) who were boarding at Ifuho-Ikot Ekpene at a time. My sister at one time got admitted into secondary school with her friend, Ifeyinwa Ikedife, whose mother, Aunty Hope Ulasi, was an air hostess with the then Biafran Airways, and who was put in my mother's care. Aunty Hope used to fly to Gabon and Ivory Coast, and would bring us clothes, so we remained well dressed throughout the war. We were also well fed. My father used to bring bags of oats, egg yolk, milk etc. All university staff continued to receive their salaries. My mum was collecting her salary and my father's own as well, while he collected his salary as a soldier. I used to take milk a lot with cracked palm kernels that I put in a bottle with salted water and would take to school for my classmates and friends. We had milk in abundance – take as much as you want.

Sometimes my older siblings and relatives attended day parties when they could. I remember them missing one party as we suddenly changed location on the day it was to be held. My mother's younger sister was so upset and really lamented over the missed party with little or no regard for her safety. Later, she was teased incessantly by other relatives. Maybe because my father was always moving us ahead, we must have taken some things for granted.

However, we still had to run for cover whenever we saw planes in the sky, though we remained fervent in the fight and positive minded. Maybe, it was due to my dad's active involvement at the warfront driven by his thirst to avenge his brother's mindless killing that we all stayed focused. We always saw him briefly in the midst of soldiers discussing the war fervently: its cause, and how it had to be won against all odds, despite the hard times and the blatant disregard of Ndi Hausa for the easterners. I remember, when 11 Div fell, Patrick and Broderick, our drivers, composed the song "eleven Div *agbasa go*" and I recall all of us singing and dancing, while driving out of the location. Maybe that is where I got my sense of humour and resilience from - great aids to survive hard times. Sometimes though, that hardiness is misread as stubbornness.

We moved to Ezinifite. At Ezinifite, we stayed in the compound of Chief Nnodu Okoye, father of Chief Leo Ike Okoye. Chief Nnodu Okoye handed over Chief Leo Ike Okoye, who was less than 20 years old then, to my dad. He pleaded with my father to ensure that his son remained alive seeing that he was the first son and too young for the warfront. Since conscription was compulsory, there were so many young boys around my father whom he protected. And that was how several enduring relationships were forged.

The mood at this point in time was uncertain as the Federal troops had advanced deep into the east. While some Biafrans were tired, a few were willing to continue but a general exhaustion was certainly in the air. The future had become uncertain, so we were preparing for the worst. Ojukwu who had a never-say-die spirit left for the Ivory Coast presumably for reinforcements.

While in Ezinifite, my cousin, Ifumi, and I saw soldiers passing by in their numbers, and we wondered why. Not long after, Major General Phillip Effiong came to the house seriously shaken and asking for "madam", that is my mum, in panic. She met him and asked what was wrong while trying to calm him down. Effiong told her the war was over. He removed his Biafran uniform and my mother gave him my father's shirt and trousers to wear, then he left. My father returned, and my mum told him what had happened. He also left. Later we heard of the Biafran surrender. Finally, the war was over. The people of Biafra had surrendered to the Federal troops. My dad was one of the very last ones to remove and bury his uniform.

The Aftermath

We returned to our hometown, Ikom, in Cross River State in a hired gwongworo (lorry) that was sent to us by my father's cousin in Ikom, Chief William Imo

Okim. I have often wondered who my dad sent to Chief Okim to arrange transport for us. Anyway, dad always thought ahead, that was his way. At a point, we no longer knew my father's whereabouts. So we stayed in a room in Chief Okim's house. While my mother's sister, Sister Akara, went home to Effraya to see her mother, my father's cousin, Aunty Enegbe, ran back to Aba to her Igbo boyfriend, a musician, whom she ended up marrying. My father's brother, Uncle Mgbe, went back to the village. The future was bleak, and my mum would make moi moi that we would sell at night with bread, which I did innocently and happily. Then a month later, my dad resurfaced to say that the Biafran officers were quarantined by the Nigerian Army, debriefed, and released in batches. While the civilians were released, some of the career officers were reabsorbed into the Nigerian Army, Air Force or Navy at the rank they were in 1967, and suffered a lot of stigmatization. I recall in 1981 when my dad and I visited Lagos and stayed with one of them, Wing Cmdr. Ita Ikpeme of the Nigerian Air Force, one of those officers visited and was scared to discuss the war. He did not want any mention of his involvement in the war for fear of further stigmatization as they had suffered a lot and been passed over for promotion.

My dad told me that he came face to face with Obasanjo during debriefing. While signing his discharge card, Obasanjo asked him if he knew one Late Major

Akpet. My father replied that the man was his elder brother and that his execution was the reason he enlisted and fought in the war. Because he was largely seen as a traitor by his people for fighting on the Biafran side, my dad had to prove himself after the war by starting work afresh in the Cross River State Ministry of Works. He left the UNN lecturing job.

Sometimes I wonder how it might have been had he gone back to Nsukka or if his brother had not been killed, seeing that his contemporaries were Obasanjo, Wushishi, Danjuma etc. Would I have remained amongst the Igbos in Igboland or lived outside Cross River State? Would I have had better opportunities?

Federal troops commandeered my father's car, a red 404 Peugeot Saloon, after the war. My father, who had driven this car since 1964 and throughout the war, came back without it. Luckily for us, the car was later found abandoned somewhere in Ikot Ekpene, and so we recovered it. The federal troops also took over my grandfather's house in my village, Okuni-Ikom, during the war. We heard that they so terrorized my uncles because my father was fighting on the Biafran side, that one of his cousins out of fear dropped "Akpet" from his name.

I also recall my father telling us about the stupidity of believing in African Juju. Once, a few Biafran officers hid up in the hills to watch the advancing Federal troops to assess their strength. To their amazement and amusement, the troops were led by a female native doctor. Had they enough ammunition, they would have successfully erased the whole regiment.

I got some mileage from my father's war experiences, and the lasting friendships he made during the war. He had so many friends – Profs. Nwogugu and Ezejiofor, Nduka Eya, Sam Nwoye, Ebitu Ukiwe, Emeka Omeruah, Nwowo, Eze Peter Okpoko, Chief Ekenedilichukwu, Assam Assam, Anietie Okon, Leo Ike Okoye, Brown Okeiyi, Goddy Oputah etc. The younger ones, he referred to as "his boys". Throughout my stay as a Law student at the University of Nigeria, Enugu campus, it was home away from home with Chief Nduka Eya and his warm wife, Prof. Regina Eya, as my guardians. Barrister Goddy Oputah was friend to my mom's secretary, Mr. Brown Okeiyi, of CEC. These were all brave men who fought for the cause and survived the war. They always recognized and appreciated my dad's sacrifice and contributions. His experiences endeared me to the Igbos who till tomorrow have accepted me as one of themselves. Those days were difficult and dangerous, but the experience was interesting and has helped shape my life and charted a different course for all of us.

I also recall an incident that occurred in 1970 at Ogoja where my father worked immediately after the war. After the war, most of the ex-Biafran soldiers had gone back to school to catch up. Quite a number of them enrolled at Mary Knoll College, Okuku-Ogoja,

Cross River State. While out in the evening, they had an altercation with some Nigerian soldiers who goaded and taunted them. About two or three of them who were involved and unarmed, beat up the soldiers who were about fifteen in number and ran to our house to hide. My dad went to the barracks the following morning to resolve the issue. The commanding officer said he was embarrassed that his men who outnumbered the ex-Biafran soldiers could be dealt with to that extent. He had put the soldiers involved in the guardroom. My father was so proud of his boys, and jokingly told the officer in charge of the barracks at Ogoja that this was the caliber of soldiers who fought on the Biafran side with little or no ammunition apart from bravery, courage and determination.

About the Author
Geraldine Akpet-Ekanem is from Ikom in Cross River State. Married with children, she is a Lawyer and is the Head of Service in Cross River State.

THE BOMBARDMENT OF ENUGU

By Raymond Obiamalu

"*Nnem oo! Nwanyi Nnewi-Ichi oo; Ndi Awusa atugbue nu anyi na bomb oo.*" These were the words I uttered as a terrified, traumatized, 4 year old boy during the nightly bombardment of Enugu, our beloved Biafran Capital, starting from 1967. At night time, we would be on our balcony watching with dread and a sense of foreboding, the incoming streaks from bombs, and the smoke trails from the meagre air defence batteries.

The Journey Home to Nnewi

It was on a Sunday that we hurriedly departed Enugu. I have vivid memories of what I came to mentally file away as "The Case of the Piping Hot Pot of Rice." You see, as was the case with a lot of families, Sundays were rice days. That fare was usually accompanied by a tomato stew chock full of beef, chicken, and other manner of protein. As a child, that was my favourite meal. On that fateful Sunday when the air bombardment got too intense, my father made the decision that it was time to leave Enugu. As far as I could tell, it was not planned. The Sunday began like any other. I do not recall if we attended Mass that day, but I know I was looking forward to my usual Sunday meal. The pot of rice was ready, and I believe the sweet smell of the stew was already wafting through our third floor flat in the nondescript, three-storey building located in Uwani, Enugu. All of a sudden, dad arrived with a 911 Mercedes haulage truck and all hell broke loose. We started packing our belongings into that truck. We had to leave most of our furniture, furnishings, and vital documents behind. To my young mind those articles were entirely disposable. What I could not bear was the thought of leaving that piping hot pot of rice behind. And so, after all five of us children had been shooed into my dad's Peugeot and the truck fully laden with our home effects, I went back upstairs to rescue the pot of rice. Of course, my four-year-old mind had not quite worked out how I was going to lug that large piping hot pot down three flights of stairs. All I received for my resourceful troubles was a burn on a rather intimate and tender part of my nether region. To crown my humiliation, my poor mom had to climb those stairs again to retrieve her wailing son who was suffering from the pain of the burn inflicted by the pot. That experience left a mark borne to this day as a mark of Cain. On the journey to Nnewi, we encountered at various points, the harrowing scenery of burnt out cars and dead bodies. We travelled through Milliken Hill; then Oji River, and on to Awka, Nkpor Junction, Oba, Ojoto, Ichi, and finally Nnewi.

When we arrived at Nnewi, the joyous sight of my grandfather met us, which had a calming effect on all of us. His mere presence instilled a feeling of safety in me. In very short order, our family compound was filled with multiple families and we had to adjust to a cramped compound. My father built a poultry farm so that everyone had access to eggs and protein. There then began the establishment of basic routines for our individual family, including daily morning and evening prayers. It was also then that I was introduced to the dreaded outhouse or pit latrine. That was one of the more unsavoury aspects of our sojourn in Nnewi.

Our dog, Kelly, was my constant companion and a sorely needed reminder of more normal days. I literally slept and ate next to my dog. As time went by, we began to run out of basic supplies, and the daily trips to the various markets began to yield less and less. My mother had to go to what became known as Afia Attack. I recall missing my mum terribly whenever she was away. To this day, I still do not know what caused my near-death sickness during one of her many absences. All I can now recall is that I was very ill. I could not keep anything down. This lasted for several days. Then one day, I opened my eyes and there was my mum. Her heart wrenching wailing woke me up. She kept crying and comforting me. Her presence was all it took for me to perk up. The icing on that wonderful sundae was the soup she made for me which I had never tasted before, or even at any other time thereafter. She called it *ofe crencre*. To the child that I was, that soup was made especially for me. I savoured it. Years later, after the war was over and we were back in Enugu, I would ask her to please make that soup again and she would look at me quizzically and say, "*nwam, onwero ofe ana akpo crencre.*" As the years have gone by, I interpret that event differently. I now believe the soup made its mark because of a confluence of several factors. A boy simply needed his mother. And when he got her back, he associated everything that had to do with that reunion with some mystical quality. Simply put, mothers are sacred!

My sister, Doreen, had to grow up fast. Meal preparations became Doreen's main chore during Mama's absence.

Losing Kelly

It was on a late afternoon like every other afternoon during those days spent waiting for the madness to end. A fawn-coloured dog ran into our compound acting strange. Kelly was resting as usual by my side on the top of the front steps. He jumped up and began growling. With all eyes fixed on the interloping dog, Kelly leaped down the stairs and pounced on the strange dog and a mortal fight ensued. I heard cries of the words "*Nkita ala*" and a new English word "rabies" uttered. While the dogs were fighting, my father ran into the house. No one attempted to separate the dogs because of fear of this strange dog and its equally strange behaviour. Father emerged moments later with one of his shotguns and jumped down the front steps. He did not appear to be afraid. He ran to where Kelly had the other dog pinned down and aimed for the dog's head. A blast, a short whimper, and then, nothing. Kelly was whining; clearly injured. I jumped down the stairs to my pal and there were puncture marks on his shoulder and belly. Dad told me to go wash him. He said to use disinfectant in the water. I went to the poultry and collected some disinfectant from the cache used in the poultry to control infection. Poor Kelly kept whimpering as we washed his wounds. A day or so later; when I woke up, I could not find Kelly. I went looking for him with my younger cousin, Maryann. I saw Kelly with his leash and collar tied to the front gate. Dad would not let me near him. I began to cry, asking my father why I could not go near him. He said, "He's got the rabies from that mad dog." Kelly just kept on moaning, groaning, and growling. My older cousins and my older brothers forced Maryann and I to the back of our compound. I was so distraught; I wanted to go to my dad. But they would not let me. My grandfather came and took me to his quarters. Then I heard a single shot. I ran out from Grandpa's room toward the front of our compound and dad was not there. Neither was Kelly. We children were never allowed to venture outside the compound unsupervised, so I had to wait for him to come back. When he eventually did; I saw his eyes were raw. That was the first time I saw his eyes like that. The only other time during that war when I saw my dad's eyes look that way was when Grandma died in my presence from what I thought was a cough. I never saw Kelly again. I think it was after the loss of Kelly that I became ill. Those were dark days during a very dark time.

A Boy Discovers a New Friend

As an adult, I now understand why I went to the poultry and adopted a young chick after Kelly's death. I was lonely during that war. Kelly's companionship kept me distracted from the constant tension and the fear emanating from the adults who seemed to know more than they were telling us children. As the days went by, the chick started changing colour from that almost golden colour to a bright white. The chick followed me everywhere. It slept outside our bedroom door, just like my grandfather's big male goat slept outside his door. Grandpa's goat was tame. It actually seemed to understand whatever he said to it. My Grandpa called him "*Nna anyi*," which means "Our father" in Igbo language. When Grandpa began his ventures outside the compound for his regular chores, he would usually say to the goat, "Nna anyi bia" and the bearded goat would follow Grandpa out of the compound. The rest of Grandpa's many goats, sheep, and free ranging hens and cockerels, went about their lives on their own schedules. Now and again Grandpa would instruct us to *"jenu gbo nni ewu,"* which meant for us to go and fetch all manner of fodder for the goats. This was our cue to go forage for food to feed the goats in the backyard pens. Our usual task was to use long strings to pierce and impale dried cassava leaves, which we would collect from our front farm. Whoever brought home the thicker load earned my Grandpa's effusive praises. Being the second to the youngest in our compound; I never won that competition. However, Grandpa always made sure to offer me praises for my efforts. Whenever he addressed me, it was always with a loving twinkle in his eyes. I adored him and loved being with him. I would accompany him whenever he left the compound. Sometimes dad would try to object that I was too young to go with Grandpa on a specific trip, but Grandpa would just shush dad up. I called Grandpa "Papa *Nnukwu*" and my poor dad "Papa *Obele.*" In the Igbo language "*Nnukwu*" is big and "*Obele*" is small. My poor dad had to contend with that junior status until grandpa died in 1975 while I was a student in secondary school. His death and what happened to his old goat is a tale for another season.

Sunday Ritual

Both my grandpa and my dad were devout Catholics. We

never missed Sunday Mass. Going to Mass was always a harrowing experience. It was at those Masses that the conscription of young boys and men would often take place. The gathering presented opportunities for Biafran soldiers to forcibly take anyone who looked big enough to serve in our armed forces.

During one of those Sunday Masses, my oldest late brother, Henry, who was barely twelve or thirteen years old was conscripted. The poor lad was simply too tall for his age, so he stuck out like a sore thumb. My father had to go to the local army barracks in Nnewi to retrieve him. Until my brother's death in 2012, it never occurred to me to ask him how that brief experience was. I regret not asking him about the experience. However, like a lot of things associated with that awful war, it seems as if a lot of us decided to just banish any thoughts about it. It was too painful an experience. The Igbo attitude seems to be "what's there to gain from excavating the past?"

Part of our weekly routine required all the young ones to make the trek to our local river, which we knew by the name "*Mmili Agu*", loosely translated as "Leopard's Water." My guess is that in days of yore when we still had plenty of leopards roaming about, the locals would have routinely seen those felines at that watering hole. My recollection of that "river" is that it was not particularly big enough to qualify as a river. It did tend to swell during certain times of the day and during some seasons. It was where I learned the rudimentary aspects of swimming. My dog paddle was enough to keep me afloat.

Dad's Near-Death Experience

There was an event which solidified my dad's belief that I allegedly had mystical qualities. This was of course paired with the belief that I was, also allegedly, a reincarnation of my grandfather whose name was Anselm Okonkwo Obiamalu. His "*Afa Otutu*" was "*Agu Enwe Oyi.*" *Afa otutu* in Igbo is a nickname either conferred when a title is taken, or conferred by one's father or kinsmen. In some cases, one may take a name themselves and that becomes their afa otutu. *Agu Enwe Oyi* means the "Leopard which has no friends." He was a man of "bilious disposition" as my father would describe him. This was a description I dispute without any reservation. To me, he was a teddy bear. Indeed, during that war, I received more tenderness from him than from my dad.

On the fateful day, my dad was in our front farm tinkering with the yam stalks which were lined in furrowed rows. I think he must have been staking them with sticks of wood. This was the usual way of ensuring that the yam stalks had something to twist their vines on as they grew.

It was late afternoon when I went to him and began pestering him to come inside to tend to one of my needs. My dad's pet name for me was "Tata *Obele.*" (Little child).

As an aside, *Tata* was a name I endured well into puberty, much to my enduring chagrin, sigh! My usual flailing response to being called Tata was to remind everyone that my name was Raymond. I suspected the adults took exceptional delight in hanging that name on me like a mark of Cain. When I would not stop pestering him, dad said to me "*Tata Obele, rapunum aka, biko.*" Which meant "Little Tata, please leave me alone." But I would not stop. After a short while when he realized that I was not going to let go, he reluctantly grabbed my hand and started walking back with me toward our compound. As we neared our front gates; we suddenly heard a sound we had come to know so well. That sound is hard to describe. I've heard it said that it's a bit like what one would hear when a tornado approaches - a whooshing or whirling/roaring type of sound. We knew to associate it with an approaching fighter jet of the Federal Armed Forces. Those dreaded jets tended to fly low. They also tended to attack during daylight. The Ilyushin bombers terrorized us at night-time. Upon hearing that sound, my dad stiffened and literally picked me off the ground and dove for the corner of our compound wall that had some banana and plantain plants which provided us with some cover. He then covered me with his body, which meant I could hardly breathe. For some strange reason, I knew to not make a sound. All I heard was this whirling sound and the accompanying sound of the crackling of dismembered wood. After a while, the sound stopped and dad got up and lifted me up. He was gazing at me intently while inspecting every part of my body. Thankfully, I was okay, and so was he. But what took our breath away was what we saw when we looked at the rows of yam stalks he had been working on. They appeared as if someone had dismembered the entire row at the waist level of an average adult. My dad then looked down at me with a look I will never forget. He carried me into our compound, and I clung to him desperately, trembling. Years later, he would recount that tale and then he would add "that's when I knew you bear a charmed life."

About the Author

Raymond Obiamalu is from Nnewi in Anambra State, Nigeria. He is an Attorney and lives in Los Angeles California with his family.

A WAR PORTRAIT

By Godwin Meniru
(From the collection, War Stories in Verse)

I stand in for her, now that she is gone, to
Talk about us, the flabby shrunken breasts flapping in
The fierce wind that still buffets us, as

I listlessly grab one then the other trying
To coax out what has run dry as she doesn't
Have any more life to give even when the
Competition is halved as the earth claims
The other me who shared my journey up till now.

Why show this photograph now, fifty years on, you
Ask? Surely those things happened a long time
Ago and should be forgotten, all done, as past, rather
Pat, isn't it?

And my shrunken head, a skeleton covered with
Brown cracking skin, and my bloated abdomen, filled
With water and liver, and boots for feet.

It is an incomplete photograph, a family portrait,
missing

A father, fighting for us, who later comes home with
half a Brain, the other half filled with other thoughts.

But it is still my portrait, a family portrait I will
continue to Cherish, showing our family history,
because there is
Nothing else I have from a life that has me now living in

Another man's land, where my rights are respected and
My children can become presidents, or whatever they
Wish, since we truly belong. We are not your internal
exiles, whom

You don't want to see, and their portraits that still
surround you, as
They continue to cry from hurt that will run for many
more lifetimes.

BECOMING BIAFRAN:
A CHILD'S ODYSSEY THROUGH BIAFRA

By John Mozie

Imust have been about three when we arrived Port
Harcourt from England in 1966. My mother and her
brothers had been born in Port Harcourt and had lived
there all their lives. My grandfather owned a big house,
180 Bonny Street and I can still remember playing in the
vast living room downstairs. It was only natural that we
had come back to Port Harcourt.

My mother and I made the journey by boat, and
my father had stayed back in Yorkshire to tidy up and
come back later. He was to come back to Port Harcourt,
only to be posted to Calabar, a coastal town about 140
miles from Port Harcourt. My life in Rainbow Town in
Port Harcourt was idyllic. My mother's brothers all had
homes on the estate, purpose-built and so very neat
and tidy, what would pass today as a white-picket fence
residential area in the West. Life for me at the time was
peaceful and my immediate worries did not stretch

far beyond playing and extended bedtimes. Between constant visits to Leventis Port Harcourt for lunch and playing in the estate, I cannot recall a sad moment. The family was changing as well. My mother's youngest brother, John, got married, and I suddenly had a new Aunt. My cousin Ngozi also arrived in January 1967, giving me hope that soon I'd have a new playmate. Her arrival also saw me spending most of my waking hours at my Uncle Kirian's house, as I willed her to grow up and start walking so we could play.

I also recall that it was during this period that I developed a fondness for cars and a curiosity about them. I recall getting into my Uncle Kirian's car and somehow managing to roll it into the garage door. The memory is all a bit fuzzy now, but I distinctly recollect being told off and having to go to bed very early. That deterred me for a long while from messing around with cars until I reached my teens.

It was also in Rainbow Town that I met Achuzie, the Biafran Colonel, who also lived on the estate with his son. His son was slightly older than I was at the time, but we fast became friends, and rode our bikes around the estate whenever we could, especially when mum was at work. Alas it only lasted a few months before all our lives were to change. His father the Colonel was to become quite an influential officer in the Biafran army.

One of my enduring memories of Port Harcourt was meeting General Emeka Odumegwu-Ojukwu. As a child, I was taken to meet him at BMH hospital where my mum worked. He was paying an official visit to the hospital and my mother was allowed to bring me to work so I could see him. He picked me up and placed me on his knees and asked what I would be when I grew up. I did not miss a bit as I declared, "soldier" to much applause by the adults gathered to meet him. The applause died when we got home and my mother 'persuaded' me to reconsider my career options. I do not think I can quite remember the conversation at the time, but I know that as I grew up, I never quite felt any inclination to mention wanting to join the military ever again. She was that persuasive.

I cannot quite recall what went through my mind at the time, but I remember being in awe of the big man who placed me on his knees. His beard and military bearing made him look big and invincible, and there was an air of complete confidence about him. All the adults stood whilst he sat on a chair, confident, resplendent in his army uniform, master of the room, a commander, unquestionably. Right then, I wanted to be just like him when I grew up.

The music ended in 1968 when Port Harcourt finally felt the pinch of invading Nigerian forces. I recall leaving our home and starting the long walk out of Port Harcourt. My mum had tied a few possessions in a wrapper and placed it on her head. She tied my cousin, Ngozi, on her back, and with my heavily pregnant aunt in tow, we started the long walk to Aba. As we were leaving, my mum would not let me take any of my toys. "Why not?" I asked, and she replied, "We will soon be back, they'll be here when we get back". Thinking about it now, I am not sure what was going through mum's mind at the time. Did she actually believe this would all be resolved quickly and painlessly or were they words hurriedly uttered to quell the discomfort of a little boy? I will never know. Fate, however, made those words famous last words. That was the last time I ever saw either Rainbow Town or my home.

My uncles found us on our way to Aba, and we completed the journey by car. Aba is 40 miles from Port Harcourt, and I do not quite think we could have made it by foot. I don't recall complaining much, but I suspect that for a child of about four or five, and a woman in late pregnancy, a 40-mile hike would have been quite a challenge.

There were many families doing the same thing, a human caravan of people trooping out of Port Harcourt. My uncles had met us just as we were leaving Port Harcourt. They were "combing", a term at the time that meant very little to me, but I was later told that as part of the civil defence effort, men were meant to comb their areas in a bid to flush out enemy spies and forestall the invading army. At that stage, one would have thought the damage had already been done.

Aba was a very brief interlude and I really cannot say

how long we were there. I do know we did not remain too long. My mother's older brother, Uncle Matthew, lived in Aba with his wife, Aunt Sara, and their children. It was to Uncle Matthew's that we went, and I recall that his house and Aba were my first taste of the change that was happening in my life as a result of the war. We must have got to Aba in the early evening. Soon after, my aunt asked me to go take a shower and get ready for dinner. I walked out expecting to meet a bath with water "mixed" to my liking, hot water made slightly tepid with cold water. Instead, a cold bucket of water and a bar of soap were in the middle of a communal courtyard, and I was expected to shower right there and then, in the open. I looked at my aunt with "you must be joking" in my eyes, scoffed, turned, and started marching back to the house. Aunt Sara is one of those no-nonsense ladies you really do not want to mess with, so with little ceremony, she grabbed me, stripped me and gave me my first cold bath. As I howled in both humiliation and indignation through the entire experience, I got absolutely no sympathy from either my mother or my uncles. My cousin, Ifeanyi, a baby at the time, looked on with a bemused expression on his face as his mother got on with the task of giving me a brisk and cold wash. At the end of it as I got back to the house, still crying, I got a stern telling off and told unceremoniously to shut up. I had never seen either my mother or beloved uncles like this. The threats of smacking and flogging sounded quite real so I recoiled and shut up, eventually whimpering until I slept. My world had changed and the war had found me.

After that incident, I fell in and simply towed the line, eating what others ate and protesting as sparingly as possible, or not at all. For me, the incident was both poignant and pivotal in a sense. It laid to rest the surrealistic and cossetted seams of my pre-war existence in Port Harcourt, living in a world my mother painstakingly constructed for me, inured from the practicalities of the world outside my enclave. As a four or five year old at the time, the shock of a cold bath in a bucket in a courtyard in full view of strangers must have been an incurable shock and a bridgeless chasm from the world I had left behind, a world where I had my bath run for me, and would simply refuse to have it if the water's temperature was not acceptably tepid. That world died that day, in the courtyard of my uncle's home in Aba, and never found me again. What changed that day, was never replaced. For the rest of my life until the day my mother died, it was drummed into my head that there was a greater purpose to life beyond the petty comforts of my own needs, stretching to circumstance and empathy for the needs of others.

Aba held very few memories for me and I have few other recollections of it outside playing and meeting other members of my family who lived in Aba at the time. I would also begin the journey of learning to live as part of a community in Aba. Every morning at the crack of dawn without fail, an older cousin would go out and sweep the entire compound. Whilst too young to sweep, it was my job to gather the dirt neatly left in mounds at the four corners of the compound and dispose of them. I also got involved in picking sticks and wood to fire the stove for the evening meals. Beyond these chores, I was pretty much left to my own devices provided I did not leave the compound.

It was not long before we fled again, further into the hinterland, presumably in response to the approaching Nigerian Army. I recall that my Uncle Matthew and his family did not come with us as he went with his wife back to her own village. Uncle Kirian, Aunt Kate, my cousin Ngozi, went somewhere else whilst my mother, Uncle John, his wife, Aunt Angie, and I headed off to Ekwulobia. I will never know why the family split up at the time and I'm sure I asked but cannot remember now what response I got. Perhaps it was to reduce the risk of being taken out in a single hit if we were all together, or perhaps it was simply exigence, I will never know. It was also telling that at the time I did not know where my grandfather was, and no one seemed to know. War did that to you, and like a mother hen you gathered up those you could find and kept going.

We settled for a long while in Ekwulobia, Aguata, where my real education into surviving in Biafra started. The compound was big with rooms built in a huge circle around a big courtyard. My mum, Uncle John, Aunt Angie and I had two rooms. I remember that one of the bedrooms also doubled-up as a living room. There was no electricity so we used a variety of bush lamps called mpanaka, crude lamps with cloth wicks powered with palm oil. Evenings were either spent in the courtyard in the company of other children with an adult telling fables, or just sitting at home with the adults listening to BBC World Service on the latest news on the war. Those evenings spent at home were quiet for me. At this point I was the only child in the family and I was always told to be quiet whilst the adults listened to the news. I must confess at the time I would rather have been playing. Yes, I knew there was a war on and things had changed, but as a child it really meant nothing else to me beyond that.

I remember that it was in Ekwulobia, Aguata that I was finally introduced to the art of communal eating. Living in a large compound with lots of other different families, the women would get together to cook lunch every day, and present large pots in the middle of the compound. All the children gathered and ate out of these pots. The garri, a cassava paste quite common across Eastern Nigeria, was always too hot, the soup scalding. If you were retiring or sensitive to communal feeding you would starve. Literally. And I nearly did. I recall the first night in this strange place. Usually, food was placed in large communal pots in the middle of the compound and the children would all gather round and tuck in. The older bigger kids would muscle their way to the outer circle very close to the big basins that held the garri and the soup pot, while the younger ones jostled for position between them. Right from the onset the little kids were at a disadvantage and the entire exercise was a struggle predicated mostly on the bigger kids giving you a chance to grab a handful of piping-hot garri and negotiating a safe passage to the soup pot. As you may well only get one pass at the garri mound, the adept kids who all seemed to me quite oblivious of the heat the garri generated, would grab large handfuls at their first pass, and then gingerly pass the little balls that would be dipped in soup through their fingers. It really was an art, and one you had to learn quickly to survive. I simply could not get into the spirit of the community meal, and even more crucial, lacked the skills to do it. I had always eaten off my own plate and chosen my meals and had never quite taken to garri anyway. I would see my mother eat it on occasion but it held no interest for me, nor was I forced to eat it in Port Harcourt.

So, I went home and that night demanded dinner. Mum obliged. Night two. She obliged and gave me a gentle lecture about rationing and joining the communal feeding station as she contributed to it. Third night, I starved. I came home hungry again and was told simply, that there was no food. I will never know whether my mum was serious or simply wanted to jolt me back to reality but going hungry that night did the trick. On day four, starving and craving any food, I jostled, blew on my garri, ignored dirty fingers, and ate like a native. I learned to fight, ignored jibes of "oyibo" and claimed my place. As the other kids saw me mix and eat with them, they began to accept me as one of the boys, and I began to make friends in the compound. I picked up a lot of skills from the other kids who grew up in the village, like how to build a hut from palm fronds, and how to thatch the roof of a small mud hut.

My mum, because she was the district nurse, also had access to Caritas supplies and one of the staples of the time was egg yolk, a powder that came in bags and was meant to be the egg substitute at the time. I absolutely hated it and it became the one and only thing my hungry stomach simply said no to throughout that war. There was also stockfish, Cod treated in salt and dried, which became a delicacy during the war and is still a big draw in the Igbo community to this day. It made little sense to me then because it was dry and didn't give me much pleasure in the eating. It lacked the fleshiness of, say, chicken that I used to know. However I knew it was gold-dust because the adults would eulogise every miserly two small cods they got with the relief, when they got it, and when it was cooked, someone would give me a small piece from their soup bowl and glare at me expectantly for the grateful "thank you" that showed I appreciated the gift and even bigger sacrifice. I did then, and do now.

News was at a premium for the adults, and in every

compound the adult men gathered around transistor radios tuned low, to listen to BBC World Service for news on what was happening. I remember anger and rage at Nigeria and Britain, and murmurs of propaganda at the time. I remember that batteries were also at a premium and people did all sorts of things to keep batteries alive, including sunning them and connecting radio wires to them externally. Also, white cars were anathema, and many folks found household paint and painted their white cars darker colours so they did not stick out for planes looking for targets. People would also cover their cars with palm fronds when they parked, to avoid enemy planes bombing or strafing the cars. Nigerian fighter pilots actively and consistently targeted civilian enclaves. On many occasions we would actually abandon the cars and jump into the bush when caught on the road by air raids.

In Ekwulobia, Aguata, I learnt to hunt. We fashioned slingshots from discarded rubber and attached them to wooden handles, and hunted birds and lizards with them, using pebbles as our bullets. I was not particularly successful at shooting slingshots, but it was good fun! Occasionally one of the boys would be hit by 'friendly fire' and there would be tears and a lot of recrimination from the adults. My mum started seizing and destroying my slingshots and I had to find ingenious ways of hiding them.

I was also forbidden by my mum from eating the

coterie of nameless creatures we caught, but when she was out at work, I still hunted with the other boys. It was on one of these occasions that we blocked a hole and dug another hole, hunting bush meat. Most rodents and bush animals always had two holes and we would seek out the holes and man one and then chase the animal through the free hole, forcing it to come out of the hole we manned, into a trap. On this occasion we dug the hole to find what we believed would be a grass cutter underground. As we dug, Chuchu, a rather chubby boy and the son of the local bank Manager, was designated to put his hand in the hole for the bite that proved we had quarry. He was bitten. Eventually a big black snake showed and we ran. Chuchu got sick and I remembered my mother warning me of snake venom and how quickly it could kill. Fearing my friend would die, I had to tell my mum what we had been up to. Fortunately, she had anti-venom and delivered it to the boy and saved his life. As for me, I do not think I sat for a week. Mum was very cross and I was sternly punished and smacked for good measure. I think I learnt then that no meant no. I also think that this experience honed my deep-seated dislike for snakes. To this day, I do not see the need for them, nor do I understand people who keep them as pets. Years later, that dislike would be buttressed even further when my friend Henry was bitten by a snake when we were at University and died from an adverse reaction to the anti-venom treatment. He was only 18 at the time.

I remember the air raids that left craters all over the village, and the sirens that sent us scuttling into bunkers as the jets buzzed overhead. I also remember my mother's cousin who came to visit. I never saw him again because on his way home, the car he was travelling in was bombed. Wherever you went you saw carcasses of cars and homes either strafed by machine guns, or simply bombed. Car headlights were painted to dim their glow, and the men made fuel from all sorts of things. Unnecessary journeys were also discouraged because of the risk. As all the other cars packed up and died, the French Peugeots kept going!

The air raids were so common that everyone knew the signs and knew what to do. Each time you heard the distant rumble in the sky, everyone ran for the bunker, a huge ditch dug in the compound with steps, with the entrance covered with palm fronds. On occasions we ran into the bunker to take cover, everyone kept quiet and you could hear a pin drop.

It is hard to know now just how many people were in the bunker at any one time during these raids. The compound held many families and everyone would head for this bunker. I honestly cannot imagine how we all fitted in. The bunker also got waterlogged after heavy rains but fortunately, we never had to use it when it was flooded. It was also a favourite place for snakes to hide and occasionally you'd hear the commotion in the compound as one was cornered and killed, and the remains paraded for everyone to look at, shudder and thank God that the villainous creature was killed before it bit anyone.

After every raid or momentous occasion, children would gather and sing propaganda songs, praising Ojukwu and heaping insults on Gowon and his cabinet. One of my favourite songs of the period was one that declared Ojukwu the King of Biafra, and suggested that Gowon's wife would be subjected to a 'Kwashiorkor pregnancy' and eventually give birth to 'fighter and bomber' which would be used in shooting Gowon and Nigeria. It finished by declaring that Nigeria would never win the war against Biafra. We would heartily march to this song as we swung young limbs and held wooden branches to our shoulders, young warriors of the Republic.

It was also in Ekwulobia that I met the python. Fabled and also spoken about in the compound, I never saw it until the night I had a running tummy and had to use the toilet. My mum took me to one of the pit venues in the compound and waited outside. As I was finishing, I heard a rustle and saw this thing. I screamed. My mum badged in, grabbed me and we ran. In the morning, some men came and I saw them leave carrying this huge snake on a log. My mum went back to the pit latrine and retrieved my shorts. That defined my relationship with toilets forever: only go after a thorough inspection. I also never ever went to the toilet at night until the war ended.

If I had another bout of diarrhoea, I cannot remember, but I don't recall ever leaving our accommodation for a toilet at night until the war ended.

In Ekwulobia, there had also been a perfunctory effort to continue the education of children and I went to school once or twice. The exercise meant little to me. The classes were in open fields and were packed with children sitting on the floor and reciting after teachers who were strenuously pointing at blackboards with long canes. I know now that both lessons I attended were Igbo grammar lessons.

There were also other lessons in Ekwulobia. I learnt to have a healthy respect for the Palm fruit. Whilst the women manually pressed oil out of it for cooking, the kernel provided a veritable snack for the children and adults too. It was dried and shelled with stones and eaten. I was particularly fond of it. The palm kernel was also used for making the only body lotion available during the war, ude'aku. Another key product from the palm oil was the native soap, ncha'nkota, the black paste soap made from burnt palm fronds. We showered with water collected from rainwater or the stream, using the native soap. Ncha'nkota was not much to look at, a black, pasty blob. And of course, it had no smell either, quite unlike the perfumed soaps that became commonplace in every home at the end of the war.

What was quite instructive was the amount of industry that sustained us at the time. Men fixed roofs, built latrines, all kept farms and also distilled petrol in some cases. The women made everything from soap to fermenting cassava and also maintaining small vegetable patches which in a sense was the mainstay of our produce at the time. Thinking about this now as an adult, I can only but attest to just how impressive these adults were.

One of the most common episodes of the war was the constant raiding of homes where there were teenage boys by the Biafran army. Older teenagers were conscripted into the army, and you would see mothers wailing and rolling around on the floor as the kids were taken away. Later, families would take to hiding their sons in the bush to stop soldiers taking them. There were rumours that neighbours would tell on families who they did not get along with and reveal the hiding places of their older kids to the soldiers. As children, we'd also go out to watch the conscripts training, as they jogged singing war songs, holding tree branches and pieces of wood above their heads as if they were rifles. The Biafran army also commandeered people's cars for the war effort, another phrase I learnt from the war. However, none of my uncles' cars was ever taken, so I presume that this was not as commonplace as perhaps the lack of equipment would suggest.

I recall the bombing of Uli airstrip and the consternation that caused amongst the adults, and the anger about Nigerian planes targeting mercy missions bringing relief portions into Biafra.

Whilst there was great community in Biafra, there must also have been an underbelly of distrust as well. Thinking about it now, there were occasional arguments between the ladies and sometimes the husbands over missing poultry or livestock. At the time, this was very serious business and could well lead to fisticuffs as people accused each other of stealing their livestock.

One occasion stood out for me. In Ekwulobia at the time, not too far from where we lived, there was a chap who ran a restaurant. I know he was not Igbo because my mum mentioned he was either from Calabar or somewhere around what is now Cross River State. For some reason I simply cannot remember his name. He was a fantastic cook and I fell in love with Ukwa (breadfruit porridge) after I was taken to his restaurant. He cooked it in such a way that it had a slightly barbequed taste, and to this day no one has been able to replicate that taste for me! Softly spoken guy, his restaurant was a long open hut with thatched roof and looked to me to be quite busy at lunch time. I know we used to get takeaways from there quite regularly for a time, always Ukwa porridge, and a special treat.

And then one day the restaurant closed. Apparently, he had been accused of stealing a goat. The said goat was tied to his neck and he was paraded round the village with it. From what I remember he was also bleeding, possibly from where he had been beaten. It made no sense to me. He had always appeared comfortably affluent to me and

I saw no reason why he should steal a goat and I said as much, while my mum simply shrugged and threw her hands heavenwards in her typical 'who knows?' manner. I recall seeing the man a few times after that, but we left Aguata shortly afterwards.

The other memorable reminder of the war was kwashiorkor, the protein deficiency that afflicted a lot of children during the war. I saw it in the children around the compound, with big, hungry eyes and protruding stomachs. My mother ran a clinic and spent a lot of time working with mothers on nutrition and helping distribute aid and relief materials when they did get to us. Given the gusto with which friends roasted and devoured rodents and lizards we caught on our hunting expeditions, the hunger and protein deficiency were not imagined. Children suffered. And then there was diarrhoea which was never far away from any of us because of the poor sanitation and our own not so hygienic habits as well. There was no tissue paper for toilet, and we used mostly banana leaves. My mother would insist on my washing my hands after a bathroom break, but really the conditions in Biafra would not always allow you to be that sanctimonious about hygiene. Survival was everything. For instance, we had an earthen pot for drinking water, and would usually fill it up from water collected directly from the rain. Stream water and water that drained from the roof was used for showering, laundry, and other casual household tasks.

Oral hygiene was another challenge. We all chewed stick; a stick simply eponymously described as 'chewing stick'. I never quite got to discover its botanical name or where it came from, but people used it and scrubbed their teeth every morning like you would use a toothbrush and my older relatives swore by it. Given the state of my dentition after the war, I must have been doing something wrong.

As tough as things were, I now know that I was lucky. Most children around me were sick, and death was common. If the hunger or bombs did not get you, the snakes and disease did, like simple avoidable ailments such as tetanus, diarrhoea and malaria. There was pain and hunger all around me, but I was spared both and whatever I did see, my young mind did not retain. I was also spared the sight of dead bodies. As common a sight as they must have been for the adults, the community shielded us from that trauma. Ekwulobia was kind to us and was my first real introduction to life in what was then, rural Igboland.

We eventually fled Ekwulobia for Agulu where we were until the war ended. I can only imagine that the move was engendered by the proximity of enemy forces, but in those days, you asked few questions and did as you were told, mostly. My Uncle Kirian and his family joined my mother, my Uncle John, and aunt, and I in Agulu. At this time, we did not know where my maternal grandfather or other uncles were. I also had not seen my father since the war started.

Agulu introduced me to the Udala fruit, which was so plentiful in the place. Agulu was so much quieter than Ekwulobia and there were no air raids while we were there. I also do not recall a bunker in the compound, which would have been unusual for the time. We also had fewer children in the compound and it was slightly boring as I had only my little cousins for company most of the time. I do recall the landlord had two older boys who always fought each other with such vicious intensity I wondered if they really were brothers. But they were both good to me and I learnt a great deal about poultry from them. Just before the war ended, the older of the two was conscripted. I do not recall seeing him again until we left Agulu.

Peace at Last

We were in Agulu for probably six months. I remember going to Christmas Mass in Agulu for the first time, and our first mass family birthday celebration since the war started. All the children were lined up and we were told it was our birthday party, and to be happy. I'd never had a birthday party so found the entire episode slightly befuddling. It bore very little resemblance to what a birthday would be now, and there was no cake. Thinking about it now, it would have been difficult to organise, and probably the adults' effort at providing my cousins and me with a sliver of normalcy in the midst of the hardship that was the war. My cousin, Njideka, had been born in Agulu in August 1969 to much hope and jubilation by the family. My uncles Kirian and John drove up to Enugu to confirm it was safe and in 1970, the family finally left Agulu for Enugu.

We had survived the war. And I saw my father again for the first time since 1967. We had been separated when the hostilities started, and my family had presumed him dead. Later on, we were to reconnect with my grandfather, who had somehow left Port Harcourt for his hometown in Umudioka, and thankfully, all my uncles had also come home safely. The slow journey to rebuild lives had begun.

No one in my family ever discussed the details of the war with me. For them, the experience was simply too painful, and too stressful. But one thing stood out for me: from that moment on, my mother would dismiss every presumed governmental infraction as the result of the peculiar treatment reserved for *"ndi'emeli'li'na'gha"*. We all moved to Enugu, at the time the capital of East Central State and even as young as I was, I saw very little difference between Biafra and Enugu. In the aftermath of the war, there was no running water or electricity in parts of Enugu.

Also, quickly after that, a new phrase entered our diction: 'armed robbery'. My young and befuddled mind tried to imagine rubber bands 'armed' and going around causing huge havoc in the population. That wasn't a stretch really, because in Biafra we had all had slingshots fashioned out of rubber bands and wooden handles, generically referred to as 'rubbers'. It took another year before I got to understand that the robbers who were armed were bandits and not humanised 'rubbers'. In 1970 and 1971, cars were snatched and homes raided, in some cases violently, by armed robbers. As the killings continued, the only difference was that there were no more air raids.

The Cousins L to R: Nkiru, John and Ngozi (now late), 1970

I was excited though, because as tough as things were, there were also some novelties and moments of pure joy, like coming back from school one day to discover that the children's bedroom in Kano Street was now adorned with Vono beds and mattresses! My first bed since 1968. What joy it was hopping on the soft mattress and springs. Then there were also other pleasures like the introduction of electricity, soft drinks (on special occasions like Christmas) and Trebor sweets, Goodie-Goodie (so good they named it twice!) and of course the revelation in Jollof rice called Tomapep. Just driving past the billboards with the pictures of the perfect Jollof rice dish made you hungry all over again.

Many years later, I would read Ekwensi's '*Surviving the Peace*'[1] and feel the anguish and dissonance the adults must have felt as they struggled with the aftermath of the war. Whilst formal hostilities were over, the struggle was by no means over. What with the lawlessness which appeared to have overtaken the East and the privation occasioned by the federal government's decision to only grant people from Eastern Nigeria £20 from all the deposits they had in the banks before the war started, it would be a long time before peace came back. But for me as a child, life at the time held just possibilities. The war had taken so much from us that it is sometimes hard to put into context what was lost: education, opportunity, even the leisure some may well take for granted today. Nothing brings this to mind more than my first visit to Lagos in 1971. My uncle John had moved back to Lagos and his job with the Nigerian Customs Service. My mum took me over to visit him during one of the

---

1   Cyprian Ekwensi, January 1st 1976, Heinemann Educational Books

school holidays and while we were there, went to see an old friend of the family, Dr Green, who was at the time a Lt. Colonel in the Nigerian Army Medical Corps.

Dr Green had been my mother's boss at the Braithwaite Memorial Hospital Port Harcourt, where my mum worked before the war broke out. We spent the day in his office at a huge military hospital where he was the commander, and went on to his house that evening, at Ikeja GRA in Lagos, for dinner. I vaguely recall at the time that he had just lost his wife. He had two sons, David and Samaila, with David being about my age and as children do, we played all evening long. When we were asked to come in for dinner, I discovered television and cartoons for the first time in my life. I was so enthralled by the magic of Tom and Jerry that when my uncle and my mum declared it was time to go, I impetuously responded that I wasn't ready. I can still hear Dr Green say, "leave the boy alone", and I was, until we got home. I can say that after the smacking I got that day, I never ever said 'I am not ready yet' to my mother for the rest of her life. She made the point quite firmly, and I got the message. However what is poignant was that this was 1971, and it was the first time in my life, at 8, that I came into contact with the magic of television.

Within a year or two of the war ending, Gowon and his wife, Victoria, paid an official visit to East Central State. We all dressed up in our school uniforms, polished our Cortina school shoes and with white knee-length socks, lined up, waved flags, recited the Nigerian anthem and welcomed Gowon, our glowing head of state, to East Central State. As children, we were in absolute awe of the exquisite good looks of our first couple. I could not stop staring at Victoria. She certainly did not look like she had ever given birth to anything, much less the infamous fighter and bomber of my earlier chants. To my young eyes, I felt as welcome in my developing and hopeful country as Gowon felt in Enugu. I also recall my mother calmly dismissing the visit as 'Gowon coming to check on us to satisfy himself that we were still alive'. *Ndi'emeli'lin'agha.* Even at that age, the irony was not lost on me. The same chap that spear-headed the most vicious war against the East that had caused so much pain and destruction, was in a Rolls-Royce State car right in front of me in Enugu, smiling, young, handsome and benign like a happy uncle. How was that possible? The irony! I simply wondered to myself how adults could be so complicated. Even my headmistress looked more menacing at Monday morning assemblies than this young and handsome uncle smiling at me in his General's uniform and white-gloved hands.

The war drove privation and even as a child, I had a very deep sense that things had changed. It simply was not the way it used to be. I had no formal education to speak of during the war and when I started school in 1970, I had just turned 7, which was 2 years later than the usual start year for primary school. But even all that, I was still very lucky. There were so many people who had lost far more many years than I had, and as I sat in classes with some chaps close to their teens at the time, I am not quite sure that in retrospect, I fully appreciated just how lucky I was. I recall we would tease these chaps about their ages and being stuck in the same school years as us, and some of them would give you a good hiding if they caught you. Now I can only imagine how frustrating and utterly unjust it must have all been for them, and the courage it took to get to start over again, for everybody. For the most part, everyone got on with the business of our new normal the best they could.

The war also robbed many of us of precious memories. Not just the children, but the adults, too. The parents lost properties, family heirlooms and sundry other irreplaceable family memories. All my baby photographs went in that war, and I never saw my parents' wedding pictures, nor my photographs with my godparents. I also have no idea what any of my grandparents looked like apart from my maternal grandfather, Peter. He had retired to his house in 180 Bonny Street Port Harcourt before the war broke out and had looked forward to spending his retirement in his house. In 1970 my mother's younger brother Raphael, also presumed dead in the war, turned up at our house in Kano Street in Enugu. He had survived the war and had gone to his father's house in Bonny Street. The house had been 'given' to another family by the Federal Government as 'abandoned property' and the new owners had allowed him to take my grandfather's photograph which was hanging on the wall. He came back and found us in Enugu, clutching this framed photograph of his father in one hand, his briefcase in the other. As for us, all we took as we left our home in Port Harcourt, was what my mother could fit on her head.

There is a significant part of my life and the lives of others like me that we simply cannot easily recount because the records simply vanished. We don't know, the history is sketchy and records simply don't exist. All my childhood records went with the invasion of Port Harcourt, as did family heirlooms, precious photographs, recorded history of who one is and how life started. To this day, I have never seen any photographs of my paternal grandparents, or my maternal grandmother. They remain mirages clouded in the generic explanation of strangers. Today, most of those strangers too, are gone.

And we have lived with these holes in our souls all our lives, with my mother's words, 'ndi'emeli'lin'agha' still ringing in my ears to this day. I also still cannot answer my youngest daughter, Chiemelie's, abiding question': "Dad, what did you look like as a baby?"

About the Author

John Obinna Unachukwu Mozie is from Obosi in Anambra State. A Lawyer and writer, John is the author of the book *The Enchanted Gift*. He lives in England with his wife Adaora, and their three daughters.

SHOCK OF SEPARATION

By Gloria Ekaette Etekamba Umoren

I was born in 1961, and so when the Nigeria-Biafra War broke out in 1967, I was barely 6 years old. In 1966, my mother, late Madam Adiaha Daniel Edem, was a nurse at the General Hospital, Ikot Okoro in present day Oruk Anam LGA of Akwa Ibom State. My late father, Professor Daniel Akpan Edem, who was then a primary school teacher, had left his wife with three young children (me being the youngest) to go to the United States of America to study. The plan at the time was for the rest of the family to join him in the United States. That never happened as the war came and put paid to that plan.

So, at the outbreak of war, my mother had 3 children aged 14, 13 and 6 to raise alone, with my sister being the oldest, and my only brother who was 13. My childhood was peaceful and uneventful until people in uniform arrived the village and started using the hospital field for parades. Children (boys only), who were friends with my brother, were given white t-shirts and shorts and taught how to march and hold long guns. The hospital field was visible from our balcony, so I recall spending fascinating times watching the parades. I was so envious of the boys being given guns and taught marching. This turned out to be my first taste of gender discrimination. Curiously, my mother would not let my brother join the parade, although he was eager to, seeing that his friends appeared to be enjoying themselves. As time went on, the men in uniform who I later got to know were soldiers, would disappear with the boys and a new set of soldiers would arrive at the village with new kids for training. There was an evening when we saw an aeroplane, then a large bowl of fire erupted from it with a bang. I was too young to rush to see it, but it remains etched in my memory. To this day, I still panic when an aeroplane flies over my house.

I have dim recollections of actual discussions by adults. For instance, I heard them talk about food not being enough in places. I did not know where, and I was not affected. We were still eating. I did not know why there was no food in some places. As the war raged on, it became apparent that Ikot Okoro, our little village, was no longer safe. The distant sounds of bombs and shelling were getting nearer. People were deserting the village and seeking safety elsewhere. It became commonplace to see strangers with heavy loads and tired feet passing through the village, and it dawned on everyone that these refugees were heading to the hinterland.

My mother made the quick decision to send us into the hinterland under the mistaken belief that the soldiers would never get there. Along with all her worldly goods, she entrusted my sister, aged fifteen, with the responsibility of looking after my cousin, aged three and my precocious seven-year old self in a remote village. Now looking back, my brother was not with us possibly because my mother was scared that he could be conscripted as a child soldier, and so decided to keep him with her. Among my mother's worldly goods was her sewing machine with her name boldly inscribed on it. My sister protected us as best as any 15-year old could. We lived in the bush and ate only coco yam and palm oil for months. Then one day, we rebelled against my sister and stopped eating. Coco yam and palm oil were not the luxuries we used to know. It is hard to imagine how she coped and the weight of responsibility she must have borne at such a young age.

The war was much fiercer in the hinterland than it had been at Ikot Okoro. Faced with two starving children, my sister decided to take us back to Ikot Okoro. So with just the clothes on our backs, we left without my mother's sewing machine. I recall that we took cover a lot on our way. My little cousin was on my sister's back a lot of the time as she was so young.

On our journey home, one incident remains etched in my mind. We were waylaid by a lone soldier in the bush. He struggled with my sister, but she escaped and ran, leaving us with the now frustrated soldier. We stood there crying. The soldier escorted us out of the bush to the main road and left us there. I cannot recall how we reconnected with my sister, but we all continued on the journey.

As we got into Ikot Okoro, my sister decided to take the longer route possibly because it was the main road rather than a bush path. Her near-rape experience made her realise that perhaps it was safer. Stubbornly, I decided to take the short cut. My sister and cousin arrived before me. When I eventually arrived home, I met my mother crying or rather wailing. She was sure I was dead. I recall so clearly her asking no one in particular what she would tell my Dad. That struck me because my Dad's black and white picture hung in our parlour. So, I thought to myself, why was he not here with us?

We reunited as a family but my brother was not there. Apparently, my Mom's brother had taken him away for safety. Thus, it was only my mother who stayed in Ikot Okoro. By 1968, lots of people had taken refuge in the hospital. My mother being a nurse became handy for those white people that used to come in aeroplanes with relief materials. Since we lived in the camp (hospital premises) and my mother was part of the Relief Team, we never suffered kwashiorkor or any other form of malnutrition. We also never wanted for clothes as we lined up like others within the camp to receive the largesse from the white people, who I now realise were members of International Red Cross Society.

Remember my mother's sewing machine? Well one day, someone who knew my mum told her that he had seen her sewing machine, and when he attempted to retrieve it from the person who had it, they had demanded money for its safekeeping. My mother gave the informant the money, and her sewing machine came back to her. She lost everything else to war.

In November 1969, my father returned to Nigeria armed with his PhD and took an appointment at Ahmadu Bello University, Zaria, as a lecturer. That same year, we relocated from Ikot Okoro and joined him. In 1970, the war ended and our lives returned to normal. My sister went on to follow in our dad's footsteps and would become a Professor of Education, whilst my brother is a Veterinarian with his own practice. Our little cousin is now a nurse in Canada.

We are the lucky survivors of this conflict that took millions, including many children who could have grown up to help in the constant effort of building and developing Nigeria.

About the Author

Gloria Ekaette Etekamba Umoren MNI (nee Edem) is a Lawyer and former Solicitor-General and Permanent Secretary in the Akwa-Ibom Ministry of Justice. She is married with children.

MY LIFE IN BIAFRA

By Onyekwere Uzoma Ogan

My earliest recollections of life in Biafra are pleasant ones. Most of my extended family fled to our ancestral hometown, Item, after the war broke out, and it was fun exploring the village with cousins that I had never met and engaging in activities that I had never experienced, like taking daily morning baths in the stream in front of the family compound or hunting in the forest for birds and rodents with our catapults and bows and arrows. At night, the children would sit on the floor in a circle after dinner and listen to moonlight tales told by older relatives. Our parents tried to create some semblance of normalcy for us kids, so they set up a school at Atanko on the other side of the stream and insisted that all of the children must not only attend school, but also help out with chores in the house or at the farms, to discourage any form of idleness.

My first real experience of the war came when there was an air raid and the school at Atanko was targeted. I ended up in a ditch in the bushes with my older cousins, Chima Ogan and Oriaku Imo. After the plane had disappeared from sight, the grownups went around the village calling out to the children who were all too frightened to come out from their hiding places in the bushes where they had taken refuge.

The relative peace and tranquility that we enjoyed at Item was shattered one afternoon when my father suddenly appeared in the family compound from the war front and announced to his shocked siblings that we all had to leave Item immediately. My father worked at the Research and Production Unit (RAPU) of Biafra that was responsible for producing armaments and other essential needs for the war, and he had the rank of Lt. Colonel in the Biafran army. His position made him privy to information that was not available to most, and so he was able to warn his siblings that Item was about to fall into the hands of the federal troops in a matter of hours. The family would be caught behind enemy lines if we did not escape immediately.

I saw my family's escape out of Item through the innocent lens of a rambunctious child and so it was very exciting to me. I can only imagine how traumatic it must have been for my parents, my uncles, aunts, cousins and older siblings though. We literally drove in a convoy through the battlefield with bullets flying in every direction and retreating Biafran soldiers running around in a panic. One of my uncles was so frightened by the gunfire that he could barely drive his car and he inadvertently slowed the convoy to a crawl until he was relieved of his driving responsibilities by my mom who was still young and dare devilish at the time. My father in his Lt. Colonel's uniform and wielding his Madsen submachine gun which, in my childhood imagination, I could not wait until I was old enough to shoot, drove in front of the convoy, and he was able to see us through the numerous checkpoints set up by the Biafran soldiers. Thankfully we all managed to escape without any casualties. I never did find out why my grandmother did not escape from Item with the rest of the family. I can only imagine that it had something to do with her age or her not wanting to abandon the house she had built with my grandfather which was one of the few storied buildings in Item at the time. Ironically, that same house was rigged with bombs by the federal troops and blown up just a few days to the end of the war while my grandmother was hiding out in the bushes. The story that I heard from one of my older cousins is that someone had informed the federal troops that my father was one of those responsible for the production of *Ogbunigwe* which had wreaked so much havoc amongst the federal troops throughout the war. The blowing up of my grandparents' house at Item was punishment meted out to my family for my father's transgressions.

Due to my age at the time, it is difficult for me to remember the exact sequence of events that occurred during the war or the timelines. But I do know that as the war progressed and more towns in Biafra fell under the control of the federal troops, we moved constantly to places like Umudike, Isu, Mbano, Owerri, Emekuku, Arondizogu etc. What I do remember clearly is the generosity of the families that took us in and shared the little they had with us. I would like to mention especially, the Obasis at Isu, the Amadi-Obis at Emekuku, and the Anezi-Okoros at Arondizogu. If I have omitted any other families, I ask for their forgiveness and blame it on my age at the time. I do, however, remember our time at Umudike partly because of its historical significance which I did not understand at the time. Our direct neighbour to the right at Umudike was Colonel Eze who was one of the most senior army officers in Biafra and who commanded troops at different fronts during the war. His daughter, Yvette, would come over to our house virtually every day to play hide and seek with my sister and I and it was from Yvette that I first heard the nursery rhyme, Milk, Milk, Lemonade, that described certain parts of our anatomy in interesting ways. Colonel Onwuatuegwu, who was also one of the most senior officers in Biafra, lived in the house that was next to the Ezes or perhaps two houses away. His wife was a good friend of my mother's and she visited our family regularly. At Umudike, there were frequent air raids and we always ran to the bunker that had been constructed either behind the Eze residence or the Onwuatuegwu residence for safety. I was too young then to know the role that Tim Onwuatuegwu played in the first coup that occurred in the history of Nigeria, but having read so many historical accounts of the events that led to the Nigerian Civil War later in my adult life, I cannot help but feel sad whenever I remember the time that we spent at Umudike.

By the time we moved to places like Isu, Abba, Mbano, Owerri, and Emekuku, things had gotten really bad in Biafra. My family had it better than most and we were still able to get some protein in our diet in the form of dried stockfish tail that we got from the relief agencies and charities that flew in supplies at great risk, despite the blockade that had been imposed by the Nigerian government on Biafra. I do remember some of the other kids in the compound pleading with my older siblings and I to share some of our morsels of stockfish with them in exchange for things like palm kernel and corn on the cob. But even for us, meat was rare, and till this day, as a result of the deprivation we all suffered during the war, I still have the habit of not eating the meat on my plate until I have finished eating the rest of the food, so that I can savour every bite of the meat at the end of the meal. Over the years, I have discovered that many of my friends who grew up in Biafra also have this habit. I do not remember seeing much of my parents during the period that we spent at Emekuku since my father was always too busy at the war front and would only drop by sporadically after several weeks to check on the family. My mother spent most of her time at the local hospital nursing casualties from the war back to health which, sadly, included a lot of kids that were suffering from Kwashiorkor.

I did attend school at Mrs. Udeozo's nursery school at Emekuku but I barely remember anything that I learned back then. Many years later, when I was attending boarding school at Federal Government College, Enugu, I bumped into Mrs. Udeozo in front of the Hotel Presidential at Enugu, and I am thoroughly ashamed to say that I pretended to be somebody else and that I did not know who she was. I still remember the hurt expression on her face when she called out my name and I acted the way that I did. She was obviously excited to see one of her old pupils from her nursery school teaching days at Emekuku and I was surprised that she even recognized me after so many years. The dilemma that I faced at the time was that I had jumped the fence at boarding school illegally and gone to swim at the Hotel Presidential with my friends when I should have been back at school attending class like my better-behaved schoolmates, who included Mrs. Udeozo's daughter, Ada, who was in my class. Dr. and Mrs. Udeozo were friends of my parents and I knew that if I had acknowledged to Mrs. Udeozo that I was who she thought I was, I would have been reprimanded right away, and my parents would certainly have heard about my truancy. A couple of years ago I spoke to Ada Udeozo and I made her promise to apologize to her mom on my behalf for the hurt I caused her many years before. The other thing that stuck out in my memory about our time at Emekuku were the efforts made by everyone to hide my older sibling, Chidiebere, from the Biafran soldiers who at the time were conscripting even children that were in their early teens. I can only imagine how terrifying it must have been for poor Chidiebere. Abba, Mbano, and Owerri are a blur to me, but our time at Isu was full of excitement, with my siblings and I getting into a lot of mischief with the Obasis. I recently reconnected with Emeka Obasi and he shared little details of our time there that I had completely forgotten. He even remembered how devastated my parents were when they received the news that Uzuakoli had fallen to the Federal troops. It seems someone close to my family had died during the battle for Uzuakoli and Emeka had vivid recollections of watching my mother cry uncontrollably on hearing the news.

Our departure from Emekuku, just like our departure from all the towns that we had lived in during the dying months of the war, was sudden and hasty and it was prompted by the heavy artillery bombardment that we could hear in the distance from the ever-advancing federal troops. The artillery bombardment would almost always be followed by the clattering sound of light firearms as the Biafran forces engaged the federal troops in combat. By this time, most of us children had become accustomed to the sounds of war and we all could point out the difference between the "*kwapu, kwapu, kwapu,*" that came from the light firearms, and the "*unudum,*" that came from the artillery fire. We also understood the message that came with the loud sounds that we heard, which in Igbo translated to, "leave, leave, leave, all of you." We had also mastered the derogatory songs composed by the propaganda unit of the Biafran government, some of which helped to form the negative image that was imprinted in my head right up until the end of the war. The typical Nigerian soldier who was Hausa was tall, dark as night, with two horns sticking out of the back of his head.

I have very few recollections of our time at Arondizogu, which was where we lived when we heard the news on the radio that the war was over. But I believe that our time there was quiet and relatively uneventful. I suspect also that it was short because I do not remember forming any close friendships with any of the young children in the neighbourhood before we left Arondizogu. I remember that the mood amongst the adults after it was announced on the radio that Biafra had surrendered was somber. One could also sense some relief that at least the war was over, and people could now finally begin the difficult process of putting their lives back together. Personally, I was heart-broken, not because I was a diehard fan of Biafra, but because I had to watch my father flush my beloved Madsen submachine gun down the pit latrine behind the compound, and with it went my fantasy of ever firing that weapon.

We moved into a flat at Garden Avenue, GRA, Enugu, shortly after the war ended, and my parents enrolled all the children at the All Saints Primary School that was within walking distance from where we lived. I still remember sitting on a cement block and holding my black slate in a makeshift classroom while waiting for classes to end so that I could run outside and wait in line for the beans that was served to all the kids out of a huge drum as part of the government's feeding program. My father and some of his colleagues were summoned to Lagos by the Nigerian government for about a month, where they were debriefed and interrogated on the roles they had played in Biafra. A couple of months after we moved into our flat at Garden Avenue, the family was reunited with Theophilus, who used to live with us before the war, and who had searched the entire city of Enugu before finding us at Garden Avenue. To everyone's amazement, Theophilus informed my mother that after we fled Nsukka at the beginning of the war, he had dug a big hole in the backyard of our house and buried all of my mother's valuable China and silverware which my mother had lost all hope of ever seeing again.

During our brief time at Enugu, I finally got to meet up close not one, but two live Nigerian soldiers, and to my utter disappointment, I discovered that they were neither very dark, nor tall, and they certainly did not have horns sticking out of the back of their heads. But I was pleased to find out that they were friendly. My parents had met and befriended the GOC of the Nigerian troops stationed at Enugu, Lt. Colonel Mamudu, who later became Governor of Gongola State and was one of the few northern officers who protected Igbo officers during the counter coup of 1966. My mother mentioned to him that she had not seen her family in almost three years due to the war. She was from Illah in the then Mid-Western State which had been under the control of the federal troops for most of the war, and this explained her inability to see any of her family during the war years. I can only imagine how worrisome it must have been for both my mother and her family at Illah, not knowing who was still alive or dead. Because there were still a lot of military check points on the roads at the time and due to the high incidents of armed robbery, Lt. Colonel Mamudu assigned a Land Rover and those two very friendly soldiers to my mum, and we were able to make the long journey to Illah where my mother reunited with her family and I met my maternal grand-parents for the first time. The trip to Illah allowed me to see firsthand some of the destruction and devastation that had been caused by the war. All through the journey, the roads were filled with refugees returning to homes that they had not seen in years and carrying their entire worldly possessions on their heads. At Oji, we were delayed for more than an hour while an army bomb disposal unit detonated an unexploded ordnance that had been discovered by the roadside. But the most exciting part of the journey for me was crossing the River Niger by pontoon since the bridge that linked Onitsha to Asaba had been blown up during one of the fiercest battles that had taken place in the entire war. Shortly after our return from Illah, we left Enugu for Nsukka where my father resumed his position as a lecturer at the University and my mother got a job as a nurse at the Bishop Shanahan hospital. And for us kids, life finally returned to normal.

About the Author

Onyekwere Uzoma Ogan is from Item in Abia State. He is a Lawyer and lives in Los Angeles where he has a practice, with his wife and two children.

REMEMBERING BIAFRA

By Nnaemeka Nnolim

In the Beginning

At what age does one remember childhood? My earliest recollection was with my father in a canoe. We went to Obudu Cattle ranch and the cows seemed enormous to me. They stared at me with those big eyes that frightened the daylights out of me. We merely sat in a canoe for pictures, but it stuck with me. I also remember my tricycle. For some reason, a photographer was detailed to take pictures of me, which I did not like. My childhood was seemingly filled with posing for pictures. You see, those days the photographer had to adjust my face, raise my chin, place my hands, legs, tell me to pose, say "cheese," and smile, and then, snap. It was the same with barbers, and those razor blades. Any mistake was unthinkable.

My father was a Divisional Officer in the early 1960s, and he travelled a lot. He was serving at Obudu when I arrived, and we spent quite a while there and in the surrounding areas. So I extend brotherly love to anyone from Obudu, Ikom, Ogoja, Afikpo and all those areas where duty to serve took my father, especially Obudu. For some reason, over fifty years later, Obudu still has a special place in my heart.

Unlike today, there were no hotels available at that time, so my father's house served as guest house to all manner of visitors in transit or relations who came to stay. So, with an army of fawning relations, and doting visitors, my childhood was spent in jolly company.

I do not remember the month or year exactly, but we were now living in Enugu where my father worked. One day I noticed he looked very worried. I could also see usually happy neighbours going about their businesses also wearing forlorn looks. Some others were engaged in heated arguments. Then I heard the word "*agha*" meaning war. My nannies could not explain clearly what war meant. They had never been involved in one. Neither did any of the numerous visitors to my father or relatives know exactly what it portended. What does "*agha*" mean? My childish thoughts interpreted the looming fight to the ones people on our street or better still, my colleagues at school engaged in. I had even seen people bleed from these fights. Was this what war was all about?

My father became gloomier as the days dragged by. This coming war must be serious for my father not to buy me presents or the usual bread. He appeared withdrawn and often hugged me tightly without saying a word. And not getting the familiar response from "Daaaddy …", I would burst into tears. In the past, these tears would attract pacifiers of biscuits, bread or promise but now, my crying and wailing were simply ignored. Everyone in the house just continued as if in a trance, as if I were not there. What is wrong with everybody? I wondered. Then I heard the songs. I did not know what they meant at the time. It was years later when the war heated up that I understood the words of the songs:

Ojukwu nye anyi mma (Ojukwu give us machetes)

K'anyi gbuo ndi Hausa (so we can kill the Hausas)

These songs were soul stirring, and often made people smile for the time-being to make up for the horrendous stories told of mass killings of fellow Igbos in northern Nigeria, sometimes enroute to eastern Nigeria. There were a few shiny eyes, and I could see my father's driver skipping for joy. He wanted to join the army to avenge the slaughter of innocent Igbos. As a child, I could not fathom what was going on. My father remained solemn, and my mother undecided on what to do. You see, we were just a small family - my sister, my brother and I.

But things were happening around us with some of our neighbours packing their belongings, presumably getting ready to leave. I noticed this because when I peeped from the window of our house, I could see them packing up.

Then suddenly, the alarm came. I saw myself on

Awgu road heading out of Enugu with some of our belongings. There were too many people on the road that day. A lot of them on foot, or on bicycles, motorcycles, and some driving cars. The road was packed, and if I remember very well, a terrible traffic gridlock. When I asked why, I was told the Hausa army was close to Enugu.

Then I saw myself in my village. I met so many people; I did not know I had that many relatives. My grandmother doted on me. I can still smell the smoke from her pipe to this day. She always lit up by picking red hot coals from the fireplace which never burnt out, with her bare hands. I would sit on the steps of our home waiting for granny to pick a burning coal and expertly place it in her pipe. Her fingers never got burnt. Magic! Minutes or was it seconds later, her pipe would be belching out smoke, with that accompanying smile on her face. She would then tear off a piece of fish or meat hanging over the fireplace for me to eat. Soon, my sister would come yelling for hers. You see my father's home in the village then, was a bungalow with a garage outside the house. Four or five rooms in all I think it was with a living room. With him being the first person to graduate from university in the town, our family was the cynosure of all eyes. My aunties loved me. As children, we were always busy playing in the sand all day and at moonlight games far into the night. All I heard were stories of an uncle who voluntarily joined the Biafran army. A lawyer by profession, I remember his visits so well. I admired his camouflage uniform and shiny boots and helmet, and he was always smiling, my uncle Anthony. Later, long after the war ended, I got to learn that every kindred in Umuchu was mandated to contribute a male child to the war effort. Anthony went of his own volition. Voluntary to start with, the mode of joining the army was to change as the war progressed.

Etched in my memory, I seem to recall that it was on a particularly dark night that my grandmother, Anderline Asine, went into hysterics. We, my mother, sister, brother and I, had finished dinner when granny's wailing cut through the late evening air. We all trooped to Pa Simon's home to hear more wailing. The war had come to me at Umuchu. My Uncle Anthony, the Barrister, the soldier, was dead, killed in action.

Living the War

Volunteers who joined the Biafran army were regarded as heroes by the community, until the army recruitment drive started, and no one wanted to be a hero anymore. I remember so well the many occasions my father's younger brother would hide in the rafters of my grandmother's room; or of the house, or would be running to the Ubo forest to evade being forced into the Biafran army. We children had nothing to worry about but as soon as the Biafran army truck came into view, young, able bodied men would run into the thick bush, even on major market days. Fifty years on, *A n'achu army*, is now used to describe situations of immediate need to escape. I did not know it then, but jealous, envious, or covetous friends, neighbours and family members used this method to send unwilling young men into the Biafran army and ultimately to death. Newly wedded brides lost their husbands this way. So many lost lands, economic crops or worse, saw their children starve to death. Just the threat of reporting to the army was enough to make young men, husbands and later in the war, mature men, quiver. Some of those young men who did join the army voluntarily or by force, wangled their way into the civil defence force and terrorized everyone. I witnessed this. My father's house is on the way to the stream. Young women usually in a group, at first or second cock crow, stealthily walked past on the way to fetch water. My uncle, Matthew, allegedly suffering from *atingbo* or shell shock, waylaid some ladies coming back from the stream. In the melee, Uncle Matthew grabbed a machete and cut down a prized paw-paw tree. He was in the civil defence force. Years later, my father told me the full story. Apparently, someone let slip the information that Uncle Matthew, considering his large size, should be in the army. My father being a senior civil servant had procured a psychiatrist's report making Uncle Matthew unfit to serve in the Biafran army and recommended him for service in the civil defence. When this information leaked, to substantiate his psychiatric status, Uncle Matthew attacked some poor innocent woman and cut off our source of vitamins and fruit.

The war was in progress.
There was scarcity of food.
Everyone was hungry.
Discussions were now in whispers,
There was much talk of relief. What was relief?

In the meantime, every inch of my father's home was occupied including the garage where Mr. Anyaegbunam's Mercedes Benz was parked. Both sides of the space between vehicle and garage wall were sleeping quarters. Beyond the front bumper was Mr. Anyaegbunam's sleeping area. I know because I stumbled on him sleeping one afternoon. After the war, I saw with my own eyes Mr. Anyaegbunam's black Mercedes Benz loaded on to a lorry. Pushing it up that ramp into the lorry took all available hands. Our living room was occupied by two families, and so was every other room except that occupied by us, and my grandmother's.

Gradually our stock of food went down, and I was initiated into eating cassava leaves. Of course, there was no salt; even my grandmothers caked salt; so, we all ate first and licked the pinch of salt on our left arm. This meant that we children went on hunts for lizards, grasshoppers, crickets and the occasional okra, pepper, and termites. How to catch termites? It started with a serious hunt for elephant grass, collected in palm sized bundles. The expedition led to an ant hill and the elephant grass was pushed into holes for the ants to bite.

It was then gradually pulled out onto a plate, cup or any receptacle. This process was repeated until there was enough to make soup. But while at it, my friends and I usually crushed the head first and plunked into our mouths. I still remember the taste.

Rat was a delicacy and we usually celebrated when we caught one. The same with lizards, the red-headed agama lizards, or the plain ones. When we caught them, we would cut the head off and roast them, after gutting the body and removing the insides. Salted and eaten with red palm oil, these creatures became a major source of protein for us. The same could also be said for the snout beetle or sago palm weevil, locally known as *Akpa nkwu*. To catch these delicacies, one must know how to climb a palm tree with or without support and put up with the pain of stinging ants that usually lived on the palm trees. *Akpa nkwu* hid in crevices that only the initiated could find. When roasted, and eaten with palm oil, we all felt the pain of harvesting them was well worth the effort.

One day, I woke up to the announcement that all zinc roofed houses must be covered in palm fronds. This was to prevent enemy planes from seeing the shining zinc roofs reflecting the sunlight and bombing them. I did not know the meaning of this until the first enemy plane flew past. We all ran to the nearest tree as directed by civil defence. The noise was frightening, and I later heard my mother and others wailing about the havoc caused by the plane. It killed many people at a market in a place called Okigwe.

News came from many sources, including the Biafran grapevine, popularly referred to as "radio without battery." These were simply rumours spread to uplift the morale of civilians or to stave off hunger, or in some cases, plain lies concocted to cause mischief. But at the time they were convincing. Another was Radio Biafra. To the sound of heavy shelling and machine gun fire coming through the radio, an announcer would coolly proclaim that it was Biafran forces decimating the enemy. It was also at this time I saw my uncle dipping expired batteries into salt solution, connected with wires into a radio set for power. I did not understand what the radio was saying but was particularly intrigued by the number of people clustered around it. Of course, children were not allowed to come close, but I do recall that when the battery went out, he again dipped it in salt solution to recharge it. Only then would we children be informed of the progress of the war. It was around this period I heard the word "sabo" which meant saboteur. Anyone suspected of the slightest infraction, real or imagined, was labeled a saboteur. In essence, fraternizing with the enemy. Thus, a man coveting a neighbour's land, wife, or simply out of sheer jealousy or envy would accuse another of being a saboteur and the accused was promptly drafted for army service and the land or wife exchanged hands in his absence. As I look back today, I shudder at the injustice meted out to the innocent and the underprivileged in Umuchu at the time.

Around this time, along with other children, I was out hunting when I learnt of my father's visit. He arrived in his midnight blue Peugeot 403 saloon car with the top half of his car's head lamp painted over in black. There were too many visitors, and apart from that first hug I never came close to him until the next morning. In the morning he tried to start the car but for some reason it simply would not start. For the first time ever, I saw the jack handle inserted through a hole in front of the Peugeot 403; a quick twist and the car roared to life. Having surmised that the battery was either low on fluid or simply run down, there was a quick hunt and scavenge for coconuts. Apparently, coconut water acts as brake fluid. A friendly visitor sold my father three coconuts in exchange for cornmeal.

On that trip, I learnt that we were to accompany my father to his base at Owerri. We left that night, and I could see the car headlamp shining on the road. Fortunately, my father was always explaining his actions to me as I do to my children today. In retrospect, he never expected to survive this war and I was to learn a lot more at Owerri. We drove at night he explained, to avoid air raids and with the top half of the vehicle headlamp painted over, we could never be sighted by an enemy plane.

We arrived Owerri safely and settled well in the Shell Camp compound. I was happy to be with my father and a cousin, George. It was also in Owerri that I experienced my first close call with an air raid. I had seen the devastation they caused in the past, but had never witnessed it first-hand before Owerri. Prior to this air raid, my father showed me around the compound particularly the bunker; with the explicit instruction to run into it whenever I heard an airplane or sensed any danger. With him never being around, I busied myself understanding my new environment and getting back into hunting. It was a wonderful experience seeing flowers and plenty of grasshoppers and lizards. These lizards were not so easy to catch as I was hunting alone. The bunker itself was a huge pit reinforced with palm tree trunks. The same with the roof, only that above ground the tree trunks were covered with earth, more earth and grass. I also had meat after a long period of not having had any during our sojourn in the village. The source, my cousin explained, was from the deadly exploits of brave Biafran soldiers who planted ogbunigwe mines to stop advancing enemy troops. The enemy knowing that ogbunigwe mines were buried on their route would drive cattle ahead to detonate these mines before attacking. But our gallant troops laid excellent ambush and massacred them as well as carried off the beef for distribution to Biafrans. This was wonderful news to me. The enemy is killed, and we receive a lot of scarce meat. The war could continue! And according to George, Hausa cows were very big, meaning plenty of meat, and they had gigantic horns!

Into this quiet life came this air raid. In my mind's eye I can still see the plane. It flew low, and the frightening sound saw me run to the bunker to meet a huge snake uncoiling itself from a beam across the roof of our bunker. George grabbed me and sprinted outside stopping my immediate junior sister, mother and neighbours from approaching the bunker. I have not forgotten that snake to this day. When it was killed, it measured six feet four inches. I was approaching my sixth birthday.

I do not recall when my father came back, but do remember his crushing hug, and for the first time, he let me use his camp bed. There were other dividends too. For a start he let me accompany him to buy petrol. Everyone called it petrol can and I do not see those kinds of containers anymore. They were made of steel, painted green, and had three hollow bars on top for easy grip. On the side was stamped a number.

Again, at night, we drove off and I woke up later to see my father talking to a man smoking a pipe. He showed me these massive tanks with a huge fire beneath them. At the other end, coming out of a pipe was what everyone queued up for. There was some pushing, shoving, angry verbal exchanges, and at last our turn to get petrol.

We had barely got back home when everyone went into a panic. My mother was hysterical. George was busy packing our belongings. In Owerri, my mother had given birth to a child, so we also had a baby with us when we left for our hometown, Umuchu, that night. The dangers and the need to be always prepared were so consuming for adults who lived through Biafra that until his passing, my father always had a half tank of petrol inside all his vehicles. He later explained to me as I got older and used up the fuel in his cars without replacing the petrol, that with half a tank of petrol, he could drive away from danger before thinking of refueling. This message has not been lost on me since that date.

Unfortunately, we had two flat tyres on the way to Umuchu. There were no vulcanizers, but we pushed the Peugeot 403 saloon car from the outskirts of Owerri to Umuchu, a distance of fifty kilometers. The impalpable spirit of the war took over. Once people saw my mother cuddling a baby surrounded by myself, a sister and George, they threw their bags on to the roof rack and pushed.

Accompanied by songs which in the jingle of the "Bab Ballads":

"I shall carry to the catacombs of age,
Photographically lined
On the tablets of my mind,
When a yesterday has faded from its page"
One song goes;
Ojukwu bu eze Biafra
Edere ya n'aburi
Awolowo, Yakubu Gowon

Unu enweghi ike imeri Biafra
Biafra win the war
Armoured car, shelling machine
Heavy artillery ....
(Ojukwu is the king of Biafra; It was written at Aburi;
Awolowo, Yakubu Gowon; you cannot defeat Biafra)

Back to Umuchu

The Umuchu we came back to was a catastrophe. The
primary school, churches and every available space were
occupied by refugees. Lizards, rats, and grasshoppers all
seemed to have disappeared. Twenty persons instead of
three or four now chased after a squirrel-sized animal.
Palm kernel had replaced foofoo for lunch. Cassava
was nonexistent. Everyone trooped to the relief points
for succour. There were no cooking fires anywhere. Even
in our compound. I could not smell stew or soup being
cooked or warmed. No fried onions. The only source of
food was now relief. This lack of food introduced a new
disease – kwashiorkor. Children, adults walked about
with oversized heads and/or stomachs on spindly legs
with owlish eyes. Their hair was dirt brown and they
seemed to be constantly accompanied by flies. Hovering
above were the vultures! It was not uncommon to see dead
bodies at the primary school, church, along the road or
on the way to the stream. They were quickly buried. No
one wailed or mourned anymore. I lost count of bodies
quickly wrapped in cloth, mat, or palm fronds before

burial. Babies, toddlers, children, adults, male or female. Parents abandoned children who could be seen opening their mouths full of flies without a sound coming out, dropping dead along the road. Adults moped about and everyone waited for relief.

At the first cock crow, we all walked to the relief center and waited for food. When it came, it was in the form of corn meal. Yellowish, tasting horrible, but everyone was scrambling for it. Then salted head of stockfish, condensed milk, used clothes. I took special interest in the treasured stockfish because my mother had to soak it in water to distill the salt it was preserved in. This water was further boiled, and the result was the treasured salt in cake form. There were also tinned fish much like the sardines of today. One had to queue for hours to have a sliver slapped on our outstretched plates or palm. You had to grab it quickly, cover it and step aside for supplement in tablet form to be thrown into your mouth and go behind the queue to start all over again. You had all day as the queue stretched far into the distance. If you were not careful and this happened to me, this tiny sliver of fish would be stolen right before your eyes and popped into a hungry mouth. Indeed, I have not forgotten nor forgiven my clansman who stole my fish. He is still alive, and we do meet occasionally, but at the back of my mind is always my lost fish.

On the home front, my grandmother was our tower of strength. She manufactured all sorts of food for us and made lots of native candles and black soap from palm waste to light up our home at night and soap to wash with. My mother and her group I remember, soaked used hair threads in kerosene, and spread them out in the sun to dry for reuse or sale.

For food, anything that could get through one's mouth would do. Maybe due to the scarcity of food or plain social anomie, there were a lot of family arguments. I vividly remember an altercation between my mother and grandmother which resulted in my lily livered, war-dodging uncle assaulting my mother. This feud is still on today albeit tempered with age. I also recollect another war-dodging uncle from my mother's side invading our family home. And because he and others were dressed in borrowed army uniforms, it resulted in a stampede as all able-bodied young men on sighting their army trucks, ran into the forest. They came with tins of corned beef which grandmother forbade me and siblings to eat and till today, in my mind's eye, I can still see the tin of corned beef on the steps of our home being devoured by a neighbour's cock. To this day I still have great difficulty with eating corned beef.

By this time, people were dressed in rags. There were no new clothes. The flow of secondhand clothes from relief agencies had dried up. Men grew their hair (afros) and spotted bushy beards.

Then one day, I noticed everyone appeared subdued. I was told the war was over. Biafra had been defeated.

There was panic as we did not know what to expect from the enemy. How would the godogodo treat us? Did they really eat people? Was it true that they captured women including Reverend Sisters? Women were hiding themselves and their children. We heard that the Nigerian soldiers captured women and they were never to be seen again and that they shot the men. I did not know why at the time, but along with other children, I was ordered to get palm fronds and wave whenever we saw Nigerian soldiers, and smile. So the day an army truck rolled along our village road, we all waved palm fronds vigorously with shouts of "one Nigeria."

Postscript

I came back to Enugu surprised to find my father's house in one piece albeit pock-marked with bullet holes and his prized books scattered on the floor.

Winston Churchill advised, "Never, never, never believe that any war will be smooth and easy, or that anyone who embarks on that strange voyage can measure the tides and hurricanes he will encounter. The statesman who yields to war fever must realize that once the signal is given, he is no longer the Master of Policy but the slave of unforeseeable and uncontrollable events. Antiquated war offices, weak, incompetent, or arrogant commanders, untrustworthy allies, hostile neutrals, malignant fortune, ugly surprises, awful miscalculations – all take their seat at the council board on the morrow of a declaration of war. Always remember, however sure you are that you can easily win, that there would not be a war if the other man did not think he also has a chance".

Fifty years after, there are still questions about whether we as a country, learnt anything from the errors of our past.

About the Author
Nnaemeka Nnolim is from Umuchu in Anambra State. A Businessman and media Executive, he lives in Enugu, Nigeria, with his wife and children.

THE GREEN MEN

By Roz Amechi

The events leading up to and during the Nigerian civil war were my earliest memories and I witnessed them as a very small child. My father, Peter Akolisa Amechi, was an Igbo man from Onitsha and my mother was from Guyana. My parents met and got married in England when my father went abroad to study Electrical Engineering. In 1966 my family, which consisted of my parents and three children, my sister Margaret, my brother Michael and I, returned to Nigeria from the United Kingdom where we were born and had been living.

Prior to the war we lived in Port Harcourt in a small flat with a balcony from where my sister and I viewed the world. We spent so much time on that balcony overlooking the streets. My mother would sit there with us sometimes either plaiting our hair or teaching us to read and write. In the evenings when my dad came home, he would come and sit with us there for a while and then go into the sitting room when his friends came to visit. His friends came almost every evening. They would talk in loud voices debating some great event that was about to happen. Our neighbour who lived in the flat downstairs often came up to join them. His voice was the loudest of all and he always seemed angry when he was talking. His voice would overpower everyone else's and he spoke like he had all the answers and wanted everyone to listen to him. Once in a while he would let others air their views and then he would jump up from his chair and start shouting so that no one else could get another word in. The debates always seemed to end in a big argument and you could not really tell who the speakers were angry with. There was a sense of foreboding and uncertainty which increased as the days went by and my dad and his friends got increasingly agitated during the debates. Sometimes they would listen to a broadcast or the news on the radio first for a while and then they would start the debates. Something was brewing and despite the laughter that accompanied the debates, the adults all seemed worried about it.

One evening I was sitting on the balcony with my sister, Margaret, watching the people go by. It was our favourite pastime as the streets were always busy and something was always happening with the neighbours or the street sellers. On this particular day, however, several people were running down the road shouting and chanting and waving leaves and branches. There was a sense of urgency and panic in their movements and instantly I knew something was happening and that my parents would want to know about it so I went to get my mum. She came out and looked at them for a while and then she went back in to call my dad. It was early evening and my dad had just come home from work. The visitors had not come for a few days and there had been an uneasy calm. Something was about to happen. My dad came out onto the balcony to see what was going on. 'What are they saying Pete?" my mum asked. My dad listened for a minute and then he said something like "It has started". My mum understood what he meant. They were both stunned and quiet.

We all stood there for a while watching the commotion downstairs. It was getting a bit rowdy. That was also the first day I saw the green men. They were all dressed in green and they wore hats that looked like green plates placed upside down. They wore green masks and I imagined that their skin was also green under the clothes. They were covered in green leaves and they looked fierce and menacing. For the rest of my childhood I remembered them as the green men and I only found out what they really were after the war when I was much older and asked my dad about them.

Some of the green men carried sticks and some had guns as they marched down the streets beside the crowds of protesters. Their presence seemed to instil fear in the already agitated people but the protest continued as we watched from the balcony. My parents went back into the sitting room. I heard my mother ask, "What does this mean?" My father seemed a bit uncertain. He sent my cousin, Ifeoma who lived with us, to call the loud neighbour downstairs. The man started shouting from the staircase. "You see, this is what I have been saying since. You see. I said it". His voice was loud but it was not as forceful as before. There was a certain resignation in his voice now as he accepted that things were about to change and not necessarily for the better. They discussed for a while about what they had to do next and the consensus was that they would wait and do nothing until things were clearer. They switched the radio on and listened to the broadcast that confirmed that Biafra was now a separate country. The other usual visitors did not come and after the broadcast our neighbour went back to his flat. My parents were quiet but pensive and Margaret and I joined in their mood. We sat quietly, no noise and no playing.

A few weeks later our lives as we knew it changed forever. My mother was baking in the kitchen and as usual we all sat around playing and watching for when little titbits would come our way. This varied from the mixing bowl which we would lick clean to the little 'testers' she made on the side for tasting. My dad walked in and called my mum out into the sitting room. He told her to start packing because we had to leave immediately. I heard my mum say "Now? Why can't we go in the morning?" My dad said "We have to go now. Just bring a few things for the children. We will be back in a few weeks. It's not for long".

My mum turned off the oven. There was no time to clear the things in the kitchen. She packed the cakes she had made and some other food items. A few clothes were tossed into the suitcases and then we loaded them into the car and got ready to go. Margaret asked where we were going and my father said, "we are going to visit relatives in Enugu". They made it seem like it was a holiday trip but my sister and I could sense the tension. The loud neighbour came in our car with us. He had a small bag and he locked up his flat which he expected to return to in a few weeks. None of us ever saw that flat again.

As we went out into the city, there were other fleeing families like us. It was like a mass exodus. There was a stream of cars loaded up with people's possessions. Then there were also crowds of people carrying bags and walking down the streets. The green men were there looking fierce and herding people. It was terrifying seeing them up close like this. I could see why everyone was afraid of them. They seemed angry and handled people roughly. Horns were blaring, people were shouting, it was a chaotic scene. Everyone was heading in the same direction, the Biafrans were going home. We drove for a long time and eventually we (the children) fell asleep. When we woke up, we had arrived in Enugu. Our neighbour was no longer with us. My dad must have dropped him off on the way. It was late at night and my Aunty Nneka and Uncle Henry Molokwu (Nwakaibeya) came out to meet us and take our things in. They were so pleased to see us but there was the same air of uncertainty and foreboding. The adults spoke about Biafra and what was about to happen and they made plans. There were a couple of visitors but there was none of the shouting or loud debates we used to have in our flat in Port Harcourt. People spoke quietly here while they decided what next to do.

The next day someone came early in the morning with the news that "Oga" had died. This seemed to be devastating news. My dad and my uncle were crying. In a short time, the house filled up with mourners. My sister and I played on the porch. We did not know who Oga was but there was so much sadness around us. Then my aunty, Margaret Molokwu, came with a car full of children. This was more like it, enough of this sadness. The children came tumbling out of the car and we all hugged, happy to see each other again. We knew something terrifying was happening but we were too young to understand what it meant and how it would affect our lives. For now, we just wanted to play.

The mourners did not dwell too much on the dead man. A little crying was done after each mourner arrived and then they would start talking about Biafra and the impending war. It consumed them. As the number of children grew, our noise level increased until the adults got fed up and banished us to the bedroom. Aunty Margaret was in charge of keeping us all quiet. She declared that it was siesta time and made us all lie down on the mattresses laid out for that purpose. No talking was allowed and a smack was promised to any erring child. Just to ensure that we knew she was not playing, she delivered two sharp smacks to my sister, Margaret (who is named after her) and my cousin Maryanne (her daughter) who were still talking after several warnings. I was lying next to my cousin, Aunty Benny Molokwu. We called her aunty because she was the youngest sibling of the adults but she was really a child like us albeit older.

Aunty Benny was quite excited about our arrival. She had heard that we lived in England and had recently returned from there. She had many questions for me so as she lay next to me, she began to ask them. I was very fascinated with this older and very beautiful cousin. I really wanted to impress her even though I did not really remember much about England. We had been back for several months and had been living in Port Harcourt but anything that would make her interested in me was good so I made something up. Aunty Margaret caught me answering her questions and warned me to stop talking but I still went on to answer the next question which earned me a sharp smack. As I started to cry, Aunty Margaret followed it up with "If I hear 'pim', you will get a real smack". That was not a real smack? The crying stopped instantly and in no time, we were all asleep.

We stayed in Enugu for several weeks. My father had to report to the secretariat for posting. All Biafran men with specialized skills were expected to offer their services and register with the war effort. My father went away for a while and it was difficult for my mother to cope outside her own home and in the midst of people who mostly spoke in Igbo, a language she did not understand. She had three small children to take care of and with my father away she was quite overwhelmed. Sometimes I would find her crying in the room alone but she always tried to put on a brave face when we were around to shield the true nature of our situation. There was not much time to brood, however as the days passed into weeks and the threat of the Nigerian army's impending approach became a reality.

My dad had just returned from his training programme when we had to move again. The Nigerian soldiers were approaching. There was talk of Nsukka 'falling'. I knew Nsukka was a town but I did not understand how a town could fall. We had to go because it was expected that Enugu would also 'fall' soon. My mother started packing again. There not much to pack as we still only had the few items, we had left Port Harcourt with. My mum had to drop her usual meticulous standards of dressing us in clean clothes every day. Water was not always available and we had so few clothes. The lack of structure around us made it impossible to prevent us from getting ourselves dirty. At this point everyone was focusing on staying alive and there was so much uncertainty about how long the war would last.

We arrived at Onitsha in the middle of the night. My dad didn't have a house in Onitsha at that time so we all stayed in one room in my great grandfather's house in Oboli Eke. My great grandfather, Akwue Chugbo Agbapulonwu (aka Akwue Onyeocha) was a red cap chief and a very powerful man in Onitsha. He was handsome, tall and fair in complexion and very fond of all his children and grandchildren. My grandmother was his first daughter and had died early when my father was still very young. A few months before she died, she had sent my father to live with her cousin, PNC Molokwu (Nnanyelugo) in Ekpoma and he remained there and grew up with PNC's family after she died. Her other two children, (my dad's siblings), Cecilia Ononye (Akaenweokwu) and Ikem Amechi went to live with Akwue. Even though my father was far away, Akwue monitored his progress as he finished school and went to university in the United Kingdom. My dad told me later that Akwue was the main reason that he was in a hurry to return to Nigeria after he completed his studies in the UK.

Akwue was extremely pleased to see us. At 97, he stood tall and strong. He had named us all and he called us by the Igbo names he had given us after we were born. There were so many people living in his large compound, so many relatives to pamper and take care of us. The next morning, we began to explore our new surroundings. Once we were bathed and fed, my brother, Michael, and I went out of the room to play outside. We had moved around quite a lot in the past few months and my sister, Margaret complained about the constant moves. She did not like meeting new people and she clung to my mother all the time.

The chaos and uncertainty made it impossible for us to continue with our lessons so we played all day every day. There were several children in the compound and we played with them. At least twice a day (sometimes more) the sirens would go off to warn us about the air raids. Once the sirens sounded, the adults would gather us all and head for the bunkers to wait out the bombing. From the bunkers, you could hear the bombs falling in the distance. Sometimes it sounded so near and the noise was so loud even the ground would shake. When it was so close, we would pray that it would not be our house this time. We would wait in the bunkers until the sirens sounded again and then we would know it was safe to come out. Sometimes after we got back, there would be wailing somewhere in the distance. Someone's home had been bombed or perhaps someone had not made it to the bunker and died during the air raid. The news of those who had died filtered through very quickly. Then people would go to the homes of those who had lost someone and commiserate. Those who lost their homes would move in with relatives or neighbours. No one knew who would be next and survival was key.

During our stay in Onitsha, my father went away again. It was more difficult for my mother in Onitsha because she was not very familiar with the environment. She did not really know the relatives in Onitsha and communicating with them was a challenge. My dad was training young boys who had been conscripted in Ozubulu and once in a while he would come back to bring us food items like milk and flour and other things that were becoming difficult to get. Food was scarce and people were beginning to feel the effects of the war but in Akwue's compound we were relatively well fed and cared for.

At the beginning of October 1967, we received the news that the Nigerian soldiers were advancing and we had to move again. Everyone was running. It was like the exodus from Port Harcourt. Some were in cars; others were walking but everyone was on the move. We loaded our few belongings into my dad's car. He had returned from Ozubulu to move us from Onitsha. There was no time for long tearful goodbyes. No one said goodbye, it was 'till we meet again" and we were all hopeful that we would gather together again soon but no one knew for certain. That was the last time we saw Akwue. He died the next day.

Some of the old red cap chiefs and other old people

stubbornly refused to leave. They sat in front of their houses watching the chaos and waiting for the Nigerian soldiers to come. They claimed they were too old to run and live outside their comfort zone. They said, 'they will meet us here when they come' and they did. When the soldiers came, they killed some and left others to die of hunger and starvation. The remains of their bodies were discovered sitting in the same position when their relatives returned at the end of the war.

Uncle Henry and Aunty Nneka whom we had stayed with earlier in Enugu were, by this time living in Umuahia. That was our next destination. Many of the cities and towns had 'fallen' so Umuahia was crowded. We had become accustomed to living like nomads constantly moving trying to avoid the Nigerian soldiers. As we travelled there were several checkpoints. The Biafran soldiers were looking for young men and boys old enough to be conscripted, who had not yet joined the army. As we drove by, we saw some young boys who had been dragged out of their cars and were sitting at the side of the road waiting for the officers to take them away. Their families sadly were sent on without them and some would never see those families or their homes again. However, my family was spared that trauma as my brother was too young to be conscripted. My father had to show evidence that he had already joined the war effort and he explained that he was taking his family to Umuahia.

We arrived in Umuahia later that same day. My mother was much happier to be in Umuahia with Aunty Nneka. Despite their wide age difference, they were very fond of each other. Aunty Nneka did not have any children at this stage so she gave us her undivided attention. So many people were on the run from their homes so all 'safe' places were crowded with relatives. Since there were many people to feed and food items were becoming scarce, we had fewer meals per day. Apart from that we were quite comfortable and well taken care of.

We maintained some level of stability in Umuahia. Again, we tried to settle into our new surroundings. There were other children in the compound and neighbouring houses and my mother elected to teach them since all the schools were closed. They came every morning for classes. Michael and I did not have to join the classes initially but my mother made me read to her every day. Margaret was becoming rather quiet and broody but she had to join the classes because she had started school before we left Port Harcourt. Every day Michael and I would go out to play but we had to stay close to the house and once the sirens sounded, our nanny, Chinyere, would come and drag us to the bunker.

After a few months, the effects of the war began to have a greater impact on our lives. It was early 1968 and the war was quite advanced. Food was being rationed and the number of people living in our household had increased as most of the neighbouring towns had 'fallen' and more people had moved to Umuahia. At this point we ate once a day and most of the children were thin and emaciated. We could not go out to play any more as we had to conserve our energy. People came to beg for food frequently but we didn't even have enough for our household and the women always sent them away. Aunty Nneka and some other women were in charge of cooking and feeding everyone. Sometimes when they were cooking, she would call my brother and I and a few smaller children in to drink the water used to cook the meat. There was very little meat and most times we did not get any of the meat with our meals so the nutrients from the meat water would sustain us. We did not like drinking the meat water and we often tried to get out of drinking it, but Aunty Nneka always insisted. It was her way of keeping us healthy.

One of the major hazards that traumatized me as a child was the constant air raids. It took a long while to get used to the sound of the sirens and the bombing. As months passed, the raids became more frequent and were a constant disruption to our lives. By July 1968, I had joined my mother's little school which had grown considerably. There were some other mothers who had also volunteered to teach some classes but it was difficult to concentrate with the frequent air raids and we seemed to spend more time in the bunkers than in the makeshift classrooms. Once the sirens sounded, there would be a mad race to the bunkers and people often sustained injuries from running to the bunkers. The bunkers were quite awful, dark, and wet with rodents and dangerous insects like scorpions. Nor was it restricted to the daytime, sometimes we were woken up from sleep to run to the bunkers because there was an air raid in the middle of the night. There was simply no peace.

One day, the sirens went off and everyone started running to the bunker. In the usual panic and chaos, I must have turned the wrong way and found myself alone in the farm at the back of the compound. It was a small farm with vegetables like ugu, waterleaf and okra but it seemed very large to me at the time. I started heading back to the house to see if I could find someone or get my bearings. Even though I didn't really understand how much danger I was in or what would happen if I didn't make it back to the bunker, I was scared because I had never been outside alone and I wasn't sure which way to go.

I heard the leaves rustle and sensed the movement before I saw him. It was a green man lying in the vegetable patch. I froze, I could not move. I was terrified. I watched him and he watched me. He did not move either, only his eyes moved. I did not know why he was there or what he was going to do but after staring at him for a few seconds I ran off. He did not come after me and there was still no one around. I slowed down as I approached the house. I saw a stick on the ground and bent forward to pick it up. The stick raised its head just as I reached forward and at that same moment someone grabbed me from behind. It was Chinyere. She had realised I was missing and came back for me. When we got to the bunker, she told my mum she had just rescued me from picking up a snake with a big head. I had no idea what a snake was or that I could have been bitten by it and no one bothered to explain.

Later that evening I told Chinyere about the green man. She did not seem to understand what a green man was but she was interested enough to investigate. She wanted to know exactly where I saw him so we went together to the back of the house but he was not there anymore. The vegetable farm did not even look like someone had been there and I wondered if I had imagined it. However, she told me not to tell anyone what I had seen. That was when I started having nightmares about the green men. In my dream I would find myself in a vegetable farm and all the vegetables would jump up and turn into green men and people would be running around screaming in fear; then I would wake up. It was the same recurring nightmare and it went on for many years even after the war ended.

Our living situation got worse by the day. Between the raids, the uncertainty and the starvation, my mum's nerves were getting really frayed. We hardly saw my dad who was training cadets in Okigwe. When he came to visit, my mother told him about the incident with the snake and how I got lost on the way to the bunker. My brother had also been left behind on one occasion when everyone was in the bunker. No one even noticed that he wasn't with us. We found him eating in the kitchen when we got back, totally oblivious of the potential danger. Earlier, on the way to Umuahia, he had broken his arm and had to wear a cast for several weeks. By the time the cast was to come off, his arm was so emaciated it was swimming around in the cast. We had all become very thin and weak. My brother's head looked larger than the rest of his tiny body and his eyes seemed really large in his head. Margaret had become moody and miserable and I kept getting into one difficult (sometimes dangerous) situation after another. My mother was worried for her children and the end was not in sight so my parents started talking about moving again.

I told my dad about the green man. He smiled and asked me if perhaps I saw him in my dream. I said "no, I really saw a green man". I described what I saw and where I had seen him. My dad asked Chinyere and she said she had checked but there was nothing like that. She said the fear of the snake must have confused me. No one believed that I had seen a green man but I think Chinyere knew which was why she asked me not to tell anyone. The next day my dad left promising to come back soon and take us away.

One evening I followed Chinyere as she went out of the house. It was almost dark and she slipped into the small farm at the back of the compound. She had been disappearing a lot and she could never account for her whereabouts when my mum asked her where she had been. I followed her quietly. As we got into the vegetable farm, I saw someone come out of the shadows. It was a green man. She was not scared and she did not run away. She went up to him and they walked off together. I ran back to the house but I did not say anything to anyone. I waited for her to come back so I could ask her about the green man but she never came back. My mum called and called for her but she was nowhere to be found. It was clear that she had run away because her bag of clothes was gone too.

When my dad came back a few days later I told him that Chinyere had gone off with a green man. He laughed, "Is it the same green man you saw in the farm the last time?" They all had a good laugh. No one took my 'green men' stories seriously but no one could explain how Chinyere had disappeared either. My dad had come to take us away so my mum was busy with packing our things. My mum seemed rather excited about this particular move. Aunty Nneka tried to dissuade her from leaving but my mother felt this was a necessary move for the safety of her children and for her own sanity.

When we were ready to go everyone came out to say goodbye. We packed all our bags into my father's car. This time we only took our clothes and personal items, nothing else. All the children that my mum had been teaching were there and some neighbours too. These were not happy times and there was a sense that things were about to get much worse. We cried and hugged everyone as we got into my father's car. Again, it was not goodbye but 'till we meet again'. In all this uncertainty no one was sure of anything. We just prayed that we would see ourselves again. When we arrived at the airstrip at Uli, there was only one small aeroplane there. It had British Red Cross written in bold red letters and a large red cross symbol. It was a small cargo plane used for bringing food relief and medical supplies. It had a few seats inside but was not really designed for carrying passengers. There was another family, a man, woman and two children already seated in the plane. My mum and dad talked for a while and then the pilot said we should strap ourselves in because we were about to leave. My dad got up and I said, "come on daddy, you have to put on your strap". He said "I'm not going with you. I have to stay and fight in the war". This was devastating news. We all stared at him in total disbelief. We had thought we were all going to be together wherever we were going. What would we do without him? I said "you have to come with us. If you stay here the Nigerian soldiers will kill you and we won't have a daddy anymore". At this my dad burst into tears and we all started crying. It was not hard to imagine him being killed as several families around us in Umuahia had received news that they would never see their dads or brothers again. They had been killed in the warfront.

He tried to explain that men were not allowed to leave but his explanation fell on deaf ears. I asked him why the other man could go with his family, and then the man got up and said he was not travelling either. His own wife and children started crying too. It was a very emotional scene. Families were being torn apart and we did not know if we would ever see each other again. The pilot came around again and said we had to go as it was getting late. He looked sympathetic and gave us more time to say our goodbyes. Margaret started screaming and clung to my dad. She was particularly close to him and she said she wanted to stay back with him. He assured us that the war would soon end and that nothing would happen to him.

He and the other man left amidst our screaming and crying. My aunt, Cecilia Ononye, told us later that he visited her immediately after we left and he was in a pitiable state. Parting with us, was for him, the most difficult part of the entire war. To distract us my mum gave us a few treats she had brought along for the trip but we had no appetite to eat anything. Even my brother who never said 'no' to food would not eat anything. We cried ourselves to sleep and woke up just as the plane was landing in Equatorial Guinea.

There were so many people at the airport when we landed. They did not know us but they were curious to see the new refugees from Biafra. The people were very kind. They gave us bread and milk to eat and little plastic dolls to play with. The British Red Cross staff brought out some clothing and blankets and then took us to the refugee camp. There were several other Biafran families in the camp, mostly foreign women married to Biafrans and their children. The families were waiting to be shipped out to their countries of origin or any other country they could reside in till the war ended. My mother was originally from British Guyana but had lived in the United Kingdom for many years and possessed a British passport so that was our destination. Most of the women intended to return after the war but my mother was adamant that she would never return. The horrors of the war had left her, and in fact all of us, quite traumatized.

The refugee camp was not home but it was clean and there was food to eat. In the mornings we had ground rice porridge which we liked very much. To this day, ground rice porridge reminds me of the refugee camp in Equatorial Guinea. We also did not have to worry about the air raids and running to the bunker anymore. It was such a relief not to hear the mournful sound of the sirens and the falling bombs. The uncertainty was still there and we missed our dad but we were safe. We played with the other children in the camp until their families left one after the other. New families arrived from Biafra to join us and each family awaited their turn to leave.

The Home Office was responsible for evacuating

us and other British families to the UK. My mother accepted to refund the cost of our evacuation once we were settled in the UK. Finally, the day for our evacuation came. We thanked the Red Cross volunteers and said goodbye to the remaining families. This time the plane that took us was a proper passenger plane with relatively comfortable seats.

When we arrived in London, it was cold and wet and dark. A far cry from the sunny Biafra we were used to. We seemed to have gone further away from my dad and the memories of all the relatives we had left behind. We stayed at a hotel for a few days while my mother looked for a job and found somewhere for us to live. As Biafran refugees, we received some government assistance which made it possible for us to live until my mother got a job.

Our first home was a two-room apartment with shared bathroom facilities. My mother did not like to share a bathroom so she bought a huge tub which she put in the middle of the living room for us to bathe in. Kind neighbours who heard that we were Biafran refugees brought blankets and other items for us so we soon settled in and started school. As we arrived in mid-winter, it was dark when we woke up in the mornings and dark when we came home from school in the evenings. The cold was unbearable and we did not have any friends. All the moving around was taking its toll on us, especially on Margaret who did not like change.

I was still having nightmares about the green men but I did not tell anyone about it.

We came home one day to the news that our mum had had an accident and would have to go to the hospital for an operation. We were not yet in touch with any relatives living in the UK so arrangements had to be made for us to go to an orphanage for a couple of weeks while my mother went into hospital. We packed a few things and my mum dropped us off there before she went to the hospital.

We soon got settled into the routine of the orphanage. My brother, Michael was in a different section with the boys so we didn't see much of him except during mealtimes and when the children gathered in the common room. Margaret was very worried about whether my mother would come back for us or if we would be abandoned like the other children in the orphanage. All the moves and upheavals had made her sullen and quiet. She thought about things deeply. She was always reading and though she did not say much, she knew things. Whenever I was puzzled about anything, I would ask her and she would know the answer. She seemed to me like a quiet embodiment of wisdom and seriousness, the total opposite of me. I was carefree and did not worry too much about anything.

One evening all the children were laughing and playing in the common room and my brother and I joined in. My sister came in quietly and gazed at us for a while and then she asked me to come with her because she wanted to tell me something. As I followed her reluctantly to the bedroom we shared with a few other girls, I wondered if she had received some bad news. She seemed more grave than usual. We sat down and she stared at me for a while and then she said in the most solemn voice "you know that daddy is in Biafra fighting in a war and he could die there and you know that mummy is in hospital and might not come back from her operation. Should you be laughing with the other children at a time like this?"

I looked at her, not knowing what to say. I could hear the other children laughing in the common room and I wanted to get back to them but I could not just walk away. I knew she was right but I really did not want to think about these weighty matters right then. Fortunately, I was spared having to respond because the Head came in and asked us why we were there and sent us back to the common room. After that Margaret said nothing more about my carefree manner but whenever I saw her, I could feel her disapproving stare following me everywhere I went.

A few days into our stay, the orphanage was abuzz with arrangements for a Christmas party for the children. The older children prepared performances, songs, poetry, and short dramas. There was also to be a dancing competition and other forms of entertainment. There was an air of excitement as we all prepared for it.

I put my name down for the dancing competition. On the day of the party, participants were invited to the dance floor for the competition. I could feel my sister's disapproving eyes watching me but I ignored her and stepped onto the dance floor. It was mainly white music like Tom Jones and Lulu. The judges liked my movements and I won a prize for best girl dancer. I was thrilled and I ran to my sister and showed her my prize which was a large book, '100 Fables'. She was not pleased that I had participated but she liked the prize and she spent the next two days reading the entire book; it took me two years or more to read it.

When the two-week period was up the Head sent for us. My brother came along looking scruffy and unkempt. My sister looked at him disapprovingly and commented on his scruffiness. She hardly ever spoke to him. She considered him rough and unruly. Unlike my sister and I who were regularly commended for good behaviour, he was always in trouble and getting into fights. I was fiercely protective of him though. I helped him tuck his shirt in and tied up his shoelaces to make him presentable enough to see the Head. It was good news. Our mother was out of hospital and would be coming the next day to pick us up so we were to pack our things and be ready. The Head spoke kindly to us. She treated us differently from the other children because we were paying guests and ours was a short stay but we could see that the orphanage was no holiday camp for the other children. We said our goodbyes and left with our mum the next day.

Over the next couple of years, we moved several times. First, we went to Corby where my mum got a teaching job. For me that was the worst place we ever lived in. The school was all white. We were the only black children in the entire school. The children were not accustomed to black people and were clearly uncomfortable with our blackness. They called us nigger, gollywog, monkey, and a host of other names. If bananas were served at lunch time, it was open season. We told our mum that the children were cruel to us but she said we should ignore them. She taught us a 4-line poem to recite when they start but it was not a practical solution. My mother did not encourage emotional displays. She felt we should toughen up and deal with it. She had enough to worry about with the war, not knowing if we would ever see my dad again and having to raise three small children on her own. We stopped complaining and kept our misery to ourselves.

I had no friends in school. It was unusual for me as I always gathered a host of friends wherever I went. Margaret did not care about not having friends; she preferred to read anyway. During break times I played with a girl called Susan who no one liked because she was always unkempt. They called her names too, so there we were, the two class rejects playing together. One of the children told me they would become my friend when I lose all that blackness and become white like them. Susan told me that if I scrubbed my skin really hard, I could scrub the blackness off so I tried this whenever I took a bath. I told my sister my plan for becoming white. She looked very doubtful, "I don't think you can become white from scrubbing" she said but I didn't believe her. She really was very negative sometimes.

During the summer holiday of 1969, we went to London and attended a rally for Biafra. There were many Biafrans there who were either students or families that were living in England. There were also other supporters who had no ties whatsoever to Biafra but were moved by the sad pictures and news on the television about the genocide in Biafra. The speakers made moving speeches asking for help and support for our soldiers. It was good to see so many black people. We told people that our dad was a Biafran soldier and was fighting in the war. We received letters from him regularly and we wrote to him every week. Sometimes we would not hear from him for quite a while and we would be really worried but eventually we would get letters from him. He always sent a separate letter to each of us. My brother never wrote, (he could not read or write) but sometimes he would get a letter too and we would read it to him. Sometimes some of the writing would be blotted out. We asked my mum who did that and she said perhaps the Biafran officers blotted out information that they did not want to fall into the wrong hands. We were always happy when we heard from my dad and for days we would read and reread our letters, exchanging, and sharing. It was like a bonding session and sometimes we would cry because we missed him so much. After some time, I really could not remember what my dad looked like. We did not travel with any pictures and the memory of his face had grown dim. I just remembered that he was always smiling but I really could not remember what his features looked like. My brother could not remember anything about him at all but we all missed him.

We moved to Grimsby at the beginning of the next school year. My mother got a better job and we had a nice house with a garden. My mum had found her feet and our lives were much better. The horrors of the war were becoming a distant memory but in forgetting the sadness we left behind we were forgetting the people we loved and the Igbo language we had picked up while we were there. The loss of the memories was as devastating to us as the loss of the people including my dad. Sometimes when we could not sleep, my sister and I would talk about Biafra and try to remember the names of the people we knew and some of the Igbo words. Try as we did, we could not remember the Igbo words or even the names of the food we had been used to. We remembered *"kachifo"* (goodnight) and *"kedu"* (hello). We repeated the words we remembered over and over again so we would not forget but by the next time we would have forgotten a little more. My sister and I had become quite fluent in Igbo while we were in Umuahia because of the 'school' we attended but we forgot most of it while we were in England. It added to our sadness and sense of loss. I still dreamt about the green men; I had not forgotten them. After a while, my memory of Biafra was all about the green men and nothing else, not even my dad.

In Grimsby we met a Biafran family, the Aghanyas who introduced us to the Biafran and Nigerian community in Grimsby. We spent a lot of time in their home especially at the weekends. Being with other Biafrans helped us remember and stay in touch with our roots. It was also refreshing to be with other black families after operating in an all-white environment for so long. One weekend while we were there, a Biafran man came to visit with his daughter. They were visiting the UK from Biafra when the war broke out and were unable to return. The girl spoke Igbo fluently and was an instant star. We were in awe of her, a child who spoke the language of the adults. The adults spoke to her in Igbo and she responded without even uttering a single English word; the adults were charmed. When they finally released her to us, we took her outside to ask her questions. She was a bit older and remembered much more than we did about Biafra. She had not seen any of the war so her memories were of good times and not jaded like ours. She taught us some Igbo words and reminded us of some words which we had forgotten. We really enjoyed talking to her. That evening when we got home, we started reciting the Igbo words we had remembered and the new ones we had learnt so that we would not forget them again. I dreamt about the green men that night too and the sound of the sirens.

Going to school in Grimsby was a more pleasant experience than in Corby. There were several other black children in the school so our blackness was not such a novelty. We were invited to birthday parties and had play dates. Being white was not important to me anymore especially as James Brown's song "I'm black and proud" increased our awareness and encouraged us to embrace our blackness.

In January 1970, we received news that the war was over and Biafra had lost the war. There was no immediate plan to return home as the expectation was that my father would join us in England. For a long while after the war ended, we did not hear from him and we began to worry that something had happened to him. Eventually he wrote and confirmed that all was well but there was no indication as to how and where we would be reunited with him. A year passed and it became evident that my father would not join us in the UK. One day my mother called us together and announced that she was considering returning to Nigeria. We had visited some other families who had also been evacuated like the Chioris and the Ezebuiros and they were all planning to return home. Margaret did not welcome this news. She did not want to move again now that we had settled down and life was so stable. My mother reminded us that if we went home, we would have sunshine all day, every day and we would not have to stay in school till 4pm as we did in England. None of that could convince my sister and she was adamant that she was not going home. The horrors of Biafra and the instability caused by the multiple moves had not left her. My brother agreed with her and said he did not want to go either. My mother and I on the other hand were all for going home. I did not like the winters and I liked the idea of living in a country where majority of the people were black. Even though she had called us to discuss it, her mind was made up and we started packing to go home as soon as the school year was over.

We arrived in Lagos in July 1971 after almost three years of being away. We had forgotten most of the people we knew and our memories were fraught with the horrors of the war. My dad was waiting for us at the airport. There were about six men standing in a line and the airport official asked us to show him which one was our dad. All I remembered was that my dad was always smiling but two of the men were smiling and they both looked familiar. My sister went straight to my dad, she had not forgotten him. I went to the other man with the familiar smiling face, it turned out he was my Aunt Cecilia's husband, Patrick Ononye

(Nnabuenyi). The rest were strangers co-opted to trick us. It was an emotional reunion; my dad was so happy to see us again all grown up. We stayed in Lagos for a few days and then my father took us back to the East.

The trip back to the East was a journey down memory lane. Once we got to Onitsha, the memories started flooding back. We went around to see long lost relatives and we went to Akwue's house. Even a year after the war had ended, the whole town was a scene of devastation that told the story of the horror that had taken place there. Almost every house had been bombed and there were holes in the walls. Some had been partially rebuilt while others were completely razed to the ground. The people were beginning to heal but all conversation was still about the war, how they survived it and the people we had lost. Akwue died the day after we left Onitsha. He was in a car trying to leave and was hit by shrapnel near Borromeo Hospital. His compound seemed smaller than I remembered it.

My dad asked us what we remembered about the war and he was amazed at my memory and the details I recalled. I had forgotten most of these things when I was in England but once we came back to the scene of the war, all the memories good and bad returned. I asked my dad about the green men. I had not dreamt about them for a while but I still remembered them. My dad laughed "you still remember the green men?" I was old enough now to realise that there was no such thing as 'green men,' but there was definitely a memory of scary men in green. My dad said, "The green men were the Nigerian soldiers; they wore green uniforms and green hats and they sometimes covered themselves with green leaves". After my dad told me who the green men were, I never dreamt about them again.

My dad took us to Ozubulu to show us where he had trained the young boys. He said that they trained the boys on the use of firearms that they would never handle. The boys went to the war front with sticks and stones to fight well trained and armed Nigerian soldiers. At the end of each training session the boys would be excited about going to war. They would dance and sing songs about what they would do to the Nigerian soldiers. My dad never joined in the celebrations. As each batch left, he would have tears in his eyes because he knew that at least 80% of them would be killed on the first day. Our brilliant young boys who had so much to offer, had their lives cut short in a war they didn't even understand. Those who survived were either severely wounded or emotionally damaged by what they had witnessed. Boys as young as 10 years old were conscripted into the Biafran army and many of them perished in the war. Just talking about it made my dad sad.

We proceeded to my dad's house in Nsukka. He had got a job in the University there and lived in one of the lecturer's houses. Settling there took a long time especially for my sister, Margaret, who had had one move too many but eventually we got our lives back.

The Nigerian civil war took its toll on the lives of all Igbos living in Nigeria at that time. So many lives were lost. Sons, fathers, uncles who died in the war were mourned and forgotten as the years went by but the tragic impact the war had on family relationships lasted longer. Many families did not reunite again after the war. Some people went missing forever and some of the foreign wives and their children who went abroad never came back. Thankfully, our story ended in praise!

About the Author

Roz Amechi is from Onitsha in Anambra State. She is a Lawyer and Chartered Management Accountant and lives in Abuja in Nigeria. She is married with children.

INNOCENT PARTICIPANT: THE BIAFRAN WAR I SAW

By Chuba Obi

I was four years and five days old when the Biafran war started on the 6th of July 1967. These are some of my direct personal experiences over the next two and half years during which the Republic of Biafra struggled against all odds to survive.

My earliest recollection of the war was the drive from Enugu to my hometown, Ogidi. My family lived in Enugu, the capital city of the former Eastern Nigeria. Enugu also became the capital of the new Republic of Biafra. It was an unusual drive in my parents' Peugeot 403 car, with an air of panic and urgency about it. This, I later learnt was due to the imminent fall of Enugu which happened around Oct 1967. The adults were sombre and there was none of the usual family banter as they hurriedly piled both goods and children into the car and we left. The drive however was without any specific incident that I recall. Perhaps I just slept through most of it.

I recall a relatively "peaceful" but short stay in Ogidi. I guess it was only "peaceful" to the extent that I did not really understand what a war was, or what the adults talked and worried about. I was also fortunate enough not to witness some of the horrors many of my peers saw in Biafra. There were, however, the constant sounds of faraway gunfire and of course, the regular diving for cover when the air raids by the Nigerian Airforce came, which was at least twice or three times a week. Thinking about it now, it was inevitable that at some point we would have to leave Ogidi as the advancing Nigerian army drew closer.

When the day of evacuation from Ogidi came, I noticed the old familiar air of panic amongst the adults, quite similar to what happened during the Enugu evacuation. I could hear distant sounds of what I later learnt were exchanges of fire between the Biafran and Nigerian sides. We left Ogidi with those sounds getting louder by the hour. I recall the adults getting more anxious and desperate as news came through that an aunt of ours had been killed by a mortar in a local market.

We fled Ogidi to my mother's hometown, Ukpor, in what is now Anambra State. The journey was both peaceful and unremarkable, largely because I probably slept through most of it. Whatever the adults were feeling, they did their best to shield us from it. We were to spend the rest of the war in Ukpor.

Whilst I have very fond memories of my time in Ukpor, sadly there are no photographs, or any visual recordings of these important years of my young life.

Life in Ukpor was significantly more stable than it had been in Ogidi. The sounds of war were much more distant except for the air raids, the air raid warnings, and distant sounds of what I later learnt were bombs being dropped in market places.

I Knew A Soldier

Long before we arrived at Ukpor, my mother's immediate younger sibling, Uncle Paul, in his twenties, was said to have very happily and enthusiastically fled home to join the Biafran army in the Afugiri training camp, in what is now Abia state. He was a typical Igbo youth for whom Biafra was a divinely cherished and totally desired next phase in the journey of life. Uncle Paul was my symbol of Biafra at the time and since then. A determined and courageous man, very clear in his mind about the mission, he was single-minded and inexorably committed to what he saw as the mission.

He would come home on leave from the "war front," as it was referred to, driving, or being driven in what might have been a Land Rover type vehicle. He always had a bodyguard with him. Though he was not a soldier in the Nigerian army, he had attained the rank of Captain in the Biafran army. My older brother, Jideofo, and I would ask him on each visit to bring us Biafran military caps similar to the one he wore. He would agree, whilst lifting us in turns and throwing us into the air a few times. In my eyes, Uncle Paul was a marvel, a dream, a star fighting for our cause. More importantly, I think as a Biafran soldier, he was living his dream. Every time he came home, there was great joy in the household. He would have his "Madison" the Biafran synonym for the Russian AK47, which he wrote that his troop obtained from captured Nigerian soldiers.

During one of his visits, he left the gun at the entrance to the outside toilet enclosure. The toilet was a pit latrine located a short distance from the main building. Whilst he was in the toilet, my older brother, Jideofo, picked up the gun and started to play with it. I do not recall if the bullet magazine was in place. What I do recall is that there was pandemonium when people saw Jideofo carrying the gun. I really don't recall if his backside received the usual visitation of the cane customary for peculiar acts of stupidity, or if he was spared that experience, but it was the day we learnt that *egbe* (gun) was not a toy.

Uncle Paul came home regularly, and it was always a delight to see him. One day, the vehicle arrived with only the bodyguards. Captain Pedro, as he was known, had died from a sniper's bullet as he and his men rested in a bush clearing after a skirmish with the Nigerian forces.

*Captain Paul 'Pedro' Anekwe.
Biafran Armed Forces
Commander Company D,
Sector 26,
51 Brigade,
Abakiliki.
Killed on duty in 1968
by a sniper's bullet as he and his
company rested after an operation.*

Captain Paul 'Pedro' Anekwe

Uncle Paul's funeral was, in my eyes, quite elaborate. My grandmother was inconsolable. Uncle Paul was her first son. She pleaded to be allowed to go and drown in the nearby local river Nsansa (a tributary of the River Niger). My grandfather, also named Paul, had died in the fifties leaving her with eight children, and as hard as it was, she had successfully raised all 8. To lose her first son without warning, was a shock nothing had prepared her for. How could she live whilst her son lay cold in the ground? Even to this day I can still hear her anguished wails as her son was buried.

To this day, my talks with my uncle and what I learnt of him, leave me in no doubt that there was no greater Biafran in belief, spirit and in practical deed than Captain "Pedro" Paul Anekwe. We have a lovely photo of him posing with his "Madison" in full Biafran army battle fatigue and helmet. As a Biafran soldier, Uncle Paul lived his dream.

Survival To The End

School for my age group was initially held in the front building of the family home. The building is known as the Obi, and is the heart of the compound in Igboland, and usually the seat of the head of the family. I remember the teachers, Akachukwu and John Ofo. I recall a lovely song they taught us which included their names. Some of the words :

> "...*Good bye to brothers, goodbye to sisters,*
> *goodbye to Akachukwu and John Ofo...*"

We sang that at the end of the day. I can still sing the above lines. Later, my age group was moved to another location. At the new location, I recall the teaching was mostly outdoors. There were fewer of us, and the teaching was not as regular as in the obi.

A number of families joined us in Ukpor. I recall children slept together, sometimes on mats and the adults got the mattresses which were tossed on the floor. I remember the shock of the first night I had to sleep on a wooden board. I think it was a bed base without a mattress. There simply were not enough mattresses because the house was full. However, people moved on over time, and I think I got back unto a mattress.

I remember at least one visit to a food distribution centre to receive ready to eat "corn meal" rations. It was part of the war relief effort to feed Biafran children and the general population. The venue was an open field. I stood in a line with other children around my age or slightly older, holding mainly metal bowls. Some adults dished out the food into our plates as we filed in front of large pans containing the food. There were quite a large number of people, but it was orderly. No one was pushing or jumping the queues, the scene was just one orderly throng of hungry folks. The food they gave us was the semi-solid brownish yellowish corn meal dough which could be eaten with or without any sauce or soup. When it came to my turn, the servers dished my share, and I took it home. We did not eat the food at the location as the adult family members who brought us took us home to eat. I do not recall another visit to the centre, nor do I recall my elder brother going back there either, but I often heard people talking about relief packages and so knew when "nni relief" (relief food) was available for people to go and collect. Perhaps I was judged too small for the walk to and from the distribution centre. I do remember either wishing I had eaten the food right there at the distribution centre, or feeling sad, or actually crying for not being allowed to do so. Perhaps that tantrum was the reason I never went back.

One of our regular activities was water fetching

from a lifesaving stream called *Onye ma N'odi* (literal translation: "who knew it existed.") My regular water fetching vessel was a plastic container with the number '3' inscribed on it. That meant that its capacity was three bottles. I am not sure what constituted a bottle in that respect, but the vessel was just right for my strength and stamina. It was dark green in colour and it was mine. I can still see it in my mind's eye. Few contested that vessel with me when it was time to fetch water. I would fight and cry to have it. A few times, it was given to another child, but not for want of me doing my utmost best to get it back.

At the stream, there was this belief and practice that an object called oba could emerge from deeper parts of the stream and pollute the water by stirring up white clay. This could happen by someone simply chanting these words whilst standing around the source from where the water emerged from the ground:

'Oba gbalu ee, gbalu ee' ('Oba pollute it, pollute it').

I could have sworn it worked at times, as the white clay would suddenly seem to begin to melt from the floor of the stream and turn the water white. Oba never responded to my own chants, but I recall some much older people seeming to make it happen. I still wonder why.

Ironing clothes was one chore I was beginning to get introduced to. The ironing equipment was a rectangular shaped iron pot with a handle and a smooth base. The heat was supplied from red hot charcoal placed inside the pot. It was called a "coal pot" iron. Many my age and older know this appliance very well. I do not recall an Igbo name for it other than "iron" or *"ife eji ede akwa"* (literally: the object used to iron clothes). One day, I was enjoying my newly acquired skill in cloth ironing. It was on the balcony of the house. The ironing stand was the floor. There was a folded cotton wrapper spread over the floor to provide some cushioning. Then there was the iron placed on two similar sized tin cans or stones acting as the iron holder. I knelt right next to the cloth and iron and began the task. Yours truly ironed away, enjoying my new experience. With a coal pot, you have to occasionally open the pot and fan the charcoal to heat it up. I did that, but I did not click the pot cover locking mechanism into place, either at all or properly. Then, I got distracted by whatever it was at one point, as I placed the pot on the tin or stone stand. I came back to the present when the iron fell from the stand and emptied the hot charcoal on the inside of my left lap, a few inches above my knee. My oh my! Pain and shock! Rivers of tears! I had managed to burn myself. Perhaps I was not quite as adept at ironing at the time as I thought?

It was our regular guest and relative named War who administered medication to the injury until it healed. The medication was a dark coloured ground substance. He was consistent and meticulous in attending to me. He would try to distract me with his sweet stories and songs while he administered the painful substance. I have never forgotten him. To date, the scar from that burn remains clearly visible on my lap. It is not going anywhere, and I do not want it to. It is my own personal Biafran war emblem.

One of my most profound memories was witnessing the conscription of young men to join the Biafran army. As four, five, six-year olds, we were the only ones who could safely stand outside and watch the large trucks arrive, soldiers jump out, and young men of fighting age scamper away. They hid in *"uko"* (lofts), bushes, and anywhere else they could. The soldiers were menacing. If they found a man of fighting age, they would make out they were going to shoot them but they did not. They would instead, march or bundle them into the trucks and drive away. There would be sadness and tears. I later learnt that this was near the last months of Biafra, when the casualty rate was very high and the confidence in Biafra succeeding was very slim, morale quite low.

One element that baffled even the younger ones like me at the time, was that when air raid warnings sounded, we the children would be asked to go indoors and get under the bed. I recall my young mind wondering if those things called bombs could not be thrown at houses. Anyway, Jideofo and I enjoyed chatting and playing under the bed until we were asked to come out. The other instruction was that if the warning came whilst we were outdoors, we should try as much as possible to make ourselves look like shrubs. The instruction was that we must bend touching our feet with one hand, and then we were to point the other hand skywards. I think we were also told to keep one eye closed. I recall being made to practice this, but cannot seem to recall ever using it.

There were also many occasions and efforts at designing activities and entertainment for us children in an effort to create some sort of normalcy by the adults. For a while, we attended Boys Scouts meetings. The venue was a kind of clearing in the bush. There were a few other boys and our instructors. I looked forward to the sessions and enjoyed them. In my mind, based on what I heard, the activity was associated with the famed Biafran Boys Brigade movement. Oh! How a starry eyed 5/6-year-old romanticised about being in the Biafran Boys' Army. Perhaps it was for that association, and/or fear of insecurity, or whatever reasons, the scout meetings either did not carry on; or my brother and I were withdrawn by our parents.

Along with other children in the compound, we also found ways of entertaining ourselves. We would hunt and eat aku, an insect that only showed up during the rainy season, just after it rained. We would catch them in the air and sometimes eat them raw. Cooking was not required, though they could be fried into a delicious treat. Catching aku was so much fun, but playing in the rain generally, was an unbeatable experience. Naked or clothed, we would enjoy the showers, running around, shouting, and just enjoying being children. This playing in the rain was called *ogo'go'mmili*.

We also picked up craft making during the war. For instance, I learnt to make bamboo stick guns. Called *egbe sukwulu dam* in Ukpor ('*egbe*' means gun; '*sukwu lu dam*' is the sound it makes just before the 'bullet' leaves the gun. The sound is caused by the internal air pressure in the gun which fires off the 'bullet'). In Ogidi it is called *egbe ugulu* (Harmattan gun), as the bamboo trees were more available in the Harmattan season. It is also called *egbe otosi* (otosi is one of the Igbo names for bamboo). We cut and built these guns from the specie of bamboo trees with hollow stems. They have non hollow nodes separating the hollow stretches of the stem. The 'bullet' was mainly cassava plant bark nodes. Slightly chewed-up paper could also be used as bullet. The gun was fired with a particular stick called ukpodi used as the trigger. These skills kept us entertained and out of mischief, and also kept our young minds busy. We got to understand our environment well and built our own toys out of the abundance of nature's gifts.

My relatives, War and Emodi would often come round to our home in the late evenings and tell us captivating folk tales. They were mainly about adventures in obodo iduu. "*Obodo*" means "land of," "*iduu*" refers to fairies. I looked forward to those evenings and thoroughly enjoyed them. We also had some theatre as well. We attended church at St. Peter Claver Church in the neighbouring village of Umunuko. The church was always well attended. A number of times there were drama presentations in the church hall or in a school hall on the premises. The stage was made of a collection of strong tables arranged together. I never really understood the stories, but others seemed to because there was a lot of laughter. They were good relaxing occasions for everyone.

Then one day I heard *agha ebe go* (the war is over). The adults said the war was over. It was a relief to them. Some danced out of relief and pure joy, as others knelt down and raised their hands heavenwards, mouthing "Thank God" under their breaths. To me, things just seemed a lot less tense. There was no more hiding and fear. But I also quickly realised what it really meant when a few days later, I saw soldiers march past our compound. The adults told us that they were Gowon's soldiers and that they won the war (*fa emeli go*, they have won). Another uncle of mine, Edwin, survived the war, but never returned after he ran into the victorious Nigerian soldiers. His disappearance was a mystery. My grandmother, who passed away in 1996, hoped until her last breath, that he would return one day. Many thought he was a victim of post war killings by those 'Gowon's soldiers' who are said not to have spared men of fighting age they came across.

I was exactly six years, six months, and fourteen days old when the war ended on 14 January 1970. Between that date and 30 January 1970, when we returned to Enugu via Ogidi, I recall while watching Gowon's soldiers march past our home in Ukpor, my feelings of hurt, disappointment, and sadness that "Gowon's soldiers" won. I wanted Biafra to win. I wanted Uncle Paul to win. I wish Biafra had won. I regret that Biafra did not win.

Out of good fortune, I did not see the horrors that many of my peers saw. God have mercy on the souls of the departed, in Jesus name, Amen. All glory to God.

About the Author

Chuba Obi is from Ogidi in Anambra State. He is a Film Producer and Property Investor, and lives in London with his wife and 4 children.

AIR RAID AT OZUBULU

By Godwin Meniru
(From the collection, War Stories in Verse)

Obia-no! Obia-no! shouted alarm.
Off I went, running for life.
Obia-no! Obia no! Shouted again.
Peak velocity reached by this time.

My legs pumped furiously, desperately
Distancing from shiny roofs, as
The planes seemed to love our homes.
I had my siblings and cousins all in tow, as
I sensed what was coming next.

Obia-no! Obia-no! Sounded again.
We tore into farmland, seeking cover.
Obia-no! Obia-no! One last time; I
Heard other sounds enter the stage.

Wara Wara, announced jet engine planes.
Rat ta tat tat, responded antiaircraft guns.
Cha-dum, Cha-dum, pumped the Bofors.
Boom, Boom, targets bombed.
Dudu, Dudu, deep-throated cannons.

Obia-no! Obia-no! "It has come! It has come!"

I crouched under the cassava and yam canopy,
Not realizing it was not bulletproof, looking
Around anxiously to account for my charges.
I quaked and shook in terror, desperately
Praying to God, as rockets and shrapnel
Churned the ground around us.

Let this go away, I prayed, but intermissions
Were short, like bouts of diarrhoea, just
Long enough for the planes to turn around, and
Head back our way.

> *Wara, Wara*
> *Boom, Boom*
> *Rat ta tat tat*
> *Dudu, Dudu*
> *Cha-dum, Cha-dum*

Ugwuolie shopping district, hit.
St. Michael's new church under construction;
Multiple roof perforations from strafing.
Regina Caeli Secondary School Army Hospital, attacked.

And so continued the symphony of air warfare, while
We hid under green crop cover, hoping the planes would
Miss us as they came and went, unchallenged in the sky.

> Until silence, and
> A pregnant pause, with
> No idea of what lay ahead.

OMO EKO RUNS FOR LIFE: MY BIAFRAN WAR TIME EXPERIENCE

By Godwin Meniru

The sky was grey and overcast when we left Lagos in August 1966. It was early morning, and the weather was still cool. We were woken up earlier than usual and told that we had to leave for the East the same day. I cannot remember being pre-warned about this trip; just that on this morning my three siblings and I were bundled into the car, and off we went, leaving Lagos at high speed. There was no time to say goodbye to my friends at Saint Catherine's Model School, Yaba, Lagos; I have never seen or heard from them since.

Our driver, Tobias, was behind the steering wheel of my mother's Opel Rekord sedan, while my mother sat at the back. I sat in front, on the bench type seat, with my younger brother Obiajulu, who kept us occupied with wild chatter at the initial part of our journey, calling everyone we saw on the road, Hausa. This was a child of less than two years who already knew enough of the prevailing situation we were in to be mouthing discordant but hauntingly familiar themes. My two sisters sat behind with my mother, together with our two nannies. It was a little cramped in the car, but no one seemed to mind. We carried the essentials, enough to fit inside the boot.

I was six and half years then, but I clearly remembered the politically tense atmosphere in Lagos in late 1965 and into the New Year. I would hear the adults discuss reports of people being beaten up or worse, killed, depending on their political affiliation. I saw the newspaper and TV photos of the day assemblymen scaled walls, gates, and concrete building fenestrations, trying to escape from the Western House of Assembly. Then one morning I woke up to hear that there was a coup during the night.

This was the 15th January 1966 coup in which the Prime Minister of the country, Alhaji Sir Abubakar Tafawa Balewa, as well as the Sardauna of Sokoto, and twenty others were killed. I regard this as one of my first significant childhood trauma incidents, Nigerian politics associated. This was the first of many such episodes that negatively impacted my life over the ensuing three plus years, and subsequently over the last fifty years. I was shocked that someone would want these public figures, whom I also used to see on television and in newspaper photos, dead. They looked like all the fathers and grandfathers I knew then, with their danshiki, and flowing agbada robes, seen around Lagos with their families. It really struck home for this child of Lagos, this Omo Eko, in a very bad way.

My parents moved to Lagos when I was still a baby. Therefore, Lagos was all I knew in my early years. My father, who was an American trained mechanical and automobile engineer, worked with the Nigeria Railway Corporation. My mother who trained in England and was a secondary school principal until just before her wedding, worked with the Ministry of Education.

As matters evolved over the subsequent days, I came to learn more about the identity of some of the coup plotters the most prominent of whom was Major Chukwuma Kaduna Nzeogwu. The coup was foiled by Major General Aguiyi-Ironsi but I believe the damage was already done as evidenced by strife that I became aware of later on that year, which culminated in a second military coup in July 1966.

It was about this time that we were stopped from going to school by my parents. Apparently, things had become very dangerous for Igbos, both in the west and north of Nigeria. We heard of harassment of Igbos going on in parts of Lagos and a more massive killing exercise happening up north. Even my parents used back roads through safer neighborhoods as they came and went from our house in Surulere. It was soon after this that we found ourselves speeding out of Lagos early in the morning, rapidly clearing Ore and Shagamu, and settling down to a high-speed transit from the west to the east of Nigeria.

Unlike my mother's previous practice, she did not hold back our driver, Tobias, from driving fast that day. I saw him reach top speeds never recorded in my family. This resulted in our arriving at Onitsha still in daytime, by about 5.30 that evening unlike the practice on previous trips which was to arrive after dark. We stayed for a few days at Onitsha with my maternal grandfather, Paul; my maternal grandmother died a few years previously. We then moved on to my hometown at Nawfia where we met my paternal grandmother; my paternal grandfather was at Aba at that time.

My father did not make that trip to the east with us. He stayed back in Lagos for a few more days to pack up our belongings and freight them down east. He subsequently arrived a few days after us and met us at our hometown in Nawfia. He was able to compress a lot of our belongings into two Lorries. However quite a lot of things were left behind at Lagos, lost to us forever. One happy event that evening when the two Lorries backed into the family compound to offload the items, was when we saw that our dog, Bella, was one of the returnees. This was something we were familiar with, keeping us company in our Igbo heartland that was still a mystery to us Lagos kids.

It didn't take long before we had to start dealing

with issues of our homeland such as the ants and mosquitoes that bit us with a vengeance, turning our nice light textured skins into a battleground of scabs and scars. The Chemist at our mother's hometown, Ozubulu, said we were hypersensitive to insect bites, but that did not help our case. Mosquitoes gleefully dove in for their nightly feast despite the unusual smelling mosquito repellent coils that were lit all over the house every night.

This was unlike the situation at Surulere. I know we had mosquitoes there too but the density and ferocity of the bites in the East was something else. I could hear them drone around outside our bed nets at night waiting for an opportunity to bite. And they did so repeatedly, at times biting us through the tiny holes of the mosquito net when we lay against it as children often do. The story did not end with daybreak; a new set of attackers rolled in for their turn, flies, bees, and wasps together with the ground crawlers such as the agbisi biting ant. In early evening, the sand flies moved in.

There was no electricity in the village. There was no pipe borne water. Not much concrete pavements existed outside the family house apart from a tiny eighteen-inch wide pavement that was attached to the perimeter of the house. Every other place was sandy, muddy, or covered by thick bushes. Everywhere was quiet, quite different from the hustle and bustle of Lagos. And we had no friends; just a bunch of welcoming relatives and distant cousins who spoke English and Igbo with a clearly distinct accent that we were unfamiliar with. When I hear of culture shock now, I smile in realization that this was what we went through then, adjusting to life in the East when we ran back from Lagos.

We eventually got to Enugu where Uncle Augustine, one of my father's younger brothers who lived in two flats along Ogui Road, graciously let us live in one of the flats. He lived with his family in the other flat and we rapidly became friends with his four children, our cousins, who mirrored our age except for the youngest who was still a babe in arms.

My immediate younger sister, Ngozi and I were then enrolled at Sancta Maria Primary School where we continued with our education. This was a Catholic run primary school with a reverend sister as the principal. With time we started running into fellow evacuees whom we used to know at Lagos. Most had successfully returned to the east but my uncle Patrick, who was my mother's immediate younger brother, was missing in Kano after having sent home his wife and son at the early phase of the pogrom.

It was at Enugu that the full spectre of the killing of Igbos going on up north and out west hit us; we heard gory tales from those who fled east alive and saw very disturbing images on television and in newspapers. I remember we collected money and clothes at school as donation for those other displaced less fortunate easterners.

My uncle Patrick, whose whereabouts were unknown suddenly turned up at Enugu. He reported having been spirited out of Kano by one of his Hausa friends. He described how he travelled by foot off road through farmland at some stage because the roads were very dangerous. He survived by eating tomatoes and fruits he took off the farms.

We were still in Enugu when the declaration of independence from the rest of Nigeria happened on May 30, 1967. The new country of Biafra quickly started getting ready for its defence as Nigeria refused to accept her independence. Our parents bought matching shirts and trousers for all of us with labels bearing our names and hometown address sewn inside of each garment. This was to aid our reunion in case we got separated during the coming war. We were also instructed on how to crawl under beds, the dining table or staircase for protection during air raids.

My mother and aunts started civil defence training, coming home in trousers and polo shirts, and carrying wooden replica rifles. Life was tense and worrying for me then and I did not share in the general enthusiasm I heard around me regarding the possibility of war. My mother's youngest brother, Joseph, joined the Biafran army. He was my favourite uncle who was fond of carrying me on his shoulders whenever he visited us at Enugu. The last time I saw him, he was in uniform as a Captain, and had a batman. He was not as ebullient as he used to be and in later years I wondered if he had already seen action in battle by this time and lost his innocence.

We were still at Enugu when the Biafran invasion of the Midwest must have happened and unsuccessful outcome known. There was a Biafran army officer I used to know then. He had a kindly disposition and always wore a smile. He disappeared for some time and reappeared with multiple surface wounds all over his body that were painted with gentian violet. He could not even put on his shirt fully because of the wounds. Someone whispered to me that he was flogged as punishment for being a saboteur; he said it had something to do with the Midwest invasion. This was about the time we left for Port Harcourt.

We joined my father in Port Harcourt (a.k.a. the Garden City) where he now worked for the Marketing Board. We did not enroll for school when we got to Port Harcourt due to aggressive bombing of public places by the Nigerian Air Force. We were homeschooled by my mother who also worked at the Ministry of Education. She made lesson cards for us every day and was quite strict when she was in that role. We studied, supervised by others, while she was at work, but she reviewed our work and marked our test papers when she got home later in the day.

One benefit of our homeschooling was that we continued to progress academically by age and did not lose any year when the war ended, and we returned to regular schooling. This was unlike the experience of most people who lost two to three years of formal schooling during the war and started behind when the war ended in 1970.

We never personally experienced Enugu falling to the Nigerian armed forces during the ensuing war because we left before that happened. We heard of that event from Port Harcourt. The war was already being fought at Port Harcourt too, initially as air raids, but the Nigerian marines were also in the process of invading Biafra from the coastal areas. We found ourselves experiencing almost daily bombing. We had some near misses including one in which Nigerian planes shot missiles at our house.

We lived at Ihekire Street in Port Harcourt in what was a Government Reserved Area (G.R.A.). This provided posh living spaces for the middle class. The one-story duplex building with a detached three-room boy's quarters was opulently furnished with modern conveniences, thick Persian area rugs and other comforts that reminded us of what we left behind at Lagos. Our house sat close to either one of the tributaries of or the main Okrika creek. I always liked to walk the banks of the creek at low tide and watch crabs and other amphibious sea life scurry around. I loved to watch the fishermen at their craft and we frequently bought freshly caught fish from them.

I remember how amazed I was the first time I ate

fish we bought from them. The fried fish tasted so good, much better than anything I had eaten up till then. The adults smiled indulgently telling me it was because the fish was cooked so soon after being caught, without refrigeration and all other preservation steps. I also remember how I tried to start an aquarium with gifts of small fish (fingerlings or fry) from the fishermen, but they all died rapidly to my dismay. It was then that the ever-knowledgeable adults informed me that they were salt-water fish and would not survive in the tap water I used.

The cousins whom we stayed with at Enugu when we ran from Lagos visited us once and stayed the weekend. They had evacuated to Aba when Enugu fell to the Nigerian forces. They introduced us to Isam (periwinkles) and showed us how to harvest them from the shores of the creek at low tide. These were later used in making soup, but I never really became a fan of Isam soup. I did not like the "fresh" seafood odour the soup had. I did not like sucking out the periwinkles from the shells; you never knew what you were sucking into your mouth. The soup was slimy although okra was not used. I believe that sliminess, called draw, came from the specific chopped vegetable that was used in making the soup. My family subsequently made that soup once or twice more before they stopped. I guess it did not catch on with us. I must hasten to say that this is a delicacy in the riverine areas of Nigeria.

Life at Port Harcourt was heavily accented by the war. There were frequent air raids conducted by the Nigerian Air Force. From accounts of where they struck one got the impression that they did not distinguish between military installations and civilian areas. Residences, schools, markets, churches, refugee centers and other public places were bombed repeatedly and with very high casualties. I remember at least one occasion when Diobu market was bombed with a lot of deaths and wounded being reported. We rarely went anywhere else apart from church for Sunday Mass because of the ever-present threat of air raids and indiscriminate bombing. I received my first Holy Communion in Port Harcourt with Mass being celebrated by Bishop Okoye.

We had not been at Port Harcourt for long when we received news of the death of my uncle Joseph at the Nsukka sector. They said he was killed by machine gun fire crawling forward to rescue his batman who had been hit by an earlier round of the same gun. His batman survived. It was a horrible day in our house. My mother was very upset and cried virtually throughout that day and into the next day. The news had come in by about midmorning. I never saw my mother cry like that either before or after this. In my adult years I figured that since their mother died some years prior to this, my mother, who was Joseph's eldest sister, probably assumed the role as Joseph's mother. But it was a complex relationship because she also seemed to hold herself accountable to their late mother for Joseph's welfare. "What will I tell my mother that happened to Joseph?" This was one of the statements she repeatedly cried out in her dirge that went on for hours until she went hoarse. She was inconsolable; my father could not say enough *"ndos"* (sorry). We, her children also tried but nobody was able to get her to stop crying. She left for her village of origin at Ozubulu the next day for what was likely a funeral service with other members of her family. But Joseph's body was not returned from the battlefield for burial; apparently, he was buried at the warfront. No one knew the exact location of his grave.

This was another one of the clearly recognized items of trauma that I experienced during that war and it stuck with me. It persists till today, and I still miss my uncle Joseph a lot. I looked at him as a kind of big brother. I do not think he was more than ten years older than me. He was very nice to me and I always looked forward to hearing his voice then as he arrived at our house on a visit. I later tried to memorialize him in a piece that I published in my first volume of poems.

By the time we got to Port Harcourt I noticed that all vehicles had the upper halves of their front lights painted black. I was told this was to prevent reflection of car lights upwards into the sky so that enemy warplanes would not use them to locate towns and cities or even specific parts of cities. The same phenomenon happened with houses. Outside (security) lights were not switched on at night. Even lights within the house were switched off as soon as possible or lighting kept to a minimum.

Blackout curtains were installed on windows or the upper part painted black to exclude as much light as possible from leaving the house. Some people used cardboard box cutouts to cover their windows. Despite these measures there would always be passersby who would shout at your house for "lights out" or to cover your windows if they felt that too much light was still emanating from your house.

Another feature that I noticed at this time was the use of palm fronds to cover shiny metal roofs, again for the same reason of preventing detection by overflying enemy planes. I am not aware how well this camouflage of buildings worked. What I know is that later on in the war when we moved to areas that had no pipe-borne water, rain water collection became a problem because the roof water runoff was invariably amber in colour and contained particles of broken down palm leaves and fiber. We had to bathe with this water. I believe some drank the water, but we fetched our drinking water from the stream although that was not necessarily the healthier option.

We had a few close brushes with death in Port Harcourt. First was when the house next to us across the street received a direct hit from a Nigerian bomb. It was about midmorning with bright sunshine. Both mum and dad were at work and we were home playing, after finishing our schoolwork. Our minder, Lazarus, was cleaning the house and at that time was sweeping the staircase. We heard a plane droning around and took cover under the staircase as usual; that is, some of us did so. One of my younger sisters, C.C., the most militant of us, refused to join us under the stairs. Lazarus also refused, instead continuing with his sweeping. This was not a jet plane; it was what we used to call a "propeller" plane.

Next thing I saw was a bright flash of light like lightning. Although this was a bright sunny day the flash was real. This flash of "lightning" was immediately followed by a very loud blast and shaking of our building. This is still the loudest sound I have ever heard in my life. All the house windowpanes shattered immediately. Luckily, none of us was hit by the flying glass shards. My sister C.C. was not hit; that was when she ran under the staircase to join us. Lazarus somehow was swept from the top of the staircase to the bottom, apparently by the shockwave or whatever that came with the blast. The bomb blast did other damage to our house. I know it ripped out wall mounted house fittings including an electric water heater.

But the bomb did more damage to the house it fell on; I cannot remember the details, but part of the house was extensively damaged. Most sorrowful was the fact that our neighbour's son was killed in that bombing. He was either seventeen or eighteen at that time and was the only son of his parents.

People soon trooped in like they usually do, looking at the damage done everywhere and gawking. Someone must have sent word to my parents because they arrived soon afterwards. I remember the look on my mother's face before she saw us. I cannot ever forget that look. Reliving that experience now as I write this brings up a lot of emotions. My mother nearly lost her four children on that day in 1968 while another mother who lived across the street lost her only son.

I often wonder what came to my mother's mind when she got the news that her home had been bombed or was next to one that received a direct hit. What thoughts chased through her mind as she rushed home? In what state did she expect to find her children? Did the message she got include the fact that we survived the bombing? Even if we were dead the message sent to her would have omitted that fact.

People still do this in Nigeria; bearers of bad news either minimize the severity of the problem or give another reason for wanting you to get home or to your base. That is their way of protecting you from yourself until you got into safe territory where you could be monitored and restrained, if necessary. I do not subscribe to this practice; I deeply resented it when it was used on me several years later. Anyway, the look on my mother's face as she approached the front door of her house reflected pure agony and fear.

Just to emphasize, Ihekire Street was in the G.R.A of Port Harcourt, a middleclass residential area. There were no military installations on this street or around us as far as I remember. This family that lost their son was not a military family. They were Ikwerre, one of the ethnic groups of Eastern Nigeria that automatically went with Biafra. The pilot clearly targeted a civilian area.

The damage to our house was repaired, the boy was buried, and the war continued. The memories faded with time or were repressed because everything is vivid today like it was on that day just before noon when I saw my only daytime lightning flash in the absence of thunderstorms. I also had a dream a few years ago in which an atomic bomb was dropped on us at work, with buildings collapsing all around me. I woke up hot and sweating but was thankful it was a dream. I got out of bed and captured my feelings in a draft poem that was eventually completed and published as, "Bad Dreams," in my first volume of poems. Writing this poem helped calm me down that night and allowed me to go back to sleep.

My parents subsequently had a bunker dug behind the house. The first one got filled up with water very quickly, so we stopped using it. Another one was dug further up along the incline, still at the back of our house; we took cover there whenever there was an air raid. In retrospect it was a flimsy affair, probably seven feet deep with steps cut into the earth. It was covered with tree trunks and branches, leaves and soil. It was also always wet, and water still seeped in probably because of the land level and the fact that we were in a riverine area. We also shared that space with termites and other insects such as cockroaches. I often worried about snakes crawling into that bunker, but we luckily did not encounter any. A direct bomb hit would have buried us there or excavated us from that bunker, in both cases killing us. More likely, the bunker helped reduce the risk of injury from shrapnel and indirect hits. I remember once when Uncle Patrick visited us but refused to get into the bunker with us; he said he preferred watching the planes and taking cover if he needed to.

But that was before jet fighters joined the battle. Those planes came in so fast that you only heard the sound of their engines when they were already all over you. You could only get to the bunker on time if you were forewarned by antiaircraft guns going off in the distance or by air raid sirens.

I remember one Sunday evening when the whole family was relaxing on the lawn outside the house, in fact behind the house and facing the creek. Everything was fine, warm, and rosy, and my mother was telling us a story. Then the peace was suddenly broken by a shout to run for cover; "Take cover, take cover, take cover," someone shouted. We were so adept in that activity by that time that we were in the bunker within seconds but two MiG fighter planes, flying in tandem, had already released missiles that hit our house. But the missiles did not explode; this was another one of those miracles we experienced during the war.

We called in the army corps who removed two unexploded missiles from the house. One missile had partially perforated the cement block wall but became lodged in the wall. The second missile fully penetrated the wall and punctured the house water tank in the roof space. They retrieved both missiles and took them away for controlled detonation after gleefully showing them off to us. The missiles were either yellow or orange in colour; I do not think they were green in colour.

I later figured out that Port Harcourt airport was located several miles away behind our house in the distance. We were still separated by miles of creeks and marshland. At times we wondered if that was why those Nigerian planes frequented our area, but that cannot be a good enough reason. Furthermore, it has been established beyond doubt that Nigerian Air Force planes attacked civilian targets throughout Biafra and for the duration of the war.

One evening a distant relative came from Aba with a message for my father. I remember how my father's head snapped back violently when the uncle whispered into his ear, so that other people could not hear what he was saying. It turned out to be a message that my paternal grandfather, Joseph Ejinaka, had been killed that afternoon by a bomb at Aba.

My grandfather was at home in the then family house at 81 Tenant Road that afternoon when the bomb hit. The house was close to a market. Anyway, the bomb destroyed half of the building, which included the part he was in at that time. The bomb severed one of his legs. He lived for a little while but died that same day.

My father left immediately for Aba. Burial was also immediate as was done during that war. I do not know if he got to Aba before his father was buried. He soon returned to Port Harcourt in mourning. One of my cousins, Ifeyinwa, was seriously wounded in that bomb attack but survived. She still carries evidence of that bomb injury that includes scars on her face, but they thinned down with time.

Ifeyinwa turned out a nice-looking, dark-complexioned woman. She has always been a quiet one and I do not know how that experience affected her. Ifeyinwa is one of the few people in our family you could not imagine harming a fly. For her to have gone through that ordeal is still heartbreaking but I thank God she survived the bombing. I found out in recent years that more people who lived in that house either died or sustained injuries from that same bomb attack.

As the weeks and months went by the Nigerian forces got closer to Port Harcourt. You could now hear the sound of battle in the distance at night when everywhere else was quiet. The sound became even more prominent with time; I remember thinking that it was due to a cool off of the weather from an approaching Harmattan season. It is now likely to be because the fighting was getting closer to Port Harcourt. If it was not that it was about death the symphony thus created was quite interesting to listen to. The predominant sound was intermittent small arms fire going in bursts of *rat tat tat tat* repeatedly. At times, the gap between bursts got so small that it became a continuous drum roll as in *ratatatatatatatatatattttttt,* probably from automatic rifles or machine guns. But there was another continuous fire rhythm that was deeper in tone and sounded more like *drrrrrrrrrrrrrrrrrrrrrrrrrrrrrr.* This may have been what they used to call HMG, for heavy machine gun.

Then you had punctuations with, "*duuum,*" probably from mortar fire or something heavier, or the Biafran ogbunigwe land mine. Immediately after such boom sounds were heard, everywhere became quiet for a few seconds before the small arms fire resumed, initially hesitantly. This went on for most of the night but somehow, I slept through it once I fell asleep. Years later I wrote another poem, "Third Marine Commando," to immortalize that bullet filled rhythm I heard from my bedroom window that I still cannot dance to.

There was one morning when I woke up to see strange looking boats tied up behind our house on the banks of the creek. This was completely unlike what we had seen previously so I pointed it out to my parents who called up the army corps again. A platoon or whatever it was of Biafran soldiers subsequently arrived at our compound and went combing, as they called it. They identified the boats as belonging to the enemy. However, they did not encounter the occupants. Later on we heard that the invaders were captured somewhere else. The war had touched us again. Those Nigerian soldiers landed behind our house while we slept. They must have walked past our house as they went about their mission that obviously did not include us, thus their leaving us alone.

At some point it was clear to the adults that things were getting to be quite unsafe. Without warning, as usual, and planning for us to return to Port Harcourt, my parents packed us off to Aba, one evening, to be with our uncle Augustine and his family. I remember the vehicle we used this time was a Volkswagen Combi bus, dark blue in colour. They tried to fit in a brand-new Raleigh bicycle my parents had bought for my 1968 birthday, from Kingsway Stores. It could not fit in, so the bicycle was left behind. The plan then was to pick it up later, but this did not happen since my parents had to leave Port Harcourt in a hurry soon after that.

The loss of my brand-new bike was another major blow for me during the war, as I saw it from the eyes of a kid, but I never had another bike. This marked my final descent into a type of life that continued after the war, where survival was the main emphasis of life. None of those luxuries that we were used to in Lagos returned. No pianos: my mother came from a musical family and frequently sang. Her father used to be a headmaster and church organist, I heard. We also danced a lot at home. There were no more music or foreign language lessons. Never having enough for real affluence but never poor enough to be abject; always scrimping, saving and frugality; not necessarily evil qualities I must hasten to say but certainly a huge change from how it used to be for us when we lived at Lagos before the war.

My parents appeared suddenly at Aba one mid-morning looking disheveled; they left Port Harcourt in a big hurry. And no, they did not bring my bike, but at least they were able to evacuate another relative, Uncle Phillip, and his family from Diobu. I guess that was a better choice. They told of how Port Harcourt had fallen into enemy hands and the mass of humanity that thronged the roads as people tried to escape ahead of the invading troops. Toilet paper and most manufactured items had become scarce by 1968; Nigeria invaded Biafra and the war started on July 6, 1967. This scarcity worsened after Port Harcourt fell, because of the loss of the seaport and the last international airport in the enclave. People turned to using newspapers and sheets of paper from every source including used school notebooks for wiping after relieving themselves. They improved the cleaning power of the sheets by first crumpling and spreading them open again before use. Some moistened the sheets of paper with sprinkled water before crumpling to make them even better. If using pit latrines the paper went into the pit immediately. If still using water cisterns the paper was collected in bins and burnt every weekend. Still others used cups or bottles of water for irrigating themselves in lieu of "toilet paper." Those that defecated in the bush used leaves they plucked from around them. You had to be careful not to use irritating leaves (similar to poison ivy) to avoid your buttocks lighting up. Banana leaves were the most desirous. You can imagine the hygiene deficits associated with this state of affairs, especially when it came to handshakes. Even fetching drinking water from streams that flowed through several towns was problematic; people often went to wash off the last traces of fecal matter and have baths in such streams and rivers. We all took it in stride then, often cracking jokes about the practice, but you can understand why especially those with a higher standard of life pre-war found such experiences quite traumatic and noteworthy.

I will not say I saw it all in Lagos, Enugu, or Port Harcourt because I was shielded from want and a lot of social ills by my parents, and our middle-class lifestyle. My father worked for the government in various engineering outfits throughout the war, so he always brought a salary home. My mother also worked for the government, until the time Port Harcourt fell. She later started writing books with her freed-up time, after teaching us our lessons, food hunting and all other activities permissible by the wartime conditions.

But they could not shield us from the sights and sounds of war, from the frequent air raids by jet fighter planes with their guttural gut-wrenching sound, bombs, rocket fire and anti-aircraft guns. I still tasted enough danger and horrors from where I was. I saw more horrors after Port Harcourt including children with Kwashiorkor whom I heard and saw a little of at Aba. I saw much more of when we reached Ozubulu.

We stayed at Aba for a few months, but the city also fell in 1968 to the Nigerian army and we had to take off for my mother's hometown of Ozubulu. We stayed in her large family house together with my maternal grandfather, Paul, and most of his children, their spouses, and his grandchildren. We all had run from cities that were overrun by the Federal forces. When the family house became overcrowded my grandfather gave my father a piece of land in front and to the side and he built a three-bedroom house for us. I remember we had to go all over town and buy already moulded cement blocks made before the war started.

We also hunted for termite mounds all over Ozubulu and brought back to the building site. They were pulverized, mixed with water and sand, and used as mortar for building the house. I cannot remember if any cement at all was added to strengthen the binding power of the mortar. My father reported that the material from the termite mounds had been discovered by Biafran engineers to be good for building. They also used the same mortar to plaster the walls. The house was then roofed with zinc sheets we managed to buy, and the ceiling constructed with bamboo. The house was then painted. Following the end of the war the wall plaster was replaced with conventional cement mortar and the bamboo ceiling replaced with modern asbestos sheets as was the building practice then. My father left the building for my mother's family at the end of war when we left Ozubulu.

We continued to run from missiles and bombs at Ozubulu. We experienced more deaths in the family and many uncles who went to fight the war never returned home. We plugged ourselves into farming and other food gathering activities of my mother's family, adapting our diet as dictated by war conditions and availability of supplemental international food relief supplies.

Somehow, we managed to maintain a semblance of normal life in between running for cover from periodic visits by jet fighter and bomber planes. A new sister joined us in 1969 together with quite a lot of baby cousins. I would say that I came of age at Ozubulu, watching and learning a lot about my Igbo heritage, many times what I would have learnt had we remained in Lagos. For one, I was intrigued by and frequently sat with one of my great uncles, Nnaa, during his morning and evening traditional religious rituals. He spent quite some time praying and chanting. He drew white lines on his body and on the floor in front of his alter with white native chalk called Nzu.

At some stage he would break a kola nut and offer some pieces to the gods on the altar and share the remaining pieces with me. He would also pour native gin, also known as Kinkana, into a glass shot and throw towards his carved god replicas and other artifacts on the alter. Then he would pour another shot and drink and pour me my own shot to drink. Then his wife would serve him breakfast or dinner and I got a plate too. I do not know if my parents ever found out about my morning and evening rituals with my great uncle, but my aunts and uncles all knew and found it amusing. Eventually my curiosity was sated, and I moved on. At the same time, I became a Mass Server in church and received my Sacrament of Confirmation by Archbishop, later Cardinal, Arinze.

I learnt to swim, fish, farm, process harvested food crop and set traps for animals. My mother banned me from canoeing for fear of my drowning but that did not prevent me from doing so. Somehow, she found out and meted out punishment, but the activity continued with me looking out for possible spies. My father was the nice one of the two but did not interfere with my mother's physical education.

It was left to one of my great aunts, whom we called Nne and Nkemejina interchangeably, who was Nnaa's wife, to rescue me whenever she heard me cry. At such times she would wonder loudly if my mother would still be alive if she had been hand raised the way she was carrying on with her first child. Anyway, on such occasions I would escape to Nne's compound next door, after standing obediently and receiving my lashes on the palm. I would spend hours in her house with my other escapee cousins being heralded with stories of everyday life as she went about her work, smoking her native tobacco pipe from time to time. Nne was a dark complexioned wiry and cheerful woman who exuded humor in everything she said or did. We really enjoyed her company and found reasons to go over to her house several times a day. We ate and relaxed at her house until evening. Then I went back to our compound by which time my mother would have cooled off. My maternal grandmother died in 1964 so Nne acted as a sort of surrogate grandmother for all of us though she had children and grandchildren of her own. Years later my mother's disciplinary activity went one eighty degrees, and she became putty in the hands of my younger siblings; such is life.

I do not think I need to continue enumerating all I did at Ozubulu, including broom making and processing virtually every part of the palm tree into some product. I watched and participated at times in the preparation of garri, fermented cassava foo foo, flaked cassava, akamu (pap) and many other food products. That was where my interest in cooking probably started and by the end of the war, I knew how to process most harvested crops for food and to cook a lot of different dishes.

I was the first grandchild of my mother's family, so I was doted on by all members of the family. I was frequently invited to meals as I perambulated the various compounds of the extended family. Such was also the high degree of trust we had in each other in those days. Aunts and uncles watched in benign amusement as the erstwhile prep school child went native. As I wrote in one of my poems my mother was nonplussed, and my father smoked a pipe!

That is where we were for the rest of the war through 1969 and into the first two weeks of January 1970 when the war ended. We went back to Enugu sometime in April with two aging cars and everything we had in life fitting into their boots. These were what remained of two lorry loads of household items that made that run in 1966 from Surulere, Lagos to Nawfia. Everything else was left behind at Lagos, Port Harcourt, and Aba when we vacated those cities always in a hurry. The bulk of our family heirlooms was lost when someone set our family house at Nawfia on fire as the town was overrun by the Nigerian army while we were still at Port Harcourt. Our dog, Bella, was seen at the compound gates barking while the house burnt. We never saw our family dog again.

Loss of material items was not the worst thing that happened to me, and probably most Igbos during that war. Instead, we have a legacy of multiple traumas, but this is rarely talked about. We are war survivors, and the scientific literature is replete with documented trauma effects on populations such as ours. This was worse in our men who went to fight the war. The few studies that have been carried out on people of Igbo extraction confirm these trauma effects, which can be transmitted to progeny up to the eight to tenth generations. For example, it has already been shown that there is a higher incidence of eating disorders, hypertension, and pre-diabetes in Igbo war survivors. Most of us probably have either chronic PTSD or some variant because of our life of multiple traumas in Nigeria starting for me from the time of the first coup and continuing up till today. But we cover it with prayers and other avoidance measures. More constructively, the Igbos supported themselves to rebuild their destroyed cities after the war though the Federal Government also made efforts in that regard. A lot of lost personal wealth was never recovered.

It is a larger story, more than what I have written here. I am still looking back at my life and chronicling aspects of interest and importance both in poem and prose. However, everything still seems to revolve around the early mishaps of my birth country and opportunistic reactive phenomena that have seen to the virtual exclusion of my ethnic group from meaningful participation in the government of the country. It is a life in which a large proportion of the children of those pioneers who rushed back home after studies overseas, to help develop their country, and many others, are now back overseas in disillusionment. But their children are more likely to become presidents, prime ministers, and high level corporate and government officials in their refuge countries rather than in their parents' country of birth.

The Igbos are a vibrant, highly educated, and enterprising ethnic group in Nigeria. Our presence is felt internationally. We travel afar and actively contribute to the development of wherever we settle whether within Nigeria or outside the country. We re-invest the proceeds of our initial investments in communities we live in; we don't strip our host communities of value and repatriate home. We fought for our independence as One Nigeria rather than as regionalists. We only broke away as Biafrans when we were massacred in the tens of thousands and the Nigerian government did nothing to protect us. After the ensuing war ended, we agreed to the "no victor, no vanquished" dictum proposed by the then head of state and came back to contribute to the development of the re-amalgamated enmeshed Nigerian family.

ABOUT THE AUTHOR

Godwin Ikechukwu Meniru is a poet, author, and winemaker. He has productively channeled his experiences during the Nigeria-Biafra war into poems and short stories. He recently published his first volume of poems, *Journeys of Life: Poems,* which is available from Amazon.com. He has also published four sub-specialty medical science books as well as several research articles in peer reviewed international journals. Dr. Godwin Meniru is also an Obstetrician, Gynecologist and Fertility Specialist in Canton, Ohio where he lives with his wife, Maryann, and their children

A CHILD IN BIAFRA

By Nnamdi Ekenna

The Civil War was many things to many people. To us children at the time, it was just a war. By the time we were told it was over, it had come to represent a disruption to our growing-up - a hiccup in our personal history. To my father, who was at the height of his political career in the Aba Urban County Council, and almost at the pinnacle of his wealth and fame at this time, it was initially a "disturbance" in the North that would soon be quelled. Nonetheless, for safety concerns, Papa would have us and Mama removed to the village anyway. He joined us shortly thereafter. His own and many others' were not voluntary evacuations, as such. The air raids which targeted urban areas were becoming incessant and life very precarious to all who insisted on staying put in those areas.

For those of us from Eastern Nigeria – that is what our Region of Nigeria was called at the time - people returned to their villages of origin from Enugu, Onitsha, Owerri, Umuahia, Port Harcourt, Calabar, those were the big towns at the time. For many of those families, this was a second evacuation, as many had already "run" from Lagos, Kano, Kaduna, Sokoto, Zaria, Jos, Ibadan, Maiduguri, Benin, to mention but a few, in order to return home to the East or Biafra. At the time, The Peoples Republic of Biafra comprised what are now known as the States of Enugu, Anambra, Imo, Bayelsa, Rivers, Akwa Ibom, Abia, Cross River, and Ebonyi, anticlockwise on the Nigerian map. History, and the geography of those days, tells us that there were 25 Provinces that constituted the Republic.

I was about to be enrolled to begin Elementary School at Township School, Aba, when the war broke out. It lasted for 30 Months, so I was still a child at the time "they said" it was all over through an announcement on January 15 1970. The Biafran Vice President and Chief of General Staff, Major General Philip Effiong, was the one who announced the cessation of hostilities.

Out of what felt like the blues, Papa announced that he was shipping us kids and Mama from our in home Aba to Obizi, our hometown, until the "civil unrest" ended. Papa, my late father, Eze Raymond Onuoha Ekenna, J.P., Obizie of Obizi, the first crowned monarch of Obizi, was never known for hasty decisions, and was like a god with his pronouncements – his words were Ex Cathedra. Mama, my father's first wife, Ugoeze (Ezinne) Gabrieline Urasi Ekenna, who at the time was a Head mistress at St. Michael's Girls, packed us up, and we left in my father's white Peugeot 404, aka, *"opi achara."* That move to the village was the beginning of the war for me.

For the Biafran child, there are simpler ways to sum up the experiences from the war. We went from mornings of "There's health in Horlicks" to "Àkàrà and Àkàmu" (bean cake/bean balls and corn/maize pap), and from nights of sleeping on Vono Beds and Mattresses to mats on bare floors (if you happened to be one of the lucky ones). Most children of the war had little to eat not to talk of a choice of breakfast menu, and most who had been displaced and became refugee-children as a result of having "run" from their homes/residences, had no roof over their heads, not to talk of a mat to sleep on. Recounting these memories, though hurtful in certain aspects and nostalgic with respect to others, brings back the sense of how fortunate some of us were in making it out alive from the horrors and disruptions of what were supposed to be peaceful and carefree years of childhood.

A Child's Deprivations in Warfare

One of the first things that resonates with a child are the things he could not have, could no longer have, or which had been taken away. It was no different with me from the inception of the war. Contrary to the saying, we did not hit the ground running as soon as we relocated to the village. Shortly before the war started, we had moved from our residence in the town at Hospital Road to our new suburban home at Ekenna Avenue, GRA. We went from a toilet system wherein some "men" came in the middle of the night to haul away the bucket-filled feces, to a water cistern. The first shock on getting home to the village therefore, was having to use the latrines – these were pit-toilets – and despite Papa's ingenuity in making them as modern as possible, by building a sit-on box for us children, it was still a pit-toilet. Some of us couldn't manage it or come to terms with it. I held "mine" in for days, but eventually had to succumb. War gave birth to toilet retraining at an age when pencil-and-paper ought to have been the order of the day, but that would not be the only thing we had to relearn.

We also soon learnt that no friendships were permanent. As soon as you settled into one, you were yanked off to another location, and would begin sourcing for and maintaining new friendships. We children had to give up friends, hard-earned friends from birth. For me, I had to give up Maxwell Allwell-Brown from next-door at Hospital Road, Echeme, Ibe, and Robert (the Nnanna-Kalus) from next-door at Ekenna Avenue. Somehow, we were able to forge new friendships, but everything in wartime was ephemeral. You were here today and gone tomorrow, which did not make for depths of relationships. Shortly after we settled in the village, my two best friends were the two Enyinnias. I am sure one was a Nwaobia. The other, his cousin I suppose, for we were told they were somehow related, might have been an Abaribe. Enyinnia Nwaobia's dad was a close friend of my father's and he brought along the other Enyinnia's family when they "ran" to our village because Aba and its environs in which their own hometowns of origin were located, had fallen into "enemy" hands.

Soon we were enrolled into win-the-war school. Surprisingly, every phenomenon during the war was affixed with the "win-the-war" tag. It always baffled me, because the war was still in progress, it had not been won, and yet the appellation "win-the-war" stuck. Could it have been they meant "the effort to win the war?" Anyway, our school was adjacent to our town's church, St Andrew's. Mama was the Headmistress there – dare I say again, she was the "win-the-war Head Miss." Two things I recall vividly, my sister, Chioma (Dr. Achos) and I, were the brightest, best dressed, and somewhat "foreign" pupils, in our class. We were "brightest," probably not because we were the most intelligent, but because we had the privilege of Mama, who had started grooming us for school as toddlers in preparation for enrolment into elementary school before we were yanked away to the village. Also, because our parents didn't want to enroll us in any form of *"ọta-akara"* " (a rough equivalent of kindergarten), Mama always took us with her, and sat us on the floor near her desk with slates and chalk to doodle and play-around while she taught her class at St. Michael's Girls, Aba. Sitting there, in those classrooms with her, we might have subliminally imbibed more than a fair share of knowledge for our age, and carried those with us into our formal start of schooling. As far as "best-dressed" was concerned, that was a no-brainer, we had just come from town, while most of the folks with whom we were in class had dwelled in the village. I cannot remember any formal school uniform though I believe shorts-and-shirt (preferably white shirts) were encouraged for boys, and skirt-and-blouse (preferably white blouses), were preferred for girls. Somehow, it became clear we could not change clothes like we used to at Aba. We wore one item of clothing the whole day and part of the week, even after we had sweated and played in them, a thing that was never allowed when we lived in town. Looking at it retrospectively, I doubt it was just because soap and water were endangered species during the war, which they were somehow - because after all, Mama made home-made soap, *"ncha-obo."* from waste products from palm after the oil had been extracted - I believe part of it was a lesson in belonging, specified by our parents as they did not want us to feel entitled or so much different from those less fortunate around us.

Our weekends of roaming free, "I challenge you take one post" football, and other games, were taken away from us. In place of what we were used to in the town, we learnt other games and pastimes – *ncho* or *nchorokoto* (other parts of Igboland call it *Akwa Nsa* or *Ako Okwe* or *Ekwe*), I have come to learn it is called the Manchala game internationally, probably from a

Swahili adaptation. The Yorubas, I understand, were the first Nigerians to sell the game outside our shores – they call it *Áyòayó* – and it is played under different names, but the same rules and end purposes apply in all parts of Africa and the different parts of the world as well where the game is played. In our version, we did not have fancy boards, beads or diamond shaped stones, we simply dug holes in the ground, and used actual stones, or other local beans and seeds we could find as our game-pieces. It was a strategic and engaging activity from which one earned bragging rights if one could capture all or most of the other player's pieces. The other game of note was *Okwe.* We played this with the seeds of the Rubber Tree – the *Hevea brasiliensis.* I just found out this botanical name as I was writing this, (there is no way I could have known that as a child during the war). Anyway, the game went from count one to count twenty. In the first ten counts you scooped up the seeds, one-two-three, etc., at a time, and in the last ten counts you performed a series of intricate manoeuvres with the okwe seeds. If you missed any scoop or mishandled any of the manoeuvres, you would lose your turn to the next player while praying fervently they had a misstep too so that you could get another shot. The first person to complete all the scoops and manoeuvres, error free, won the game. It was a major test in concentration and cognitive skills and functions. There were many other okwe games too.

However, apart from these games and pastimes, two

major productive activities emerged for us children. One was participating in cleaning and clearing the brush around the church, a task suited to young boys, and also, picking up scraps as part of our war efforts. The first included enrolling and becoming a Boys' Scout, I started as a Tenderfoot, and it was through this aegis that I learned the Biafran anthem:

"Land of the rising sun we love and cherish ....
mi – re – mi – faa / mi –reh – mi –doo / re- re-miiii ...."

We would sing and recite the anthem and the first Scout Law before every meet and would end with singing the fourth Scout Law:

"A Scout is a friend to all, and a brother to every other Scout ...."

All this happened under the able leadership of De Blessing Abara (of blessed memory).

We had a variety of marching songs, too. The one that sticks in my memory, and to which I still hum and sing till date when on the treadmill, is the Zankarewa song. It must have been borrowed from the North by reason of "arewa" in the title, and the recurrent mention of "Amina," a predominantly Hausa female name from the Hausa warrior Queen of Zaria. The tune is upbeat, and our steps corresponded to the music. It made marching a piece of cake, in a manner of speaking. Under the auspices of the Boys' Scout, we also cut the grass, weeded around the parsonage and the Catechist's residence, the church building, and the church office. Of course, the older boys did the heavy lifting, but it was still a change of pace and a novel introduction to the otherwise life-free-from-chores that we had in town.

The second, which was adventurous and which we all looked forward to was the scrap-hunting. We went around the village and its environs, seeking out, picking up, and returning to a designated dump at the WRAP, all sorts of metals, broken bottles and shrapnel. In fact, anything that was not wood or grass. We were told this was how we must help our side win the war. Now, let me elaborate on WRAP. It was way after the War that I learned that WRAP was an acronym for War Research and Production. Of course, there was no way a child could know or relate to those heavy-duty words. All we heard of and knew was WRAP. However, we knew where the facility was, and what we were told they did in there. Next to our compound in the village is a Secondary School, Obizi Community Grammar School. As it then was, only a fence separated our compound from the school. During the war, these premises were converted to an arms and ammunition fabrication center. It did not matter how young you were during the war, if you could breathe and talk, you knew about *"ogbunigwe."* Those weapons of destruction were made next door to our compound at WRAP. From Wikipedia, I can now describe *"ogbunigwe"* as "a series of weapons systems including command detonation mines, improvised explosive devices, and rocket propelled missiles, mass-produced by the Republic of Biafra,"[1] used during the war. All the scraps we picked and supplied to WRAP were recycled and used in making *ogbunigwe*.[2] We did an excellent job. For us kids, it was an adventure in itself, scouring the nooks and crannies of the village and the neighboring communities for scraps.

One day there was a mighty explosion. Something blew up at WRAP. We heard it was a bomb that detonated during fabrication. Some mishandling must have happened, and we were told that some people lost their lives from that explosion. My eldest brother, Dede Okee, was "working" at WRAP at the time, and has been instrumental in refreshing my recollections about the incident. From what he told me, the explosion resulted from the rupture of the crude oil boiler/distiller from which they distilled petrol, kerosene, and diesel. Dede Okee was working at the plant that night, close to where the boiler was being fired. At the rupture, vaporized steam and crude oil spewed backwards through the shutter to the oven which they were about to close simultaneous to this burst. My brother recounts that his burns were minor compared to the other Tech who was working beside him at the time. The man's pain was so bad that it drove him "crazy" to the point where he took off and ran into the bush.

My brother and the other Techs chased after him, and when they caught up with him and brought him back

---

2   https://en.wikipedia.org/wiki/Ogbunigwe

to base, they discovered he had major third degree burns all over his body. This ordeal and confusion were further complicated by a simultaneous flyover of a plane close to the time of the explosion. At first, those outside the camp thought the plane had dropped a bomb until the "kata-kata" that followed from inside. My brother said they all spent the night at the hospital at Aboh-Mbaise, and the following morning, Papa went to visit them. Luckily for us, given our age at the time, we were spared all these details.

My eldest brother, Dede Okee, and those Techs with whom he worked at WRAP, were dubbed the "young scientists" who helped in putting together the innovations that made Biafra unique and great. However, my brother's proximity to that explosion from which he escaped with minor injuries scared Papa. This was his first son, about to get through secondary school at the time, so, he plotted to have my brother removed from WRAP. In fact, he went above and beyond merely plotting. Papa wanted him out of Biafra completely, and the opportunity came through the Biafran Republic counter plan to avert the rumored mass-killing of Biafran male children. Papa was a "big man," the term associated with a person who had "connections" as well as wealth. Papa could even be described as a "bigger man" if there is a term like that, during the war. He had connections with the WCC (the World Council of Churches), and another organization of which I heard very little during the war, but learnt a great deal more about when the war was over - Caritas. These organizations supplied relief to our war-torn neighborhood, and from time to time, their special planes would come in bringing supplies of mostly food and medicine.

One of Papa's cousins, I believe it was De Ferdinand Ukoha, we just called him De Ferd, a gentleman who was training to become a Medical Doctor, and who was then studying in Germany, was a volunteer to one of those organizations, along with some other young Biafrans abroad. These volunteers accompanied some mission-trips with these organizations to Biafra, maybe to assist with language and directions. I was made to understand that as the war raged on, there was an evil master plan by the Hausa-Fulani oligarchy in the North to carry out a Biblical-style Egyptian massacre of male children of the Eastern Region aged 6 years and above. When this plan was leaked to the Biafran side, the Elders and Leaders of Thought in the then Eastern Region got together and devised their own plan that empowered the Biafran President and Commander-in-Chief, General Odumegwu Ojukwu, to get as many males as possible out of the country – those not of conscription/ fighting age, one supposes. Of course, those who already had valid International Passports got the first billing. My elder brother, Dede Okee, had just done a tour of Europe, enabled by a DMGS (Dennis Memorial Grammar School, Onitsha) program in 1965/66, and so had an International Passport that was still valid. Again, I was too young to have all these details at the time, but later discussions with my brother filled in some of the important factoids from my hazy recollection. Upon return from a World Jamboree under the auspices of the Boys' Scout in Lagos, Dede Okee, was selected for the Student Exchange Program with Loughborough Grammar School in Loughborough, Leicestershire, for exceptionally intelligent and gifted students. It is worth noting again, that my brother supplied these names to me, as it is very unlikely for this to be my recollection from memory as a child. Soon after he got back from Loughborough the war started. So, through De Ferd's and other connections, Papa arranged for my brother, Dede Okee, to be removed from Biafra – at the time my brother was hell-bent, I learnt, on joining the actual combat Biafran Army – so, he was simply told he was being taken abroad so that he could learn how to be a pilot and come back to fly missions for Biafra. I later learnt this was the only thing that sold him, and that was how my brother left for England in the middle of the war, and went on from there to medical school in Germany. We did not see him again until 1974 when he came home to visit from Germany.

A lot of brilliant young men came to work at WRAP from all over Biafra. A good number of them were quartered on the grounds of the secondary school, but many others lived amongst families all over our hometown. A few resided in our compound, and one gentleman that especially comes to mind is Dr. Chi Anyiam. He was not a doctor then, though, as was later clarified to me, he was a 1st year Med Student when the war began. I later learnt he was an old boy of my alma mater, DMGS, Onitsha, and was my elder brother, Dede Okee's, Master at DMGS, where we had the tradition of junior students "serving" senior students as part of our school's tradition of mentorship. Therefore, that must have been why he was accorded many special privileges while he was living in our compound during the war. He lived in Mama Obunwa's house, I remember his room clearly, the first room on the left of the house's approach. He was fair and handsome, and I never saw him without a smile on his face. I do not know what he did at WRAP, but like I said earlier, these were young brains, budding scientists, youth who brought skill and precision to whatever responsibilities they were charged with at WRAP.

During the war, Chi Anyiam and I, (I cannot ever remember our calling his name without adding the surname), formed a special bond. He liked me, and I adored him. Part of my eldest sister's, (Adanne Mrs. Ngozi Ododo's) war-effort was to make and sell cooked food and snacks to some of the workforce at WRAP, and later, to soldiers camped at St. Benedict (a Catholic church in my hometown located in the village next to ours). Adanne's specialty was ukwa (African Breadfruit) porridge. She made or prepared other foods, but her ukwa porridge gained exceptional fame, to the point that patrons had to book in advance. We, the kids, were the carriers/delivery boys or what you might want to refer to as "ukwa mules." Our assignment was to deliver specific plates of ukwa to specific individuals. In order not to drop or mix-up any errand, we carried only one plate at a time. It became routine that I was assigned to deliver Chi Anyiam's food, and went back to pick up the plates after he was done eating. He always left some for me. That must have been part of why I was so fond of him, because most of the other patrons would "wipe" their plates clean of every morsel of ukwa. Later in life, I became classmates with his younger brother, Iheanyi, at DMGS, and also later, at UNEC, (University of Nigeria, Enugu Campus), and we became instant friends from our families' connection through Chi Anyiam.

As Adanne was doing her ukwa thing, my other elder sister, Sister we called her, (Rtd. Navy Commander Chidiebere Ekenna-Kalu, of the U.S. Navy), then a teenager, and her peers with whom she cavorted, made their own contributions to the war efforts. I chose that word "cavort" deliberately, because from what we heard; they also did a lot of win-the-war dancing called "jump," organized at the local school hall. Disco had not come in then, so their fare was mostly Beatles and the like. They "jumped" to dance away the strain and stress, the denials of war. But in war, everyone had a responsibility, no matter how young and/or how animated they were, so these teenage girls - Sister and her pals - volunteered at the French-Run Children's Kwashiorkor Clinic at Udo, the neighboring community to our hometown. Those of them who were "good" and skilled at caring for patients were recruited for bigger responsibilities farther away in other neighboring towns to care for wounded Biafran soldiers who suffered from "Shell Shock." Most of them were cared for at schools that had been reconfigured to Army Barracks and makeshift clinics. It is little wonder then that Sister, Danne Stella Amadi, Danne Noella Odibo, Danne Rita Nwogu (now Mrs. Chioma Azuonye), Danne Charity Nwankwo, and Daa Edna Osondu and her sister, Danne Edith went on to become nurses, midwives, and doctors. In war, mind you, they did all they did as volunteers, and at an age when most girls would still be trying to figure out which boy they would say "yes" to in an "excuse-me-dance" situation. Our neighbors at Aba, the Allwell-Browns, one of whose daughters, Siene, was a childhood friend of Sister's, ended up in our village. They did not stay in our compound, though; they stayed at Dr. Ogbonna's compound. Sister and Siene were thus able to continue their friendship from Hospital Road, Aba, through Township School, Aba, into the couple of years or so they shared in Secondary School at ACMGS, Elelenwa (Archdeacon Crowther Memorial Girls' School), during the war.

This brings me to Kwashiorkor. Like I have said to

many people in the past, and in some previous writings, Kwashiorkor was real; more real than many who did not see it firsthand give it credit for. Unfortunately for us "children of the war" we saw it live in our peers. In fact, two of my second cousins were amongst some of the children airlifted to Gabon because of Kwashiorkor. We did not know its origin or its causes, all we saw were fellow children with protruding stomachs, swollen extremities, especially the back of the hand and the top of the feet. To us, it looked like someone had pumped water into the ankles, wrists, and feet of those children. They not only looked weak in the face with drooping lips, but seemed to have lost colour in their skin, and apart from the bloated stomachs, hands and feet, everything else looked emaciated. We were told this disease affected children who could not get enough to eat or the right foods to give their growing bodies the nutrition needed for sustenance and a balanced immune system. We learned that starvation was adopted as an instrument and strategy of war by the enemy side, and our fellow children suffered the most for it. It was some of the most horrendous aspects of the war that my young eyes witnessed – the wasting of the children – the inhumanity of war, especially to us children, who in our innocence could not understand why the evils of war were being visited on us. It was not uncommon to see children lying disoriented, in a coma, or half-dead, by the side of the roads and on trek-paths. Unable to "march-on" with their physically weakened and confused families, the only option was to abandon those children as these families "fought" to save those who were strong enough to survive. Many children died of Kwashiorkor. Many children's growth was stunted because of Kwashiorkor. Many children suffered different ranges of emotional, mental, and physical disabilities arising from the affliction, the scourge, and the plague of Kwashiorkor. Many children did not come back home from Gabon because of Kwashiorkor.

As my sisters were doing those young-people kind of heroic things, I cannot help but remember at that same time, with great nostalgia, Mama's cakes. They were win-the-war wedding cakes, and Mama single-handedly made sure every couple that wedded during the war in our neighborhood, had a wedding cake to cut at their reception. This is nostalgic to me, because it was the beginning of the tradition of Mama having me lick up the batter on the mixer and beater she used – with a stern warning not to cut myself in the process. Her oven was a large, home-made contraption that was spherical and could be heated with wood below and charcoal on top for the overall cooking and browning of the cake. A few of the cakes came out burnt on the bottom and the sides – and the removal of the baked cake from the oven and the scraping off of the burnt part, the flattening of the tops for balancing and stacking of decks, was an event we kids never liked to miss. It was a windfall situation for eating partially burnt cake. There was not much to dress the cakes with, so Mama improvised, covering the sides of the cake with foil and other shinny papers cut from old magazines, as foil was not always available during the war. These were just for the ambiance of photographing as they were later carefully removed together with the "Mr. and Mrs." (that is what we called the Caucasian looking couple); the cake topper she always placed on top of the cakes. The wedding cakes were usually single, double, or triple decker, according to the purse of the groom. I cannot recall seeing any that were taller than three decks. Mama, we were told, only charged for the ingredients – the labor was her gift – and to the many who could not afford to pay for the ingredients, she gave them one anyway. Mama's win-the-war wedding cakes were a recurrent testimony from many of the older gentlemen who attended her funeral in April 2019. I understood what they were talking about because I too saw these things firsthand.

All those cake matters were before our brief stint at Ihiagwa. Also, we did not hang around, schooling at St. Andrew's for long, because events that followed later removed us from the village. As the war raged closer to our hometown, influx of people from all parts of the region who were displaced from their homesteads, or simply evacuating for fear of falling into the wrong hands and being killed for flimsy reasons, began to take its toll on our village. These people came with stories of what they had seen, what they had experienced, the horrors of senseless killings and the deaths of young able-bodied men, also the abduction of women and girls. So, running away from "occupied" areas, where the enemy-soldiers had infiltrated was more of a preservation move, a quest for a semblance of peace and sanity, but as was evidently obvious, there was none.

Soon, we became victims too.

Lost Memories and Stolen Innocence

Homelessness was real. A child's sufferings during wartime is quite different from what adults experience. It is a story of stolen innocence, a denial of pleasant memories brought about by the constant agonies of uncertainties. Like I said, soon we too became victims. Victims of removal from home, victims of homelessness, and victims of uncertainties regarding where and in what form the next meals would present themselves. With the stories of the advancement of enemy soldiers, drastic and immediate decisions had to be made, but strategies were as haphazard as the stories from war refugees were diverse. Before you could say "Jack Robinson" Papa uprooted and relocated us to Ihiagwa, near Owerri. This time he took only Mama and the last four of us kids, Chuks (Amara), Dr. Achos (Chioma), along with our youngest at the time, and me, to stay with the Ngokas. Papa explained to us that since Owerri had "fallen" and had been "recaptured" it was most unlikely it would fall into "enemy" hands again. Moreover, Umuahia had been designated the de facto capital of Biafra, since the "fall" of Enugu, and our hometown's proximity to Umuahia made us a target for "enemy" forces upon their entry. Papa figured it would be easier to evacuate the family, should the "enemy" forces enter and "capture" our hometown with my older siblings than with us the younger ones. It was a failed strategy, for shortly after we got to Ihiagwa, Owerri "fell" for the second time. Anyway, that was how my short friendship with the Enyinnias, and the other playmates I had in the village, came to an end. To Ihiagwa we were sent.

We were well provided for at Ihiagwa. Papa Ngoka and his family took extra good care of us, and Papa would visit, bringing provisions to the Ngokas and us, from time to time. These visits ended abruptly on 1 January 1970 when an air raid spotted Papa's white Peugeot 404 at Ulakwo on his way back to our village after one of those visits. Papa's car was riddled with bullets as we were told, and one of the bullets pierced the fuel tank which made it impossible for the car to be driven back home. They covered it with palm fronds and left it there. But by the time Papa organized a crew to go back and retrieve the car, it was gone. It had been "confiscated" (one of the words you were bound to learn as a kid during the war due to its rampant usage) and taken to the Army barracks, awaiting the "sabo" (saboteur) whose white car had attracted the bombing in the first place. The car was never given back to my father, although he was cleared from the accusation of being a "sabo" and vouched for by many respectable local indigenes, including Papa Ngoka.

Soon after the incident, we "ran" from Ihiagwa, due to its proximity to Owerri, which had been occupied again by the enemy soldiers. The thought was that from Owerri, they would begin the sacking of adjoining towns and villages, and wherever they overran, they usually left a mess of casualties, with even women and children not being spared. I have no idea whose decision it was, it might have been Papa Ngoka's, but again for safety concerns, we had to head out from Ihiagwa and seek solace in a smaller, more remote village, at least, one that was not so close to Owerri. Again, I have no idea how many were packaged to leave, but I recall our party comprised women and children from both families under the leadership/guide of a gentleman by the name of Ajọlụda. Anytime anyone called out his name, he always responded with *"ma ghịara ụdara."* I neither knew nor understood, to this day, what either the name or his response to it meant. A mystery I would have liked solved. That must have been a nickname. He was a special kind of guy, very funny, and perhaps mildly afflicted with some genetic disorder, but not in any way to have been fully mentally impaired or totally intellectually disabled. Of course, these are conjectures I made from observing him as a kid, not that I knew these things, or these scientific and clinical terms, at the time.

Ajǫlụda's leadership as our guide lasted only for a short period of time. In the confusion of war-evacuations, we were separated from the Ngokas, but somehow, luckily for us, we were never separated from Mama. As we were heading in one direction, there were people heading from that direction towards the direction from which we were escaping. We were too young to understand the dynamics of war-disorientation, but even in the eyes and mind of a child, there was something odd about the whole scenario. The most serious question in my mind was: if we are "running" from there, why are they "running" to there? And of course, vice versa. However, our training and age would not permit voicing out such questions to Mama. We just diligently followed where she led. In the noisy confusion of war, a different set of instincts must have been elevated, because no matter what was happening around us, we kids managed to make sure we never lost sight of Mama – a better way to put it might be that we made sure Mama never lost us. We hung around her for dear life, and she did a better job than a mother-hen. Whenever any of us was too weak to continue the trek, she would stop, tend to that person, encourage him and strengthen his resolve. I cannot even remember the exact words she said to us, but whatever they were, they got us going – none of us fell by the wayside.

Before we left Ihiagwa, Mama had packed some belongings; whatever she felt we could carry, according to everyone's age and strength. Initially, it was an ambitious luggage, but as we went from day to day, and the strain and stress of walking, thirst, hunger, and dejection set in, our loads were reduced. Most of the clothing Mama packed for us were given away to strangers, and some she just left by the paths for people to pick up. Most of the travels were done through back roads, we were supposed to avoid the main roads as much as possible. Before we left, Mama had also cooked an abundance of food, which we carried with us. I guess the strategy was for us to have enough to eat until we could settle somewhere she could cook new food. That was wishful thinking. We walked for days, and with nowhere to reheat our soup and stew, most of it went bad. Despite the fact that some of the food had gone bad, we could not throw all of it away, there was no backup, and in the times we were facing, "rotten" or "rotting" food was better than no food at all – so, we endured. We ended up at a village called Umulolo, Mama told us, and were readily welcomed by a local family. People were very accommodating in wartime, and most went out-of-their-way to help fleeing people. In all that confusion and total disorientation, fatigue from walking miles at a stretch, irregular feeding, having to "ease" oneself at the most unusual places, and uncomfortable circumstances, one incident remains indelible in my recollection.

Before we got to Umulolo, we were crossing a bamboo bridge that lay across a stream – I believe it was too small to be called a river. Quite possibly, now that I think of it, it was a tributary of Imo River. That is when the unthinkable happened. Typical of the cliché, it happened to me. In the confusion and all the shoving, with the hurry to get nowhere from nowhere, it turned out there were too many people for whatever load the bamboo bridge was designed.

Usually, in all our trekking, Mama would be in front, and we would follow as closely as possible, with stern instructions never to lose sight of her or wander off from directly behind her. Well, something inexplicable to me until this day happened. We were arranged to walk behind her in ascending order of age, the youngest was directly behind her, followed by Dr. Achos, then me, and then Chuks right behind me. She could not put us in front of her, to have an eye on us, for the obvious reason that we could not lead the convoy. I don't recall if I missed a bamboo slat for my footing, or was just simply listless – quite possibly the latter – but I fell through, and was descending into the stream, when a hand pulled me up, and set me back on the bamboo-bridge. It was not the "Hand of God," because it was a female that pulled me up, and we all know God is male. I know, I know – hold your horses, it's just dry humor. As soon as I regained my footing, I called out to Mama, but she could not hear me. When we got over to the other side and I told her what had happened, she turned around to thank the woman, but she was gone. Only my sister, Chuks, who was directly behind me, was able to corroborate my story. Whether the woman who saved my life was "mami water," or just another person fleeing the war in the opposite direction, we will never know. But to this day, we have remained grateful to the person, or powers, that pulled me up and saved me from falling into the Umulolo stream.

We stayed at Umulolo for longer than necessary. Mama did not get to know that the war had ended until suddenly she noticed convoys of Nigerian soldiers patrolling the tracks which prompted her to start asking questions. During the war, Mama, like many adults, got their news from whatever they were told Okoko Ndem had said. Even as kids, we knew Okoko Ndem. He was the personification of Radio Biafra, the source of propaganda for the Biafran side, and to many, the source of hope and stories of exploits of the troops at various warfronts. Most of those accounts, we were told, were embellished and exaggerated, designed mostly as morale boosters for the fighting men and sustenance for the civilians. We were too young to listen to his broadcasts directly on the radio, but in our little cliques, whenever someone told a tall tale, we usually would call such a person Okoko Ndem. Legend had it that Okoko Ndem's last broadcast on Radio Biafra was at the end of the war during the surrender by Major General Philip

Effiong. It was said he packed up Radio Biafra, which was largely mobile at the time - stationed in some pick-up truck - moving away from enemy-bullet fire as the sectors collapsed, and the enemy forces gained grounds into the hinterland of Biafra. It is said he disappeared after that last broadcast and was never heard from again, though the victors diligently searched for him. These were rumours, of course, ones that a child could neither verify nor corroborate. But for the memories of a Biafran child, it is best that those fantasies remain intact, heralding the heroism and escapades of this man. It must have been from the said broadcast that most people learned that the war had ended. It was a bit later that Mama heard through word of mouth that the war was over, and that refugees, even voluntary ones like us, were now free to go back to their homes.

I do not know how she found the guides, but after consulting, some men led us back to our hometown and reunited us with Papa and the rest of the family. Upon arrival at home, we learnt that we had been given up for dead, as the war had ended weeks before we made it home. Papa had started making inquiries, village-to-village, from Ihiagwa and surroundings, with full descriptions of all five of us – Mama, and the last four kids – and would not succumb to having an official funeral for us as unaccounted-for war casualties, until he exhausted all means of searching. Our return was as miraculous as it was triumphant. Instant jubilations and celebrations ensued, and of course, what one could imagine was the utmost relief for the adults, because from stories that circulated, many did not make it back home. We were tired, hungry, disheveled, and for the most part disoriented. We were very happy to be home, but the physical pain of the tight hugs and being lifted and thrown up in the air and caught midair caused more anguish than the joy they were purposed to elicit.

The first important thing I recall that happened was our being fed. There was some leftover food, a jollof made from some kind of millet grains, white in colour, and leaving us with the sensation of chewing rubber. This is memorable because it was our first meal at home upon our return. We later found out the food was ready and handy because our other siblings at home had "rejected" it. I must have mentioned it felt like chewing rubber. You should have seen how we pounced on this mess, how we consumed it like hungry hyenas, it was little wonder we didn't all fall sick after that. I guess our little stomachs needed something, anything, to process. These were not your ordinary seeds from wild grasses of millet; we were told they were called ojoro and seemed like processed or artificially engineered food. Thereafter, we were washed – not just bathed – washed and brought changes of clothes, and as the adults continued their merriment and celebration of our return, we slept and slept and slept. After the much-needed rest that was more rejuvenating than the food, we quite simply strode into the rhythm of things as if we never lost a beat. Childhood is precious in those kinds of ways.

Picking up the pieces on our return to Aba

At the end of the war, Papa, who like I stated in the beginning was at the height of his political powers, and at pinnacle of his wealth, was to restart life with only twenty pounds in exchange for whatever amount of Biafran money he had. We were not allowed to move back to our GRA home on Ekenna Avenue when we eventually left the village for good to return to Aba. The Nigerian Army had commandeered all the property in that area of town. Ours was reserved for the Quartermaster-General, the Nnana-Kalus house next-door to ours, was the Flag House, and Valletta Lodge, the Chukwus (Eke-Chukwu's) home was the Officer's Mess. I cannot remember to what use they put all the other existing properties on our street at the time, the Anyaehies, Tunaks, Isokas and Okwuchis homes after the war. So, we were forced to take up residence once again at 64 Hospital Road, Aba. But the good thing is that we got some of our old neighbors back too. The Anyaegbus were back at 63, opposite us; the Allwell-Browns were back at 68, adjacent to us; and down the road, Baba Tafa, Baba Iyabo, were back at 73 and 75, Moneme Bookshop and the CMS Bookshop were all back and fully functional before you got to Asa Road. Across Asa Road, the Mosque was once again flourishing, and all the Mallams were back in full force making and peddling suya, Tabu scent, incense, and amulets. Unless you looked deeper, it almost seemed as if life was back to normal.

Nevertheless, many never returned from the war - in thought, word, or deed. Many also did not physically return from the war. My Uncle, De Eugene, never made it back from the Biafran Army, my maternal grandfather, Pa Lazarus, was informed that he was killed in combat and his body was never found. After a respectable period of waiting, Pa Lazarus gathered the community and had a funeral for him. We also were told that a few children including some from our village, who were removed to Gabon, never made it back home. However, I know two of my second cousins who came back from Gabon.

They say war leaves an indelible psychological impact on children. To me, none of those lingered, either because I was too young to internalize most of the debilitating consequences or, possibly, due to the fact that most of its devastating effects were cushioned by our having lived through it in innocence and with distractions, as children. Returning to some semblance of normalcy within a short period of time after the war came to an end was, therefore, not that farfetched. I would not say the same for the adults. About three and half to four years after the war was officially over, we returned to our GRA residence at 33 Ekenna Avenue.

For me, the war ended the day we returned to GRA in 1974, by then, I had already started secondary school at DMGS, Onitsha.

One thing most children of the war will never forget - the war stole at least, a couple of years from our schooling. These lost years followed us into the University and saw us in the same class with kids who were two to three years younger than we were, and to a child, that's a whole lot of lost respect right there. Well, it came to an end. Yes, the war ended, at least theoretically, on 15 January 1970. However, in all facets of life after the war, we were still "fighting" the war and living through its aftermath. War is not a good thing. I do not like war. I do not wish war on any child.

About the Author

Chief Nnamdi A. Ekenna is from Obizi, in Ezinihitte-Mbaise in present day Imo State of Nigeria. He is an attorney and lives in Los Angeles where he has his practice. He has a daughter, Adannem.

WAR CHILD: A YOUNG BIAFRAN'S VIEW OF THAT WAR

By Chukwudum Ikeazor

The Biafran war ended on 15 January 1970. Those of us who were Biafrans, mostly willingly and proudly so, were dragged back to Nigeria to resume participation in its unity that was designed by a few foreigners. It was and still is a very costly unity whose purpose has never been fully articulated or agreed. The war left behind it, some 2 to 3 million dead - killed, bombed, shot or starved to death. Of this number, an estimated 1,000,000 were children. I was one of the lucky children that were not killed by starvation or bombs. I survived that war with mixed feelings. I felt bewildered, heartbroken, and at the same time, relieved that some of the immediate horrors of war had stopped, and I looked forward to seeing my old friends and resuming my education at my old school.

As for surviving that war in which hundreds of thousands of children died, I was just lucky and not in any way wiser, cleverer, better, or more suitable and deserving of life. It was just plain luck as in Biafra, living and dying were lotteries played every day for you by fate. If you did not do the dying, someone else was doing it. Sometimes, you knew them, and other times you heard about them. And when you did not know them or you had not heard of them, you imagined them. If you shut your eyes, you saw them. When you slept you would see them in your dreams. In Biafra, the sense, smell and presence of death, the dying, the desperation, the devastation of life and shattering of normality were everywhere. If you were not hearing the groans of pain from the afflicted - the wounded, hungry, starving and dying, you heard the anguish and wailings of widows, the mothers and the other bereaved. You could do your own crying if you wanted, pray all you wanted, and we prayed. We sang wonderful songs, prayed, and called upon God, but the journey still seemed endless.

All Biafrans lived side by side with death. In Biafra we who were children became well acquainted with death, to the point that a huge chunk of our childhood innocence was obliterated. Hundreds of thousands of children, perhaps over a million, would never be teenagers or adults nor would they ever grow old. They would be slaughtered by hunger, disease or any of the modern weapons and armaments deployed by a relentless aggressor who came from sea, land and air. Maybe a million children died, but a couple of millions more survived. Who or what chose those who would be killed and those who survived is not clear or known to me, but I survived. I carry no physical scars, but the emotional and psychological scars are branded into my soul to this day. I entered the war at age 10 and emerged aged 13. There would be no counselling for any child or any formal emotional support for survivors. The war was over, so there you are, get on with the rest of your life. And the world which we emerged into was not exactly very comforting or welcoming, but we were alive.

The duty I have for surviving the war and the debt I owe to those who fell, includes telling some of the story of what happened to those who can no longer speak because they are dead. I must also, whenever the opportunities arise, tell my story about the event, that war, the dream that was Biafra, the whys and hows, as I understood and understand them. All these are events that have impacted on my life, like nothing else ever will.

I was turning ten years old in the year 1966 when the Nigerian political crisis of the previous years boiled into military coups and blood and deadly pogroms. The year had begun with a military coup in January in which the Prime Minister, two regional premiers, a federal minister, several senior military officers, and some other persons were killed. The coup was planned and led by Majors Ifeajuna, Nzeogwu and Ademoyega, but has often been tagged as the Nzeogwu coup. Major Nzeogwu was the only one of the key planners and participants to complete his mission and seize control of a regional government and thereafter announce the coup. He became its enigmatic and most famous face.

My year 1966 had begun with a brutal lesson in politics and the acquisition of new words, the most prominent being "coup". As the year went on I added new words and phrases to my vocabulary - "pogrom", "refugee", "counter-coup", "massacre", "beheading". More words that were quite outside the expected lexicon of a pre-teen were acquired in the following years of the war. They were not happy words or words a young child should have had anything to do with. I was picking up much more than new words though, as the deadly events in my country unfolded - I was having experiences of mortal fear, bereavement, loss, fear, and some kind of awareness of my own mortality, in a way I do not think children should. My nightmares, which I was to live with for decades, were just beginning.

I had a most idyllic childhood. I knew nothing but the peace and happiness that accompany all the joyful benefits of a good childhood. The January coup did not shock me as I did not quite understand the full implications of the sudden transition from civilian to military rule or the deadly significance of the dynamics of those who were killed. My life at home and at school was not changed in any way, and so there was no major impact for us as children. When the July coup occurred, it was pretty much the same. Life at home and at school was normal and unaffected. By this time, I had already become well acquainted with the word "coup" and I understood what a military government was. I began to hear that Ironsi and Fajuyi were missing or had been killed (and so we were getting another military government). It seemed that the new way for Nigerians to change the leader of the country was by killing the one in place to make space for a new one. It was the news of the expansion of the violence beyond the targeted military officers and leaders to the streets, homes, and businesses in search of Eastern Nigerians and the flood of refugees back to the East that began to give me a sense that this second coup was a bit different.

We were not just going to get a new set of rulers and record a few dead former ones, we were seeing hundreds, even thousands of people uninvolved with politics and the military being killed. And I had something in common with them. I was Igbo and Eastern Nigerian. They were either Igbo or Eastern Nigeria or both. As a ten-year-old, I was alert to the horrors that were gripping the country. I was already an avid pretend reader of newspapers. Let me rephrase that. I loved to read the comic strips, "Garth," in the Daily Times and "Modesty Blaise" in the New Nigerian, after my father was through with them. Inevitably, I would see the headlines that stared at me, and read a few lines of what I could understand. I was quite aware when the news of the killings of Igbo and Eastern civilians in the North began to trickle in and then the flood of stories, verbal accounts, newspaper reports and television images of the dead, maimed, bewildered, dispossessed, as they flowed into the Eastern Region from all points.

I think this was the first time I started having a sense of being Igbo as a standout identity. It dawned on me at age 10 that there were people in other parts of Nigeria, our country, who were killing and harming people who were Igbo or Eastern Nigerian for being Igbo or Eastern Nigerian. And I had both of those identities. In other words, a child had to start figuring out that there were people who could kill him, just because he was from a certain part of Nigeria. I was traumatized and I knew it. If I could sleep alone, prior, with the light off, I no longer could. As if the newspapers and the television news were not enough, the Eastern Regional government, clearly a highly organized outfit, collated pictures of destruction, the maimed, the murdered, the dispossessed and the fleeing and arriving refugees, and wrote and published a pictorial book titled "Nigerian Pogrom (Crisis 1966): The Organized Massacre of Eastern Nigerians." I have a copy of this book today, but I do not look through it or try to read it. I just keep it, perhaps as one of the mementoes of the world in my youth. One of the images in that book that haunts me to this day is the picture of the torso of a beheaded man. It never left me to this day, and by the way, "beheaded," was another word I learned. I think I picked up the more fanciful "decapitated" later. I was totally horrified at the idea of a human being rendered headless.

I had never imagined a human being without a head. I had never seen a dead body before that time, real or in a photograph, and the first I saw had no head. It was taken off by some other human beings. His name was given in the book. I was made to understand from the book's text, the news, newspaper stories and from adult conversations that those who did this and other heinous things such as the murder of tens of thousands more in a variety of vicious ways, were Northern Nigerians and sometimes referred to as *Ndi Hausa,* a generic term for Hausa-Fulani people and the Muslims that peopled Northern Nigeria. It seemed the luckier of the murdered victims were those who were simply shot or stabbed to death with one or two blows. There were accounts of pregnant women being murdered in a manner I do not wish to set down in print. Suffice it to say that feticide was committed. There was an account of a stunned mother who arrived with a trainload of refugees carrying the head of her child in a bowl, basket, or some container. I saw in one of the Eastern government publications, the photograph of a man whose cheeks were slit, both sides, from his mouth towards his ears. There were pictures of all sorts of injured and maimed people: men, women, and children.

The awareness that there were people, and millions of them for that matter, who were intent on killing me and anyone who looked or sounded like me, regardless of age, simply because we were from the Eastern region, was a mindset which I had when the war began, shortly after Biafra's declaration of independence. There was fear, sense of self, desperation, and defiance. Although the formal war began on the 6th of July when Federal forces attacked Biafra (Eastern Region to them) from her Northern borders, the war against Easterners really began in 1966 with the pogroms.

One of the aspects of the war that was to stand out for me was the mobility of the population, and my family's as well. People just kept on moving from place to place as Biafra's geography changed. We moved from place to place in search of shelter and safety, in fact, in any direction away from the shelling and the terrifying blasts. Whole villages and towns were entirely emptied of their populations. I was living at Onitsha with my family before the crisis, and soon, as Onitsha became threatened by the Nigerian 2nd Division, our parents moved us to Obosi. We just came back from school one day, and suddenly, we were put in the car with some possessions, clothes, toys and some books and headed out to Obosi, some five miles away. We were not to see our school or most of our classmates again for some 3 years. We had no chance to say goodbyes to our friends and schoolmates who were so much part of our lives.

We were at Obosi when the Murtala Mohammedcommanded 2nd Division reached Asaba and performed the most infamous war crime of the Biafran war - the killing of over 1000 Asaba men. Tales of their rampage through the Delta Igbo towns, the rapes, the killings, and the arson had reached us through a flood of refugees that had crossed the Niger. We had a Delta Igbo lady staying with us at my grandmother's home. She was a refugee, having fled from her hometown. I did not know her connection with my grandmother and great aunt, Dorothy Okechukwu, but I think she was their friend and ran over to them for a place to stay. I remember her being referred to as "*Nne* John" (John's mother). Her son, John, was missing at that time. She would recount horrific tales of her escape to my grandmother and aunt as we were shooed away to prevent us from being traumatized by whatever she had to say. I knew it was very bad stuff. And this was just the early stage of the war.

One of the earliest and enduring images of the war for me was not dead bodies or anything grisly or unsettling but my sight of fear in the faces of two women I loved dearly. This was during an air raid - my grandmother, her sister, Dorothy and *Nne* John, at the sound of the approach of Nigerian jet fighters and rapid cannon shots, with Biafran anti-aircraft guns firing in return, grabbed us and ran to the space under the concrete staircase. That was the first time I heard adults saying that under the staircase was the safest place to be during an air raid or bombardment due to its reinforced nature. But that was also the first time that I saw fear in the eyes of my grandmother and my great aunt. I had not seen my great aunt cry since her husband died in 1960, although my great aunt's son, Guy, and four other cousins had joined the army. Her's and her sister's eyes welled up with tears with each thud of an exploding bomb or shell in the distance, and they would clutch their chests. My grandmother was a formidable individual, and one person I regarded as the emotional and psychological foundation of my childhood. I spent my first years of life with her until my parents returned from their studies. I had never known her to be afraid. I was badly shaken by the sight of her in distress; greatly disturbed by her situation and my helplessness. The next psychological shocker that brought the war near home to me was announced by the piercing screeches and wailings from a neighbour's house, one evening. News had come from the war front, that Adindu's father, a soldier, had been killed at the war front. Adindu was a little neighborhood girl who lived with her family a few houses away from us. The neighbourhood fell into mourning. This was the first death of one of us from the war. He was the first Biafran soldier I knew who died in combat. His widow, Adindu's mother, and his mother were inconsolable. War had come home to us. This was just within the first few weeks of the outbreak of the war. Prior to that time,

I had not quite made any serious connection between the war and death. Those who had been killed then, were just some "gallant Biafran soldiers" and "Nigerian vandals", as Biafran radio would say. They were stories read in the newspapers or heard over the news.

We were soon to leave Obosi. We had been there for a few months, out of school, away from the comforts of our Onitsha home, but still at home in Obosi and happy with relatives, cousins, and friends. Some of these were refugees from the North, and they brought back with them tales of the horrors they experienced and fled from. Obosi was at the time a frontline town. The Federals had gained a temporary foothold at the Onitsha river banks. They had devastated Asaba and burnt and looted the Onitsha Main Market. Onitsha was only 30 minutes' drive from Nnewi, General Ojukwu's hometown.

The Biafran Army threw in everything it had to deny the Federal Army, the city of Onitsha. Civil Defence units were formed in Obosi, Nkpor, Ogbaru and the smaller towns that ringed Onitsha. Some of these units also set up Boys Company units within their ranks. They mounted roadblocks, watch groups, and, very importantly, combing patrols to comb the forest and bush in search of Federal Army stragglers and reconnaissance units. They were armed with no more than cudgels, machetes, and maybe a couple of double-barreled shotguns, and several war songs. It was one of these units that my brother, Philip, and I joined, with other boys of our age.

I was 11 and my brother was 10. We were not turned back. We, with a few other boys of our age, paraded with ranks of older boys - those not quite old enough to join the regular army, and men who were too old to join the army. We were a motley bunch. Our mother had prepared a packed lunch which we placed in shoulder bags with our water bottles. At the parade ground at St Andrews's school, a man in some kind of military uniform addressed us. He may have been in the militia or the military. I could not tell the difference, nor did I know what badges of rank were. Our combing expeditions fortunately yielded nothing. Further attempts we made to join the militia were rebuffed. We were simply too young for any militia or military duties at the time. Soon after this period, our parents whisked us away to the hinterlands as the outskirts of our hometown came within Federal shelling range, and Federal jets were strafing columns of humanity fleeing Onitsha.

Although the Federals were not able at the time to progress their assaults at Onitsha, they began wild and clearly uncoordinated shelling of Onitsha and neighbouring towns and it was time for us to move again. We piled into our father's car and joined the exodus of hundreds of thousands of refugees on the roads to the hinterland. These roads heaved with humanity as far as the eyes could see. There were cars, buses, trucks, motorcycles, bicycles, and multitudes on foot, all heading in any direction away from the booming sounds of the shells.

Our first port of call was Uga, where we spent a few days with many others as the emergency guests of Roy Umenyi. It was temporary, as our entire family of eight plus two relatives piled into one room. Our grandmother found a place at Oraifite, with the Oranubas, and we later joined her there. Our accommodation there in the main house, was more spacious. We were to stay there for a number of months before we moved again.

I cannot tell how long we were at Oraifite; perhaps it was until the middle of 1968. It was at Oraifite that I first saw someone die from starvation. She was said to have been killed by kwashiorkor. I first heard that ugly word at Oraifite. She was the oldest daughter of a neighbour from across the road.

By this time, the blockade of Biafra was complete, and the food-producing zones of Abakiliki and the Obudu cattle ranch farm had been lost to the Federals or made uninhabitable from constant and heavy shelling. Onitsha had eventually been taken by the Nigerian 2nd Division, denying easy access to the other food rich area of Biafra, the Anam area. Throughout the war, we kept moving from place to place in search of safer and more comfortable accommodation. At one time, we moved to a town called Ihitenansa, as guests of one of my father's pre-war clients, Chief Orjinaedo. Although we were now further removed from the war front and distant from the constant bombing targeting the Uli Airstrip, death followed us there. More and more people were falling, not from shells, bullets, or bombs as they were in some other places, but from hunger. This included children, adults and the old. Sometimes, almost daily, bodies were carried past our window in *"ukpa"*, open caskets made from the trunks of raffia trees.

At age 11 or 12, mortality had become something I was all too familiar with. It was here that news of the death of my Uncle Sunny and Cousin Ike, came through. Sunday was killed at or near Uli, and Ike was killed at a war front I can no longer remember. He was a captain. I was confused and began to grapple again with the meaning of death or in particular, their death. Others who had died, that I knew of, were not family or people I knew well. These were people I knew. I cried several times over their deaths as I knew I would not be seeing them again, and my grandmothers and aunts were obviously hurting very deep. Strangely, I preferred to cry privately and when the mood seized me, I would go to a quiet corner or go outside the house. One evening, my maternal grandmother, Sunny's mum, caught me crying. I say, "caught" as that was how it felt to me. She saw me standing in the dark by a wall outside the house and asked me to come in. When I hesitantly answered that I was coming, and still waited for her to leave so I could compose myself, she sensed the distress in my voice and came close to enquire further. She asked me what the matter was, and I tearfully told her that I was thinking about my uncle and cousin who had been killed. She drew me close, consoled me, and said the right words of reassurance. I thought she was very strong, seeing as it was her first son who had been killed.

Every boy fancies himself a super soldier and I was no different. At 12 I thought I was now old enough to go to war, the war had dragged on enough with no end in sight. I had gotten tired of playing at soldiers, playing card games with my friends and daydreaming (I did a lot of that) about my pre-war schooldays. I would remember all my friends and classmates almost by name, and I would see their faces, wondering where they were and how they were. I missed them so much. One day, I went to the market with my grandma and by a road junction just off the market square, there was a Land Rover with some soldiers milling about. Of course, I looked long and hard in admiration and then, there he was! A boy of about my size, just a little bigger, and I knew him from primary school. His surname was Sankey or something like that. He was only a class above me, and he was dressed in full camo with a weapon I now recognize as an AK 47 slung over his shoulder. I yelled out from the window of my grandmother's car as it turned away from the market and we headed home. I could not believe my eyes. He looked so good in uniform and that was all I saw. I was green with envy. I did not see the grisly bodies dismembered by bullets and shrapnel that were part of soldiering. When we got home, I began packing my possessions ready to run a mile back to the market square to join Sankey and his army colleagues. I do not know how my father heard or found out, but I discovered that he found out about my military desires when he came at me with a belt. Did I know what war really was all about? he asked, as he directed his belt at my sore bottom. I yelled in pain. That was the end of my openly expressed desire to join the army. I do not know if Sankey was a frontline soldier or a batman for a senior commander at Army HQ. I did not care either, I just wanted to look like him and go to the war front and win the war. Laughable. I was 12 years.

For a whole year, there was no schooling so we, the children, kept busy being children. We played, dreamed of becoming soldiers, listened to war stories, helped with house chores, fetching water from the stream and babysitting our two brothers who were born in 1966 and 1967, respectively. There was time for brooding and pre-teen depression, and I found myself there every now and then as things dragged on. One time, I got a whipping from my father for that. Strange response to a brooding child, but that was Africa in those days. My father, and we so adored and admired him, was a great whipper, especially where I was concerned. I was that annoying first son with a slightly stubborn streak.

When hunger came calling, and the food was not ready, or did not fill us up, we would go to the bush or nearby farms, collecting palm kernels to crack open and get at their chewy edible insides. When you ate enough of these and drank some water, much of the void in the stomach would be filled. Some 2,000,000 people are believed to have died in Biafra, the vast majority from starvation. Many millions more would have died, had it not been for the massive food and relief airlift that defined the war. Almost every night, we heard the drone of the turbo prop engines of the relief planes and sometimes the screech of the Nigerian jets in pursuit of these unprotected quarries. Those planes were our lifelines, and we knew it. Through distribution networks organized by the foreign aid agencies, the churches and the Biafran Red Cross, the food aid got to the hungry. For some, it was too late or not enough, but for many more, it was lifesaving.

I remember some of the food items, a few of which were quite alien to us until then. Two of these new foods were cornmeal (a sort of cereal that looked like porridge, without the lumps) and powdered egg that you mixed with water and then fried like regular egg. It was quite tasty eaten or licked directly off your palm. The rest were things like powdered milk, corned beef, and spam. Sugar and salt were premium, but mostly the former, as Biafrans soon began to have to mine salt from some location.

When required, we would go to the river to fetch water in metal buckets and pans which we carried on our heads. My brother, Emeka, and I made ourselves as useful as we could, and we enjoyed the trips to the stream to fetch water. It was at Oraifite that we learned how to fish or set traps for fish with trap baskets which we made or borrowed. At some point, our parents stepped in. We had come away from Obosi and Onitsha with some storybooks. After the first trip out of any place we vacated, our father usually made one or two more trips back to pick up as much of our stuff as he could, and to bring some other relatives that could not come in the first trip. We did come away with a few books, but I had read these storybooks again and again and again until I got sick of them. My father or mother, I cannot remember who exactly, began to set up basic tests for us in subjects like English - spelling tests, sentence construction and comprehension. My father gave me a book to read, and I was aghast. It had no pictures in it, and the print was small. He had given me a novel to read. I was 11 or 12 for heaven's sake! My instructions included underlining new words I came across and figuring out their meaning with a dictionary or a query to him. What a pain.

After a while, we moved again from Ihitenansa to Osumenyi. I do not know why we moved but, we did. By this time, Port Harcourt had fallen to Federal Troops, and it was here at Ihitenansa that I first heard of Biafra's mini refineries. Our father spoke and marveled about how the refineries (wherever they were) kept his car going. The car engine oil was apparently made from the mixture of palm oil, crude oil, and some chemicals, but it worked. His car, an Nsu Prinz, survived the war.

Osumenyi was a walking distance from Uga airstrip and not so far from Uli, the main Biafran air station, and so we were nearer the epicenter of Federal night bombing attacks. The explosive flashes across the treetops provided us with nightly fireworks and the booms, thuds and bangs of the bombs accompanied by the rapid shots of the anti-aircraft batteries were like a nightly orchestra. Nightly, meant literally every night. We, the children, had been out of school for over a year at this point. The Biafran government was mindful of this. Biafra seemed to display incredible resourcefulness, inventiveness, and organizational abilities in the most difficult and trying of times. It maintained a judiciary, complete with lawyers, magistrates, and judges. Banks were in operation, post offices functioned, and letters were sent and received until the end of the war. By mid or late 1968, schools in Osumenyi opened. It appears it was a nationwide affair, as Primary Six (i.e. final primary/ graduation) exams were part of the program. We all excitedly got back to schooling again!

We were directed to resume schooling in our pre-war classes, so I went back to Class 5. School was fun and I enjoyed it thoroughly as I interacted more with more children. Every now and then, a Nigerian MIG fighter/ bomber on its way to offload its deadly payload on Orlu, Umuahia or Aba, if it could not find the Uga airstrip, would screech past at almost treetop level to avoid Biafran anti-aircraft or radar, if it existed, and we would dive for cover on the floor or under our desks in sheer terror. If we were in the playgrounds, we would run like hell to nearby trees or the greenery of farms for camouflage. Within seconds or minutes, we would hear the massive blasts of the payloads dropped on some urban center like Orlu or Nnewi, not knowing who was being obliterated. Occasionally, news would reach my parents of some poor soul, their friend or acquaintance who had been killed. It was at Osumenyi that they heard of the death of their friend, Lawrence Onwudiwe's family at Aba during a bombing raid. Lawrence went to work, wherever it was that he worked, and came back home to see his home and a few nearby houses shattered. They had taken direct hits from bombs dropped by a Nigeria Airforce fighter bomber on a sortie against the usual targets – civilian centers. His wife, all three children and his mother-in-law were killed.

By late 1969, we moved again to our final place of refuge, Ezinifite. I had no idea why we moved, but we did. We were to stay here for the final few months of the war. At Ezinifite, we were quartered in a couple of rooms in a large house inside a massive compound owned by a chief who was married to an Obosi woman. Things were much nicer here. There were other families living in the compound, and some more joined us. At the time, I did not realize that movement of those families was due to the shifting geography of Biafra. We resumed schooling here and this time, I was in Primary Six and eventually took my Primary Six School leaving exams there. I felt I did very well in every subject, except arithmetic and I remember I was concerned about the result. Other families that joined us at Ezinifite from other parts of Biafra were the Nwobodos, the Ofoles, the Okigbos and the Ibezues.

The large compound had the atmosphere of a playground during the day, and by this time we were so used to the sounds of shelling and gunfire that we hardly noticed. We spent Christmas, 1969 there. It was to be our last Biafran Christmas. On 12th January 1970, I saw my father listening to the radio with peculiar intensity. I joined him. General Phillip Effiong was reading Biafra's epitaph. I sort of got what he was saying, but my father added after the sombre speech; *"Agha ebe go"* (the war is over). Papa was very quiet for a while. There were no whoops of jubilation, but I sensed and felt the mixed feelings, including deep sadness at the sunset of our valiant Republic, fear about what the future held for us, and relief at the end of exile from our home and of the privations of refugee life.

I went outside and sat by a corner of the large steps leading up to the building. I cannot remember my exact thoughts at the time, but I almost dived back into the place of sadness bordering on depression that I had experienced time and time again during the war. I was morose and deeply hurt at the thought of the end of Biafra, this beautiful idea that we had suffered so much for, sang many great songs about, and learned to live for with the deaths around us as due sacrifice for its sake. I remembered the Ahiara Declaration, which some of the adults had spoken reverently of, and Ojukwu's inspirational speeches. I mourned my uncle and cousins again, and remembered my bereaved grandmother and great aunt. Sad as I was, I had something to look forward to with the end of the war. We would be back home to Obosi and Onitsha, and I would see all my cousins, friends, and school mates again, that is those of them who had survived. I would go back to my much-beloved school, All Saints, back to my class again with my classmates, and I would wander around the library again, smell those lovely books and borrow the ones I wanted. I missed my school so much. Some of the things I missed included chocolate, soft drinks and comics. I had survived for almost 3 years without chocolate. How? I would have my grandma close by again. I never got to join the Biafran Army, after all. I was 13 years old when the war ended. All my hopes of fighting for Biafra collapsed with Effiong's announcement. Virtually, every boy of my age in Biafra had been anxious to join up. Some of us tried to, but were chased away as too young. Some were accepted in some fronts that were desperate in the role of ammo carriers, and soon graduated to being full soldiers. Many were killed. Mere boys of 14, 15, and 16 years of age. Biafra inspired stratospheric levels of devotion and patriotism in both the young and the old.

My last act as a Biafran was burying a gun. Yes, I laid a service weapon to rest in its own grave. I will explain. Major Sam Ofole, who was married to my cousin, Ify, had come to Ezinifite with his family in the last few days or so of the Biafran Republic. Whatever his unit was must have been dissolved by that time. He was no longer in uniform. One day, before we left Ezinifite, he asked me to get a hoe or some digging implement and accompany him to the bush or farm. That was easy, there was one just a short distance beyond the side wall of the house. We were going to bury his gun, an automatic pistol. I showed him to the bush, and he selected a spot by some tree and we began digging. When we had reached a satisfactory depth, he produced his weapon which he had wrapped in something like a plastic or rubber bag. He took it out, applied some grease to it around the moving parts, and the gun seemed coated in grease. I asked him, "Uncle Sam, why are you doing that?" He told me that the grease would protect the metal weapon from rusting and that if he had to retrieve it to use it, then all he had to do was to clean off the excess grease and it would be ready for use. I just learnt my first lesson in weapon maintenance. He placed the weapon in the hole wrapped up in the bag, and we covered it up with earth. I do not know, but I imagine he made a mental note of the spot. He returned to the house, to blend in with the rest of the adult population as a civilian. He was a doctor and was now just Doctor

Ofole and no longer Major Ofole.

As soon as my father determined that we could travel, we bade our farewells to our wonderful hosts and our friends and drove off to Obosi. The journey was uncertain and there were army roadblocks. As with our flight from Obosi in 1967, the roads were busy with traffic of all sorts. People were moving back home in droves. This time, there were no sounds of booming guns and little or no panic for the most part. When we got to Idemili Bridge, to cross over from Oba to Obosi, we saw our last horrors of the war. Dead bodies in the Idemili River. Some were slowly floating downstream, and one or two seemed to be caught in the weeds by the bank. Our mother and aunt urged us to look away and covered up the eyes of the youngest ones, but being children, some of us still looked. I was one of the unfortunate ones that looked, and had that awful sight imprinted on my mind.

We were excited to return to our beloved hometown, Obosi. Many of the houses were pock-marked by bullets and shrapnel. Several had lost their roofs, but it was at Onitsha that we were to see the full horror of the war against infrastructure. At Onitsha, there seemed to be no single building with its roof left on top of it. Windows were blown out or stripped away as were doors. One of the first places I visited after seeing my cousins, was my old school, All Saints Primary. I went there with my now late cousin, Lizzy Egwu, and another person. We were shocked at the sight that met us, and I was thoroughly downcast. The school roofs were blown out. All the windows in all the classrooms were absent. My classroom was a mess. There was no furniture anymore, no bookcases, but there were a few exercise books strewn on the floor, once wet from rain, and now dried. I even saw one that bore faint traces of my name. I was badly shaken. The world I left behind when the war broke out was now gone, blown apart. Some of the classrooms seemed to have dry excrement on their floors, and I did not want to go in there. As we headed for our library, I must have known I would be hurt some more. The library was now a virtual shell, completely gutted. It was in a similar state to my classroom. I stood there, stunned, for a while. Perhaps, my mind was trying to connect the scene of destruction before me with that room, a favourite of mine, that I had last seen three years prior, and so longed to see again. I would never see it again. It was almost like a bereavement.

For years, I kept on wondering what kind of soldiers shoot at school buildings to blow them up. I could understand soldiers shooting other soldiers to kill them, because if they did not, they could be shot and killed by those other soldiers. I got that. But what on earth did a school or books ever do to anyone? What did my school do to them? Why did they shoot up my school, destroy my library and desecrate classrooms by defecating in them? I could never understand what sorts of soldiers those where, but then, I was very young and yet to learn and read of the greater horrors that human beings carry out in times of conflict, the human rights abuses, genocides and mass rapes some of which had actually occurred in the war I just emerged from. I do not think I hated soldiers as hate was probably too strong an emotion for a child, but after encountering my old school in that state of absolute destruction and desecration, I did not like soldiers very much. Years later, I read accounts of the particular "vengeance" of wanton destruction wreaked on the University of Nigeria, Nsukka, by Federal forces, when they captured the university town. They were angry at the university students' association, infuriated with the pro-Biafran independence demonstrations, and the Nsukka students' alleged membership of the intellectual backbone of the Biafran organization. I associated this behavior with what had happened to my school, but mine was only a primary school for children. Strangely enough, many years later, I was to try, futilely as it happened, to enlist into the Nigerian Army and later its Air Force.

We returned to Nigeria to make the best of what we had been forced back into. For all former Biafrans, re-integration was a struggle The aftermath of war did not include any formal trials, publicized or legislated punishment, or the feared mass executions, but there was still pain to come – beatings, shootings, killings, rapes, property dispossession and all manner of humiliations, for which there was no recourse to any law. We were rebels. We were Biafrans, and most of us were Igbo. We had no protection from the law.

Those who owned property in certain parts of the country were brazenly dispossessed of their property under the Abandoned Property policy. All ex-Biafran adults who were of working age, and who had accounts in banks, were allotted 20 pounds each by the Federal Government, regardless of whether they may have had hundreds, thousands or millions in their accounts pre-war. Life in the East, in the aftermath of the war was precarious. My family and I escaped much of these post war privations of the East by relocating to Lagos, but we heard what some of those we left behind had to go through.

I was thirteen at the end of the war, and in every sense, still a child or an early teen who wanted and did all those things a child of that age would want to do; play, play, play, toys, toys, comics, sweets, chocolate and some football, which I was not at all good at. I was a child, but I knew that I, with millions of other children who had survived, were no ordinary children anymore. We were Biafran children. We were war children. We had seen war. We had seen and felt pride and appreciation of something greater than us – an ideal, the Biafran dream. We were exceedingly proud to have been part of that story.

It is difficult to explain to others who did not experience it, the idea that was Biafra. Save for the horror of war which was a given, as we were at war, we tasted something that few Africans had ever felt – defiance of world powers, defiance of incredible odds, creation of our own Republic by our design, to our own values. We were supremely proud of a country we called our own, and which we had sought to give ourselves by our design, effort, and sacrifice. Ours was not one designed by others for their benefit and for the benefit of a few. Ours was a Republic that we were prepared to die for, and for which some 2 million did indeed lay down their lives. Biafra was not perfect. It had many imperfections, many of which would have had to be worked on if the republic had survived. However as was clearly enunciated in the Ahiara Declaration, the land of the rising sun offered us a sanctuary and a home of our own at a time we did not feel welcome in Nigeria.

As children, we heard of the inventiveness of our scientists and technicians who had ventured deep into those areas of expertise and endeavours psychologically reserved by Africans for the "mythical" powers of the white man. Totally blockaded, we built our own petroleum extraction and refining industry, giving us vehicle petrol and diesel, kerosene, engine oil, and even jet fuel. We set up our own munitions industry, set up and maintained our own mobile radio stations, ran an efficient post service, judiciary and even school system, all during a total blockade and despite daily bombings. We constructed and maintained our airstrips, with the principal airport at Uli hosting more air traffic than could ever have been anticipated. At its peak, Uli was the busiest airport in black Africa, second only to Johannesburg in South Africa. All these and more were done in wartime, without the involvement of outsiders. We had given birth to modern African technology in the fields of petro-technology, metallurgy, rocketry and aeronautics, cottage industry and manufacturing, all in war time, and we as children, knew it.

On the back of these, we emerged from Biafra, beaten, bloodied but unbowed. At her demise, I wept, but I was proud and instinctively felt I was a better person for having lived in her for those three years and imbibed her values and philosophy to the full. Today, I am extremely sensitive about the suffering of others, anywhere. Today, I am unable to look away comfortably or with ease from the plight of the afflicted, injured, bullied, or oppressed. Today, I am still a grateful person, grateful to those who came to our aid in different ways. Today, I am more concerned with humanity and much less about ethnicity or geography. I owe so much to Biafra for who I am today.

I took with me the Biafran values of "can do will do," abiding affection and value for justice, sacrifice for the greater good and for humanity. Each person was affected in particular ways that only they can express but Biafra made me a better person. This child of a long-ago war, longs for peace and safety from war, hunger, want and insecurity for the Nigerian child and for the African child.

About the Author

Chukwudum Ikeazor, is from Obosi in Anambra State. He is a retired police officer and the author of several books including *Nigeria 1966: The Turning Point* (1997) and *Laments on the Niger-Delta* (1999). He has been a long-standing integrity and transparency campaigner in the worlds of policing and public service in Nigeria and the UK. In 2003 he became one of the pioneer winners of the Anne Frank Moral Courage Award in London. He is presently working on a book covering the Biafran war with a former Biafran Army commander.

PRIDE AND SORROW: THE MEMOIRS OF A BIAFRAN CHILD

By Charles Spiropoulos

Enugu

As a very young child I had been sent from England to live with my grandparents in Enugu, ahead of my parents' return. I had travelled unaccompanied at the age of 18 months, and do not have any recollection of my journey. I loved my grandparents immensely and was sure that they loved me just as much (and my sister, Simone, I grudgingly conceded). My grandparents symbolized, for me, comfort and security.

Eagle Lodge, my grandparents' home in Enugu was an inter-generational home, with four generations of the family living as one large, happy unit, with Simone and I as the youngest of the lot. Closer to us in age, but already in their teens, were my uncles, Peter, Richard and Edward, known in the family as the three musketeers, then came my aunts, Irene and Stella, my parents, Charles and Christine, my grandparents, Papa and Mama, and my great grandmother, Nne. There was my great uncle Mike, Nne's youngest son, and other sundry relatives who came in and out on holidays and as circumstances permitted. My grandparents also had one son studying in England, my Uncle Gilbert, known in the family as Oke, and there was my uncle, Ken, their eldest son who also lived in Enugu.

It all seemed exciting to start with, the prospect of war. Nothing of its awful reality dawned on me at the time. There was talk of people who had fled the north, then I became aware of young men gathering in town, marching to patriotic songs, two of which I remember as *"Ojukwu nye anyi egbe"* translated in English as "Ojukwu give us guns" and *"Ebee ka unu si, Biafra"* in English "Where are you all from, Biafra." Everyone, it seemed, was eager and raring to go to war to give those Hausas a beating, the federal side being conflated in the public's mind with the Hausas. Unfortunately, the war soon came to us.

It began to take on a new meaning, to me at least, with the night-time visits to my grandfather by the Biafran leader, Colonel Ojukwu. We would all line up in the entrance hall to greet him, and he was always gracious and charming, speaking to each of us before proceeding to the sitting room upstairs to hold his discussions with Papa. There was a feeling that these discussions were of a very important nature, and we kept well away from the sight and hearing of Papa and Ojukwu. Sometimes, Simone and I would be permitted to stay up late to say goodbye to Ojukwu. These visits came to an end after a huge crowd gathered in front of the house one night to catch a glimpse of him as he left. I suppose that was bad from a security point of view.

Then came the air raids. And with these, came the reality of war. As a child who had basked in the security my grandparents symbolized, it was frightening to see them worried about our safety. I remember the air raids as being absolutely terrifying. As soon as one began, my grandmother would gather all of us under the staircase and while we were there, we would recite the Rosary. I always wished everyone would shut up lest our prayers draw the attention of the pilots to our location. In time, we had a bunker constructed at the back of the house, by the apple tree in front of my grandfather's clinic. My grandfather suggested to Ojukwu that an anti-aircraft gun be mounted on the roof of Eagle Lodge, but my grandmother robustly opposed that suggestion, as she said the house would become a target of the air raids.

As fighting began, my grandmother joined Lady Ibiam and a number of like-minded ladies to visit the war front to tend to wounded soldiers. My aunt, Stella, known in the family as Akuabata or more commonly, Nana, went with her. God alone knows what horrors they saw. My grandmother always went up straight to her room, and even my usually gregarious aunt seemed rather subdued after those trips to the front.

One afternoon, as my grandparents and my mother were in the sitting room chatting, I heard a loud cry, and my mother picked up her handbag and ran upstairs to my grandmother's bedroom. I made my way up there and saw Mummy on her mother's bed crying. I had never seen her cry before. I was alarmed and asked why she was crying. I then learned that they had just received news from the front that Christopher Okigbo, the well-known poet, had been killed. He was a friend of my parents' and, it seemed to me, that it had only been a short while ago that we had visited him and his family, and he and my parents were having a spirited conversation. I was sorry to learn of his death, and asked Mummy if he was in heaven, which brought floods of tears as she answered yes to my question.

As the air raids continued, it became apparent that we were no longer safe, and my grandmother worried that the house might suffer a direct hit. I remember that these air raids took place in the day but I do have a recollection of one that might have taken place in the evening, making it necessary for us to run to the bunker for shelter. I remember that it was dark in the bunker and someone had to run back to the house to get a lantern and swiftly return to the bunker. This underground retreat had a nice pithy smell like wet earth, but I was keen to return to the house as we were in the middle of dinner when we had to race to the safety of the bunker. When we came out, there was a black out and we had to continue our dinner by candle light, which I found exciting, more so, as I toyed with the idea of blowing out the candles and plunging the room into darkness. I thought better of it.

The family must have made the decision to finally leave Enugu, and it must have been a difficult one as I think we were among the last people to leave. It was made harder by the fact that we had to choose what to take with us and what we were leaving behind. I had a huge rocking horse that I wanted to take with me together with my tricycle, but it was gently explained to me that there was no space for the rocking horse. So, I endured my first major sacrifice, my rocking horse.

We left Enugu early one morning. It was a bit chilly, and I remember I had on a charcoal grey cardigan. As we stood outside the house, looking on as the cars were loaded with the few possessions that we were leaving with, Ojukwu's motorcade drove past on its way out of Enugu. He leaned out of his car to wave to us. Shortly after, we got into the cars and left Enugu for a new chapter in our lives, if not as refugees, then as displaced people.

Orlu

We got to Orlu in the afternoon and had lunch with the Okolis. Clara was Papa's niece who was married to Josephat Okoli. He was in the police force, and was instrumental to our leaving Enugu for Orlu. He had found us a house when he feared that it was not safe for us to remain in Enugu. After lunch we went to the house he had rented for us. I do not remember much about this house, but it stuck in my memory as an unpainted house. But, my uncle has since told me that it was in fact painted. Anyway, we spent only a few days there before we moved again to Holy Rosary College, Umuna. There we had the use of two bungalows that sat beside each other. The bigger one became my grandparents' and the smaller one ours.

Still feeling relatively safe and peaceful, Umuna was a joy for us the younger members of the family at least. It was a lovely place, with white picket fences and well-kept grounds. There was a big expanse of lawn in front of the houses, and a fairly large field behind, on the other side of which was a bigger bungalow than any of ours. In that bungalow, lived an Egyptian doctor, his English wife, and their young son, who I was told, was close to me and Simone in age. I looked forward to meeting him. There was, also, a remarkable priest, Father Courtney, and an equally remarkable nun, Sister Mary Clara. Father Courtney came calling with a leg of pork to welcome us.

It was at this time that I had my first taste of natural cocoa as there were a few cocoa trees around the place, and my uncle, Peter, got a few pods and let us have the sweet cocoa beans inside. Curiously, the same trees stopped producing any pods as the war intensified.

My parents did not leave Enugu with us. My mother staying back to continue with her work as a Dietician at the Enugu Specialist hospital, while my father moved with his work as a Chartered Accountant at the Development Corporation. They would come visiting on some weekends. On one of those weekends, my mother decided to take me to meet the little boy that I mentioned above. No sooner had we left the house and waved Papa goodbye as he stood at the window, than we heard the sound of a jet plane. We could not run back to the house, nor could we run across an open field. Mummy pulled me, and we ran to a hibiscus hedge that marked the boundary of the property. She made me lie down and covered me completely with her body, much like a mother hen does with her chicks, while the earth around us spat up clods of earth from the bullets sprayed by the plane as it strafed indiscriminately. I was filled with terror! The sound was loud, but Mummy lay still and started saying the Hail Mary. Just as suddenly, the plane went off to cause misery and grief elsewhere. We got up and Mummy said we had to go back to the house as Papa would be worried sick as to whether we were ok. I was too shaken to be disappointed, and we went back to the house, to find Papa beside himself with worry about us. He asked for the entire family to gather round, and we discovered my uncle, Richard, was not around, but just as we were about to think the worst, he came in with a bleeding leg and partially torn trousers. He had heard the plane and tried to jump over a barbed wire fence when his leg got caught in it. He was only too happy that this was his only injury. We later learned that the plane had struck a marketplace, killing a lot of civilians.

With that first air raid, things began to feel a little less safe. I referred to the clothes I wore on the day of that air raid as my "Gowon" clothes and refused to ever wear them again. Shortly after that, while running for the safety of a bunker when the Nigerian Air Force attacked the hospital in Enugu, Mummy was hurt by shrapnel to her eyebrow that required stitching once the attack was over. Papa sent a car with Steven, his driver, to bring her to Orlu from Enugu, and on their way, they narrowly escaped being killed by Federal troops, who wanted them to stop and opened fire on them when they didn't. By this time, the federal troops had a presence in Enugu and some of the surrounding areas, and you had to be careful or know which route to take to move in and out. My mother later told me that they had been given the wrong information about what route to take out of Enugu that day, and that she and Steven were very lucky not to have been killed. She started working at the hospital at Amaigbo, about four miles from where we lived. It was a nice feeling having my mother back with us, although I spent all my waking day at my grandparents' where I never permitted myself to be anything but a touching distance away from my grandfather.

As the air raids became more frequent, the family decided that we should construct a bunker by the hibiscus hedge where Mummy and I had hidden when we were caught out in that first air raid. It took a very short time to build, as I recall, as there was no shortage of willing hands to work. In the event, we never set foot in that bunker, as my grandparents were not satisfied that it had been properly constructed and felt it was unsafe. One thing that has remained etched in my memory of the time, is a fight that broke out among the men building the bunker, and the sadness that enveloped the kitchen because of it. It turned out that a couple of chickens had been plucked and cleaned in readiness for lunch, and the intestines and other internal bits were being thrown into a bin. It was this offal that the men were fighting over, and it was the sight of grown men in such a situation that made everyone, certainly the adults in the kitchen that afternoon, sad.

I consider, looking back now, that we were relatively lucky. For quite a while after we moved to Umuna, we had electricity, and when the supply ceased, we had for some time, two refrigerators that ran on kerosene. In due course, we could no longer find kerosene that easily and we stopped enjoying the use of the refrigerators. Life still looked new and exciting. In place of electricity for lighting, we had some tall, graceful looking Aladdin lamps. I remember another air raid, and this must have been early on in our stay at Umuna because we left the house and went to sit in a thicket of bamboo just outside the gate of the college (as time went by, we stayed indoors during air raids and hoped for the best). My grandfather had his rifle with him and was trying to take a shot at the fighter plane, much to my grandmother's alarm. She was not in the least amused, and told him that he would get us all killed, whereupon he put down his rifle rather grudgingly. My uncle, Ken, who was in the army, dropped in just before we left the Bamboo thicket and made jokes with Papa about trying to shoot down a fighter plane with his rifle, while my grandmother remained unamused.

I remember that when we newly arrived in Umuna, there was a woman who went around selling fried chicken. She was known simply as *Nwanyi okuko*, in English the chicken woman. My great uncle, Mike, was a devoted customer of hers. One afternoon we heard a huge commotion outside the grounds of the college, and we ran to the gate to see what it was all about. We saw a large crowd made up of both children and adults singing and making jeering noises. As they came close, we saw *nwanyi okuko* in the middle of the crowd with a chicken tied round her neck. I have never seen such humiliation on someone's face and I felt sorry for her. I asked what had happened, and someone explained to me that she had been caught trying to steal the very chicken tied round her neck, and was being treated in the time honoured manner of the countryside. We never saw her again.

There were no other children my age or Simone's for that matter, aside from our Okoli cousins whom we saw now and again, until our Njemanze cousins, Huguette and Lucy-Anne, came with their parents, Uncle Hugh and Auntie Germaine. They stayed with us for some time. Auntie Germaine, being French, worked for the French service of Radio Biafra. When we were naughty, Auntie Germaine would brand us "Nigerians", which to us children was the worst thing ever. There were no schools, so Simone and I had a teacher, Lizzy, who came to the house to give us lessons a few hours a day. We finished our lessons in time for lunch and spent the rest of the day either playing together or fighting or each living in their own dream world. This might explain why, today, I am quite happy being by myself for extended periods of time without the need for any company.

One day, as we were having lessons, we saw a man from the village walk up the drive to my grandparents' bungalow, only to leave shortly after with my young dog, Bubi, tucked under his arm. My mother had only recently got me the dog, but my grandmother did not want it in the family. I was in such a hurry for the lesson to end, and ran over to my grandparents' the moment it was over. My grandmother said she had arranged for a new home for Bubi, and that was that. Both Simone and I cried, and when Mummy came back from work, we told her what had happened, and she burst into tears, too. Papa then said that we could bring the dog back, and promised to work on Mama. On the weekend, having secured Mama's approval for Bubi to return, we set off with our uncles to the man's home in the village. When we got there, my uncles told him why we had come, and he opened the door to his hut wider. We caught a glimpse of pieces of meat hanging from his rafters, and we all recoiled in horror, and retreated in tears to our house. Mama was so sorry for what had happened. We children put a curse on the man and to our joy he developed a cough that remained with him until we left Umuna.

As we were very young, our whole existence was within our home. We did not, like my uncles, go exploring the place. However, my young uncle, Edward, took to making up adventure stories which kept us entertained. Evenings were spent, when I was not at my grandparents', with my mother and she would recite and teach us nursery rhymes. Now and again, Daddy would take us for car rides and we might drop in on some friends of our parents' like the Ukas and the Onyejiakas. These rides became less regular after Daddy's car, a spanking new black Audi, took a direct hit from an enemy airplane. He had just stepped out of the car to see someone when a plane dropped a bomb on it. So, from having four cars for the family's use, there were now two left, and those two belonged to my grandparents, my mother's having been written off in an accident previously.

I remember one hot sunny afternoon when there was a burst of excitement. Someone had come rushing in to tell Papa that a hunter had just shot a leopard. Not quite believing the story, Papa asked for details. Simone and I piled into the car with the three musketeers with my grandfather behind the wheel. I remember distinctly what my grandfather wore - a pair of grey trousers with a white shirt, sleeves rolled up and his sunshades clipped onto his glasses. We got to our destination, and there was such a huge crowd that it felt like a carnival. People made way for Papa to pass, and we walked toward a tree, where a leopard was indeed strapped. It looked to me like a big teddy bear. Papa asked for the hunter, and they pointed him out to us. He was a small, wiry man and was looking rather harassed himself, with not a trace of bravado about him. There he was, sitting on the ground by the side, hot and bothered, with this huge crowd around him. Papa walked up to him and congratulated him before we turned around and went back home. We speculated (at least Papa and the three musketeers did) that the leopard must have escaped from a zoo and found its way into the wild.

As time went on, we stopped eating certain foods because they were not available. I remember going through a period when I was absolutely miserable for want of bread. I went about craving it and asking for it. My mother must have been driven to despair, because she came back from work one day with the most beautifully baked loaf of bread. It turned out that she had mentioned my craving to one of the Irish nuns and she had, bless her, baked a loaf and given her. Such joy! For some time after that, the nuns would bake and send some to us.

As I said, choice of food became limited, and people began to rely on what was known as relief. These were food supplies flown in by charitable organizations, the most prominent of which was Caritas. These relief food items were supplemented with whatever you could find to buy. One of the things that came as relief food was corn meal, and this was used as fufu, accompanied by whatever soup. It could also be made into fritters. I had a rather pronounced loathing for this corn meal, and when it was served, would sit at the table looking at my food and not touching it. My saving grace was that my aversion to the wretched corn meal was nothing compared to my grandfather's, which meant that he had his pounded yam, no matter what, and he let me have some of it.

On the occasions when I had no appetite, my uncles would tease me by enacting an imaginary scene where the disease, Kwashiorkor, was knocking at the door looking for me. This both annoyed and frightened me, especially as they made it clear that my mother would be unable to help me when kwashiorkor came knocking. I had heard a lot about this disease, and it sounded scary. I put aside my dislike of medicines and made sure that I took my vitamins religiously just to keep the disease away from me. One late afternoon, a lady ran to our house with her child in her arms crying out for my grandfather. The child had kwashiorkor and before we could be stopped, I ran over to have a look. That image has remained with me all my life. The child was all skin and bone with a hugely distended belly and big hollow eyes. Just at that moment, my grandfather drove in with my aunt, Nana, and stopped to look at the child and talk to his mother. He asked my aunt to fetch some milk for the child and they fed him with it. The mother was given some to take with her, and she left. My grandfather was very upset about the child, and could not eat the lunch that had been kept for him. I often think about that child and wonder if he made it, but judging from Papa's reaction, I got the feeling that he was in a bad way. There were many other children like that poor child in Biafra. Many.

I had a dream in which a rather big snake was seen in the field beyond the Hibiscus hedge behind the house. That field was now much overgrown and reverting to bush. Playing around on my tricycle one day, I tumbled into the bush, and my mother, looking out of the window saw me and asked me if it wasn't the same bush in my dream where I had seen a snake. That spooked me, and I ran out as fast as I could. Not long after, while recovering from a bout of malaria, I was taken out to sit on the veranda behind my grandparents' bungalow, all nicely wrapped up as it had just rained. I soon heard my grandfather call out that I should be brought back in at once. He had seen a python in the bushes from his bedroom window, although it was quite a distance away from the house. He sent for the biggest man in the village, whose name, I think, was Orji. Orji came with a group of people and an enormous Bamboo pole. They went to the place Papa directed them and saw the python. Orji muttered some incantations and slowly the python wrapped itself around the Bamboo pole. They slung the pole on the shoulders of two men and left singing. Papa asked Orji what they were doing, and he replied that they were taking the python to a bigger bush. Papa was aghast and said that he had expected them to kill the python, but they told him it was forbidden to kill pythons and if anyone did, then they would have to go through the burial rites normally followed when a person dies. Papa shook his head in disbelief, but there was nothing he could do.

We began to suffer constant air raids and these were not good for my grandfather's blood pressure. He soon found a place even more remote than where we were. So, after a series of air raids, we would pile into the car and go to this haven of a place called Lilu. We would spend a few days there before going back to Umuna. My grandmother came once with us, and not finding the lavatory system to her taste, refused to retreat there with us on our subsequent trips. My grandfather would ask her to come and she would refuse and he, in exasperation, would turn to Nne, his mother-in-law, and ask her to talk to Mama. Of course, Mama's staying on in Umuna worried him, and we would always go back as soon as we could so he could be with her. I seem to recall meals there in Lilu of mostly sweet potatoes; boiled, fried, roasted and with different accompaniments, but they were a staple.

While we were in Umuna, Papa had a stroke that left him partially paralysed on the right side. With excellent medical attention and sheer will power, he recovered enough to regain the use of his right side. Papa's stroke was a huge blow, not just to him, but to my grandmother and to all of us. Mama nursed him back to relative health. I would always run up to him in his chair to hug and kiss him, so much so that each time I came into the room, he'd playfully make as if he was swatting me away, or he'd ask if he was about to die.

Dr Ibiam came visiting one evening, and I noticed that he was crying as he and Papa were chatting. I now know that Papa had told him that he had cancer and Dr Ibiam was advising him to travel abroad for treatment, but Papa was reluctant to do so. My grandmother persuaded him to travel abroad. On the day that he left with my uncle, Peter, it looked like he was still reluctant to go. Three times they left for the airport, only to come back, ostensibly because Papa had remembered something. On the third return, I went up to the car where he was sitting, dressed in a black suit with his favourite fedora on his head. I asked him if he would buy a bicycle for me when he got to London, and I was shocked to see tears fall from his eyes. My mother came out of the house, leaned into the car and kissed him, telling him to go as my grandmother was beginning to fret that he would miss his flight out of Biafra. After he left, my evenings became rather empty and I would walk around aimlessly.

It also meant that my access to pounded yam ceased, and I had to face the wretched corn meal.

My grandfather arrived in England on 4 May 1969 where he sadly died on 4 June 1969. On the day that he died, my grandmother felt so sick that she had to be taken to the hospital. None of the cars would start, and we had to send someone to Okwelle where my aunt, Nana, lived with her newly married husband, and she sent their car to take Mama to the hospital. Later, Ojukwu sent a messenger to the house with the news of Papa's death. I was taking my siesta when the messenger arrived, but was told that as soon as my grandmother saw them arriving from her bedroom window, she cried that she didn't want to see them as she felt that they were bringing bad news about Papa. I woke from my siesta to find my mother sitting at the foot of the bed sobbing quietly. I greeted her, and after asking if I had a good siesta, she told me, "Papa has died, Charles, and is now in heaven watching over us." I pictured him in the sky in his black Fedora. We both cried together for a bit, and I said that I must go see my grandmother and left to go to her. Following Papa's death, my grandmother was sick with worry on account of the frequent news bulletins on Radio Nigeria that his body was being flown to Nigeria to be buried at Ikoyi cemetery. She mentioned her fears to Ojukwu who assured her it was never going to happen. Papa's body was flown back to Biafra for burial and he was temporarily laid to rest at Ihioma Cathedral.

Lilu

As the federal troops gained ground and Biafran territory decreased, it got to the point where it was apparent that Orlu was going to fall and we had to move. My dad came back one afternoon and told my grandmother that we had to leave. I remember that he did a lot of running around to make sure that the car was in order, the driver having been conscripted into the army. He then had to go miles to get a spare tyre, and it was dark before we left Umuna for Lilu, to the house that Papa had had the foresight to rent as a bolt hole.

We lived in the Chief's compound in a semi-detached bungalow, one of several buildings in a large and beautiful compound. It was clean, but the amenities were basic. When we got there, my grandmother found out that some friends of hers had their country home nearby, although the family itself was abroad. She arranged to go there daily to make use of the facilities there.

There were no air raids in Lilu, and life was very peaceful. One of my younger great aunts, Love, would take Simone and I around the village. We went to the village square, which always smelt of palm oil, and where the men sat under trees in the evening drinking palm wine and playing draughts. We also went to the stream and the market. Lilu remains the closest that I have ever been to living a rural life, and I remember those days with a touch of nostalgia - except for the day that I was set upon in the village square by eight dogs who didn't recognize me in my cowboy outfit as I ran past, tassels and all! One day, we learnt that the war was over, and that federal troops had been spotted nearby. I remember that once, there was information that the federal soldiers were on their way, and all the ladies fled through a door in the back wall of the compound to hide. The reason for this fear among the ladies was the proliferation of stories of rape and indecent assaults on women said to be perpetrated by these soldiers. My dad went outside and tied a white cloth to the car as a sign of peace. Fortunately, nothing eventful happened, and the war was really over. My parents left to go to Enugu to check how things were and to arrange for transportation for the household and our belongings.

My parents came back from Enugu a short while later, having made the necessary arrangements such as transport, and getting Eagle Lodge cleaned and habitable. About two days after their return, we took our leave of the Chief in whose compound we had stayed. There was a large crowd of people who came to say goodbye and having done so, we left for Enugu in a short convoy of two cars and a lorry.

Enugu

On the way to Enugu, we saw the destruction wrought by the war, so I was surprised to find so much life and activity in Enugu. We had stopped to eat before going to the house, and it was dark when we got home. There were people at the back of the house who were not family. I went in and rushed to the Green Parlour, where my rocking horse had been when we left almost three years previously, but it was not there. I then went back to the kitchen and walked to where I remembered the fridge used to stand, to get some water, but touched the wall. I thought it very strange and called out to my mother. She gave me some water and took Simone and I upstairs to get ready for bed.

Simone and Charles Spiropoulos in Biafra, 1969

I woke up the next day to a practically empty house. It turned out that the house had been looted once my grandfather's death was announced. The looting had been arranged by his erstwhile steward, Okorie, who had elected to remain in Enugu when we left, and over whose safety my grandparents had frequently agonised in Umuna. My grandmother brought tears to the eyes of everyone around with her lament that she had left the house with her husband and had returned to it a widow. She also lamented the loss of almost all the family's treasured possessions, but my great grandmother and my uncle Edward reminded her that those could all be replaced. Still, the loss was devastating. Gifts from such famous people as The Queen and the Duke of Edinburgh, Golda Meir and the Pope, as well as things that had been collected over time were all gone, as was the sculpture of the eagle on the roof that gave the house its name.

Various family and friends came calling, since a feature of the Biafran war was that people moved to wherever that was safe and lost touch with some family and friends. Simone and I were enrolled at All Saints Primary School, which initially operated from the grounds of All Saints Church before it moved back to its actual site, which bore scars of the civil war. We were to be there very briefly as our parents made the decision to move to Lagos to try to rebuild our lives there.

With the move to Lagos, my Biafran days really and truly came to an end. The war had gone on for long enough that I no longer remembered what certain foods such as corn flakes or bacon either looked or tasted like, and had to be re-introduced to these, and to so many other foods which we did without in Biafra. A particular favourite was cotton candy. We had survived and prayed the happy days we saw were there to stay.

About the Author

Charles Spiropoulos went on to read Law and practised in Nigeria and in England. He lives in London with his wife, Niina, and their daughter, Mia. He is from Asaba in Delta State.

THE KILLING FIELDS

By Oka Okwara Amogu

Prologue

Accident of birth? Fate? Providence? For whatever reasons and through no fault of mine, I was caught-up in the mindless Nigerian power show that brutalized my folks and chased the surviving ones back to our homeland in the Eastern part of Nigeria. Here we felt safe, until the Federal troops showed up at our doorsteps to force us back onto the killing-fields. With dogged determination, we resisted. We fought back with all we had just to remain in the only place that guaranteed us security and physical survival. I survived. Plenty of others did too. The objective of the war was met, which was to keep us alive. I therefore emerged as an authentic Biafra-win-the-war child.

I am eternally grateful to God for that mighty favour as I attempt to recall the terrible days of the Nigeria-Biafra war. I witnessed boys and girls my age lose their lives to hunger, to disease, and to the cruelty of callous air-raids. I was aware that some boys and girls got lost in transit and during stampedes that ensued when towns and villages began to experience direct hits from artillery, mortars and bombs, and yet others were compassionately ferried out by charity organizations, never to return.

In The Beginning

I was born in Lagos in March 1961, as the first child of one of Nigeria's pioneer diplomats to the United Kingdom. That provided an elite yet modest beginning for me. Attention shifted from me when my brother, Idika, showed up in the severe Manchester winter of 1962. Then yet again to Eni, my second brother, in 1965.

In the summer of 1966, a close Yoruba friend at work in Lagos, tipped my father off, so dad left his job at the Ministry of Defense and made the long drive to the East with his young family. This was how we entered the war.

Ikom

Late in 1966, we moved to Ikom, in the then Ogoja Province in Eastern Nigeria, when my father was posted there as the Senior Divisional Officer-in-Charge. His job included managing relations with Cameroon. I recall we were treated like royalty each time we visited Cameroon.

However, our house suddenly became a beehive of activities. The grown-ups within our household, (drivers, the gardener, the washerman, the cook and the houseboys) began to mimic military gestures. The government field opposite my house turned to a recruitment ground, hosting military drills and parades to the background of morale-boosting songs. The field also doubled as a helipad. It was later I understood the reason for the sudden burst of energy. Ojukwu had declared the Republic of Biafra, and Nigeria had commenced what was termed a "police action," with the Nigerian army firing the first shots at Garkem near Ikom. The country was at war. My father was charged with providing logistic support to Major Ifeajuna who had been assigned with recruiting troops.

Ohafia

Before long, we were evacuated from Ikom to Ebem, Ohafia, and got in very late that evening. By morning, I realised we had just joined 19 others - (cousins, nieces, and nephews, aged 3 to 15). Apparently, this home had been forced by the war to host 6 "refugee" internally displaced families.

It was common in those days to see single family dwellings housing 4 to 6 families and even more. As more families joined, meals moved from individual plates to massive portions in big bowls for 4 to 7 similarly sized kids. So, for survival, I learned to eat hot food very fast. We took turns washing-up the dishes. Bathing and laundry happened down at the stream. Going to the stream was fun as we used to leave in droves of "family platoons." Our platoon numbered about 16 (on the average). The seven kilometers walk (to and from the stream) would only cease to be fun on those days when one was commandeered by soldiers to take water to their 'barracks'

For a long time, my father was away, and we did not know why. Attention dried up, things began to toughen up, and sympathies began to wane. We began to experience hunger. I learned to steal and to snare small animals and insects, roast them over open fires and relish these simple fares. I learned to fight back, and above all, mastered the art of walking long distances. The "win-the-war" slogan had just begun to gain popularity, as every effort was supposed to be targeted at survival.

More refugees poured into Ohafia, joined by battle-weary soldiers with physical injuries and mental injuries popularly referred to as "shell-shock" or "atingbo." In hindsight, I believe it was becoming very difficult for that Ohafia home to sustain all of us, especially as our numbers kept swelling with new arrivals.

Umuahia-Aba-Umuahia

February 1968, my father showed up and hurriedly moved us to Umuahia. Here I experienced my first air raid. I had escorted our neighbour to the market to assist her with taking her wares there and bringing back the foodstuff she was going to help us buy. Hardly had we begun transacting when, out of nowhere, came a deafening sound of an aircraft flying past, quickly followed by loud explosions and a vigorous earth tremor that threw up so much earth I thought I was being buried alive. The market had been bombed. There was dread, panic, and confusion everywhere. People covered by excavated earth were screaming and running in various directions. In that confusion, filled with terror, I took off running home and did not stop until I had traversed the over two kilometers to No. 80 Eket Street. I had never been that frightened in my entire life.

Despite the air raids, we were encouraged to queue street by street with our plates for meals prepared and served once daily by charity organizations, with assurances that enemy planes would not attack a place where Red Cross flags were flying. That was until the day an enemy plane swooped down on us, scattering everybody and the food, despite conspicuous Red Cross flags flying beside the feeding operations. Some vehicles were damaged, some people were injured, and my friend's house further down our street was partially flattened. Later that afternoon, as they were evacuating, I saw that my friend's arm was heavily bandaged and in a sling. He survived, although their house barely did. We later moved to Aba with my father. Nothing eventful happened there except the air raids, and the scary knowledge of my father's detention for mutiny. Apparently, his cordial relationship with Major Ifeajuna had placed him in such a precarious position that it took a concerted intervention of "Umuahians" (that is, people who schooled at Government College, Umuahia) and who were in the Biafran Army, to get him released.

[Government College Umuahia Officer Cadet Corps provided field drills and adventure training, inspiring the likes of General George Kurubo, General Alex Madiebo (GOC Biafran Army), Col Patrick Anwuna (Staff Officer Biafra Army), Brigadier Tony Eze (Commander, 12th Div), Colonel Tim Onwuatuegwu (Commander "S" Brigade), etc. to brilliant military career]

We quartered in the outskirts of Aba near Opobo junction with about seven other families. The isolated block of four luxury flats on two suspended floors with the ground floor as parking was like an oasis judging by the grounds and the quality of finish. Luckily, we were not short of food in Aba. There were also moments that stuck with me even amid the general horrors of the war, and one of those was the botched job we once did of killing a hen for dinner. On this day, we caught the chicken and tried to slit its throat. The usual practice was that we would cut the throat while holding the chicken firmly as the blood drained and it went through its death throes. Having done that, you put the remains of the chicken in hot water to remove the feathers. Trouble was that the knife we were using was not sharp enough, and we only found out when the chicken on the work-top jumped down and started chasing everyone in the kitchen, with its head dangling to one side. That, there, was the never-say-die Biafran spirit.

The incessant shelling meant we had to move from Aba. We shared a flat with another family and at night, we could see distant balls of fire. Within days, we began to associate these incandescent balls with explosions. They got progressively louder, and refugee traffic became heavier daily. On this particular night, the explosions were so intense that nobody could sleep. The fathers tip-toed around the block, talking in low tones with dread in their eyes. Lights were off, and we dared not make a sound. By the next morning, we had gathered our essentials, ready to flee. By evening, all but two other families had moved. That night we all huddled together, and my father came in late to join us. There was air raid again that night to compound the trauma from artillery bombardment. My father was part of a government campaign discouraging civilians from fleeing Aba. In the morning, he left, assuring us he would be back immediately after he got petrol. By midday, we were the only family left in the entire compound. Hunger had set in, but we could not afford to unpack in case he showed up. We were all in tears when my father finally returned after 5pm. Then it started to rain heavily as we hit the road for Umuahia. We moved at snail's pace because of refugees on foot, bikes, cars and trucks containing evacuees fleeing for dear life. We were only too happy to get further and further away from the explosions. I remember we could not continue at a point, because we had a flat and did not have a spare. It was already midnight, and we had to pass the night there. I remember the efforts to prepare a meal that night. It was terrible because the egusi could not be milled, but had to be broken into tiny bits. It was dubbed "win-the-war-soup." We continued to Umuahia later the next day after my father had the tire vulcanized.

No sooner had we arrived Umuahia than it came under an air raid siege. The effect got so severe that Government offices had to operate only from 5am to 9am. It appeared the Federal troops had sworn to bomb Umuahia into submission. Economic activities shifted to the hinterland, the town would empty during the day and fill up again in the evenings. The planes flew an average of 7 sorties daily, some days as many as 11 sorties lasting between 10 mins and 50 mins per raid leaving behind a smoking town replete with pain and misery. Fortunately, we had relief of cornmeal and salted stockfish provided by some white folk. We had to line up at critical relief service points, such as churches or military camps with soup bowls, to collect spoons of soup and cornmeal. My brother and I developed assorted types of malnutrition symptoms which obviously were never treated. We had a skin condition (craw-craw) and though it meant nothing to us, it was an extreme situation to be in having returned from the UK only 4 years earlier. We progressed to eating with metal pot covers so that when Nigerian planes raided Umuahia during mealtimes, we used the pot covers to cover our heads and dived under the spring beds if we were fortunate to be in the house. We found that we spent more time hiding in the bushes in Ahia-Eke, where we got used to trekking to and from on a daily basis from Umuahia town. The volume of heavy bombardment, machine gun and small arms fire had become so intense that Umuahia capitulated in April 1969 its suffering compounded by accurate hits from artillery shells. My father thought it wise to scramble us back to Ohafia.

Owerri To The End

Back at Ohafia, news of Brigadier Ogbugo Kalu and his 14th Div. Biafran Army was all over town for clearing Owerri of the Nigerian forces in April 1969. We were all eager to identify with him, and so I jumped at the opportunity of going to the "war front" with my father even if only to behold with awe the mien of our hero. I might even see Ojukwu.

I joined my father when the entire Biafran Public Service relocated to some school ground in Arondizuogu. For about five days, we lived in the car, with him in the front seat, me in the back seat, and our soup pot in the boot. Though there were several other car-homes close by, I could not find a playmate, so I would just loiter around but not go too far, except to get water or to toilet. My father and I had to retire early to "bed" immediately after our dinner. I used to look forward to every night in the darkness of the car, (ignoring the distant sounds of artillery shells and the staccato of small firearms), to his lessons on how wars were conducted, stories of war and battles that eulogized Erwin Rommel, Douglas MacArthur, Bernard Montgomery, Moshe Dayan, etc. Dad's super-hero status got magnified the moment I discovered a college photo of him in military fatigues, in front of a Mercedes duty truck.

When it was safe to move the Biafran secretariat to Owerri, our car could not move, so we travelled in the truck carrying the files et al. I remember it was a Leyland Truck, and I was made to sit longitudinally on the engine that protruded into the cabin. We travelled through the night, past numerous checkpoints manned by stern-faced Biafran soldiers. We camped at the Advanced Teachers Training College, (presently Alvan Ikoku College of Education), until we got our quarters at the Shell Camp.

My Owerri experience began with a lesson on the importance of salt. Nothing can be more awful than attempting to eat soup prepared without salt. My father and I were compelled to experience this after we had searched in vain for even a pinch of salt. The "saltless" experience was quickly followed by my attempt to resuscitate soup that had gone sour. My father was leaving me alone for 5 days, so he made soup that I could warm and relish. By the time I was ready to eat the soup, it had swollen and was giving out a foul odour. I broke down in tears because there was nothing else to eat except to soak the accompanying garri. Advice from neighbors to keep warming the soup without covering it did not help matters. It was a harrowing experience.

I also had the experience of hawking porridge yam in the Owerri "win-the-war" food court at five shillings a plate. This food court was open to the sky and located at the present day Rochas Conference Center. There were a few other kids my age, but most hawkers were much older people. Note that air raids had ceased to scare me. I was confident enough to watch the aerobatics of these vandal jets and the explosions they engendered, coupled with the cacophony of Biafran anti-aircraft batteries. I began to look forward to those raiding sessions

Surviving The Peace

The war ended while we were in Osuihite-Ukwa. We arrived from Owerri and moved into a lock-up shop in the market that became our apartment. Our location was experiencing a total breakdown of law and order in which Nigerian soldiers were on a rampage, harassing the populace and commandeering any females they fancied, irrespective of age. One evening about 6pm, a short man in mufti marched boldly up to the entrance of our "apartment," and demanded to search it because he had spied my mother and wanted to take her away to the military barracks. There were about five men including my father in front of our "apartment" making small talk and whiling away time as the evening wore on. When my dad blocked his path and would not let him through, he yelled, "do you know I am a Nigerian soldier?" At this, the other men began to disperse, leaving my father on his own. My dad refused to yield, and I was scared to death. Then the officer realized he could not intimidate my father unarmed, and coupled with the fast approaching darkness, he stormed off. All who witnessed the stand-off came around to congratulate my dad. We left town about 4.30am the next morning, I guess to escape an animal whose ego had been badly bruised. We walked the whole day. It was cold, dry, and I was covered in dust by the time we approached Obodo Ukwu. I was in front, carrying my sister on my back, and then I saw them: Nigerian soldiers. I froze as I waited for my parents to catch up. To my surprise, these officers spoke kindly to us, asking us to wait and ride in their truck that was leaving for Okigwe later that evening. As we waited, they offered us army rations of Beans and Yam which I wolfed down like there was no tomorrow. A roofless Bedford duty truck showed up at about 6pm, and we climbed in behind, together with some other refugees. Initially the journey was interesting, with the soldiers taking delight in "wasting" Biafran currency and rubbing in how worthless it had become, but I remember the chilly journey ended at Okigwe where we had to sleep in the open within a military camp, together with other refugees in transit. By morning, these soldiers busied themselves helping refugees with transport. We got onto a military truck that took us to Ohafia. I later learnt that the unruly, crude and wicked officers were troops of the 3rd Division under Col. Obasanjo and the kind, compassionate ones were troops of the 1st Division under Col. I. D. Bissala.

Our lives were spared, and we went back to primary school at Kpoke. Our journey to school always took us past our grandmother's house which was at the halfway point between the school and home. My brother usually never made it to school. He would always stop over at our grandmother's.

Life began to take on a semblance of normality when we moved to Enugu from Ohafia, but we will always carry with us the memory of all the Umuahia old boys who we lost:

> *Major Chris Emelifonwu (killed July 66 coup),*
> *Major Ibanga Ikanem (killed in July 66 coup),*
> *August Okpe*
> *Col (Dr) Bassey Inyang*

About the Author

Oka Okwara Amogu is from Ohafia in Abia state. Oka holds an M.Sc. in Architecture and is a fellow of the Nigerian Institute of Architects and currently chairs its Practice Committee. Married to Aderinola, they have two sons and two daughters, and live in Abuja, Nigeria. Oka devotes his time to training, supporting, and mentoring young people.

THE REFUGEE YEARS

By Meg Amechi

Sometimes when I close my eyes and think of my father, I can still remember his tears on that fateful day. My father certainly seemed quite large to me at four years old, nearly five, and yet there he was sobbing into my neck as he gave me his last cuddles. I do not think I really understood what was happening or its implications. I certainly did not understand that my father was not actually coming with us. I do not even think that I truly understood that by morning, I would be in another country, a country where I was born and which we had left by boat roughly two and half years before. My parents were living in England and had even bought a house when my father decided that he needed to return to his country of birth, Nigeria. He had achieved his Master of Engineering degree and he felt obliged to go back and help build Nigeria. He loved teaching and was keen on lecturing in Nigeria's foremost University in Nsukka.

Luckily, I loved my dad so much. So much so that when my aunts heard he was bringing us back to Nigeria on his own and wondered how he would cope on his own, I was happy to go with him and did my best not to be too much of a bother. I simply wanted to be with my dad and nothing was ever going to change that. My mum had to stay back, she was pregnant, and she wanted to give birth in London where we were living. She also had to sell the house and ship all our things before returning to Nigeria. Manage well my Dad did. He even plaited our hair, and we were very close to him. My aunties always teased us, reminding us that when we first arrived in Nigeria, we would hide behind my father whenever they spoke to us. We would cry, whilst hiding behind him, and my dad would say, *"Rapu fa"* or *"rapu ya"* if it was only me. I was the biggest culprit of all as I was terribly shy.

Once my mother joined us in Nigeria, we moved first to Port Harcourt, then to Nsukka where we were living when the war broke out. As Nsukka fell we fled, and so began our movements as a family. An engineer, my dad soon had to go to the war front. Luckily, he had recently bought a car, an Opel Rekord, so he was able to shuttle between the war front and Port Harcourt where we returned to eventually. Sometimes my mum was frustrated because we were left alone with her, and being from the West Indies, Guyana, South America, to be precise, she could neither speak nor understand any of the Nigerian languages spoken around her.

The consequence of this was brought home to her one afternoon as we were playing in the house while she was in the kitchen making a simple pudding for dinner. Suddenly, the air raid siren sounded. By then, six months in, we knew the drill. We had to make for the air raid bunker. I hated it because it smelt of fresh earth; nevertheless, my sister and I obediently ran to the bunker while my mum went back to round up my brother. He was only two and a half at the time and was incredibly mischievous. My mother was frantic. By the time she got to the bunker, she had not seen any sign of him, but she thought he might have headed into the bush with some of the older children who also did not like the bunker. When the all clear sounded, we all came out and rushed back to the house only to find out that none of the older children had seen my brother. At this point, my mother was at her wits' end, and everyone was out searching for him. Then, she went to make dinner, and there was my brother licking the bowl that had previously contained the pudding. Mum was extremely cross with him, and at the same time, relieved that he had not come to harm. But from then on, she insisted that we had to leave Biafra. I will never forget the dank earthy smell of the bunkers or the sound of the sirens.

All this led to the night on the tarmac at Uli, with my father's tears rolling down his cheeks as he imagined he may never see his family again. The next thing I remember was being in England without him. Neither I nor my siblings could talk to my mum about our worry about our dad not being there, because we soon realised it made her very upset. I later discovered we were part of one of the greatest airlifts of any war to date.

As refugees we were housed in a beautiful house in Corby. I loved that house. It had a nice garden where we could go out and play. However, that place wasn't home for too long as we moved around a fair bit depending on where my mum got a job. At first, she got a job in a primary school which my brother attended in Corby, while my sister and l were enrolled in a different school. I was not too happy about attending a different school because there was a small black dog that chased my sister and I on our way home from school every single day. It would wait for us halfway home, then it would come out from seemingly nowhere and chase us all the way home. What an ordeal. The only advice we got was to stand still and the dog would get fed up and go away. That certainly did not work. When I could see its fangs and feel its hot breath on my ankles, I would set off running once more. The first time we started at our new school we were introduced as the "children from Biafra". So of course, we were teased by other children in school especially as I did not talk much outside home.

That house in Corby was also where my siblings and I caught mumps. Within days of each other, we were all down with mumps, and my mum had to stay off work to nurse us. We could only eat soft foods and drinks and my mum was very creative in making healthy meals for us. Ice cream was a wonderful treat, especially the way my mum made it. She was also very good at making all sorts of puddings. Eventually she got a job in Grimsby as a lecturer in Law, so that meant we had to move again. I was so happy as it meant saying goodbye to our tormentor, the dog. Ever since then, 1 have hated small yapping dogs and tend to avoid them.

I loved our new house. It was actually built on top of shops, and the shopkeepers downstairs were all very kind and sympathetic. This is where I learnt the lesson about being a big sister. Once we went out to play, and came across a road that was being tarred. The workers had gone home for the weekend, and left the big drum covered up with a smaller bucket which still had dregs of the tar in it. I was attracted to the smell; I felt I had smelt it somewhere before, but from the look of the tar, it was obvious it would stain clothes, so I stayed away from it. My brother and sister kept going near to the tar bucket. They stirred the practically empty bucket with sticks and ran at each other waving the sticks. By the time we left the road behind, they were covered in tar. I decided it was time to go home, and as my mum opened the front door, I brushed past her very quickly. As she turned to look at me, wondering why I was so hasty in getting through the door, she did not notice my brother and sister creeping in behind her covered in tar. I was watching them intently, and my mother turning to see what I was looking at, saw my brother and sister. The best way I can describe the noise that left her lips was a squealing scream. She could hardly believe her eyes. I tried to absolve myself of guilt and told my mother exactly what happened, and l also, told her that I had warned them not to play with the tar bucket but that they would not listen. My mum caught hold of me and gave me a beating with her slipper. I was extremely miffed that I got the slipper and my sister and brother got off seemingly scot free. My mum then gathered them up and put them in the bath. When I saw the way she scrubbed them within an inch of their lives, I think I got off with the lighter of the punishments. As my mum came to tuck us into bed, she told me "that I had to help her with my brother and sister." I had to be more responsible in the absence of our dad. She said she had beaten me out of frustration because she was trying to do everything all by herself. I felt ashamed and vowed to try and be more responsible.

We eventually moved to a very small bedsit flat in Grimsby. It had no sitting room and all our nice furniture seemed to have disappeared. I thought maybe my mum knew the flat was too small to house it all, but now, I believe she knew at that point that we were going back to Nigeria. At first, she did not tell us that this was why we were in temporary accommodation. Before we finished the school year, however, she told us that the war in Nigeria had ended and we were going back once school broke up because our dad was alive. I was so happy. We went to Peterborough to get passports and all my siblings were put on my passport.

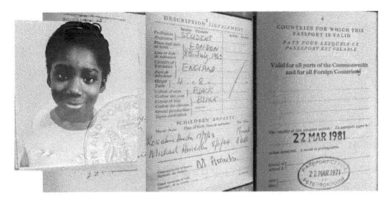

Meg Amochi Passport Photo Page, 1971   *M. Amechi Nigeria Passport pages 1971*

Getting on the plane to Nigeria was exciting, it was the first time we could actually remember travelling by plane. Before we left England, we visited some of my mum's friends in London. They too had flown back to England during the Biafran war and mum knew them well and kept up the friendships when we all returned to Nigeria. The plane touched down, and the familiar heat-driven smell filled the air. We were escorted into the terminal; got our passports stamped and walked into the luggage hall. As we headed out, there were several men reaching out their arms saying, "It's me, I am your father come to me." It was all so emotional and confusing as there were so many of them. I walked past them till I saw a man with a tear laden sparkle in his eyes and a huge smile. I instinctively knew this was my dad. He hugged us all and carried my brother in his arms. I was so happy! Home at last.

Two days later, we travelled down to the East. As soon as we got to Asaba we began to see bullet-riddled houses. We crossed the river Niger and Dad took us to our hometown, Onitsha, to see some of his relatives. Again, more bullet riddled houses. So, we asked our father where the holes came from, and why there were so many. He explained that this was the result of the war, and told us a few stories about what happened. He clearly did not like talking about the war and how he had survived. We later learnt of his true bravery while working at the war front. My father had helped build bombs in workshops and also ferried them to the war front and set them up for use. He helped move people caught up at the war front, especially my aunt who was an active businesswoman, and other relatives as well. The very next day we travelled to Nsukka. I was sorry to leave, as many of my cousins were there.

My dad had already set up our home in the University of Nsukka Campus. We had a lovely childhood in which we were allowed to explore around and about, and play with other children who introduced us to the area. It was the summer holiday, and we had a lot of fun and adventures. One day, my friends and I found a bag in the boy's quarter, it contained a large chunk of soft white rock that tasted so sweet. For a while we would make excuses to go to the boy's quarters to seek out the sweet rock. My dad's nephew caught us and reported us to dad, and he had it cleared out, telling us that it was milk that had been used to keep Biafran children from starving and was now unsuitable for human consumption because it had gone hard. So many precious memories of smells, sounds and feelings which have remained with me to date.

Postscript

I decided to contribute to this project despite only being in Nigeria for about six months after the war broke out. I hope my contribution will show a contrast to stories told by those who stayed through the entire war. My two siblings, Roz, Michael, and I spent the rest of the war in England. Although we were safer, I had abiding memories of the war that stayed with me for quite a few years: the fear of shooting, sounds of bombing and sirens in particular. I really hope my children read the entire book.

About the Author

Meg Amechi is the mother of four adult children and lives in England. Only one of her children has ever been to Nigeria. Her children all live in Colchester. Meg is also a grandmother and enjoys spending time with her family.

CHILD OF WAR

*By John Mozie **(2020 Collection)***

I should be in school
Or at least safe at home
Home used to be the place
Where joy and laughter rang out
We never quite had a lot
But I was too young to measure my lot

Guns boom as if against my soul
Then again, it could be bombs
Loud noises and occasional screams
The dying and living seem to merge as one
My parents tell me we're at war again

Home is where the currents turn
Chased to shelter in lands anew
Friends and strangers on common grounds
Far away from homes we once knew
Then come the strangers from afar
Bringing with them full bags of chow

I am a child of war, I now know
Caught up in a cause that I do not share

Holes and craters mark my path
My future measured in cups of chow

What life holds for me I do not know
Fancy clothes and healthy foods
Are the stuff of other people's dreams
My life is measured on a day by day
As I look to a tomorrow I cannot see

As I chase for chow with arms stretched out
Nudged along by my mum so weary
Head as big and tummy heavy
What I feel I cannot say
Nor do I care that the flies stay with me
All my tomorrows are honed into now
A warm meal to stave off the hunger

EPILOGUE

By Amaka Efobi-Oguejiofo

The Aftermath

Bia nulu onu anyi o, Nna bia nulu onu anyi o... I used to hear the plaintive refrains of this song as a child growing up just post war. I didn't understand the associations it had with the Biafran war though, until much later.

I was born into upheavals; arriving on the 7th day of November in 1965, just as the bitter Nigerian crisis that led to the civil war was brewing. The crisis chased my parents from Ibadan where I was born, back to the rainforests of Oraifite from where they both hailed. When war finally erupted in 1967, I was less than two years old. Our departure from Ibadan was both sudden and dramatic. We left the same day that the then Nigerian military Head of State, Major-General J. T. U. Aguiyi-Ironsi was executed at Ibadan in a counter coup launched by Nigerian soldiers of northern extraction. This was mid-1966. As soon as the news of the Head of State's assassination trickled in, my parents left Ibadan same day, headed due East.

For me, the greatest trauma of war has nothing to do with any direct memories I have of that terrible time in Nigerian history. It has little to do with any sights and sounds of war because, actually, everything I know about the Nigerian-Biafran War, I heard from older family members. So, for me, the greatest trauma of the war remains the mystery of how inexplicably, a child who was five years when the war finally ended in 1970 has no memories whatsoever of that period. Zero. Nothing. It is as if a giant hand reached out and erased a chalkboard containing my memories of the war years. Apparently, the trauma from what was one of the most terrible armed conflicts in modern history must have gone so deep that my mind shut down to protect itself.

My father, Chris Efobi, worked with UAC, Nigeria as a senior manager and would eventually become their head of operations in Eastern Nigeria during the civil war. He barely managed to sneak out from Lagos alive having returned there briefly after taking us to the village. He was on the list of Igbos who were earmarked to die in Lagos, post coup number two that killed Ironsi. Papa just managed to cross the Niger Bridge back into Biafran territory before it was shut down.

Our war years as a family involved keeping one step ahead of the invading Nigerian Armed Forces. We went from Ibadan to Onitsha, then to Port Harcourt, until my mother elected to remain in Oraifite while my father moved from place to place to fulfill his obligations to the Biafran government. He was superintending at the Uli and Uga airports for the Biafran government at a point, in addition to working to secure UAC assets that they left in his charge. Somehow, he wore both caps simultaneously and survived it. So for much of the war, my parents and consequently my family was separated. Half the time, this half did not know what was happening to that half. Were they alive or dead? They had to wait and find out. The biggest problem was not even the air raids which were terrible in themselves, but the systematic starvation that took the lives of thousands.

The songs of that era take me back to those days lost to clouded and, like I said, virtually nonexistent memories. Sometimes, I have what seem like flashbacks, but when I look at them closely, I realize they are powerful mental images I have composed from my parents and older siblings' tales of the war years. I still hear the tune of *Akpu nkolo deme, osisi kwelu nmadu lie nni* - "thank you Cassava, the crop that gave us food." And my family tells me it's yet another relic from the war years. The lyrics speak to the deprivations and sheer starvation that came with the Biafran conflict. I remember that directly after the civil war, we would pick Cassava leaves (apparently for food), but then soon afterwards, no one did that anymore as things got better. I heard tales about eating water snakes called *ukolo* while we sheltered in Oraifite, and as it happened, people also ate the red-necked male Agama lizards which they gave a nickname, Military Police. Beleaguered Biafrans in my village even roasted the sacred python of Ifite-Oraifite for food as hunger bit harder daily.

Just after the war, I can see in my mind's eye, burnt out vehicles dotting the landscape here and there. They were leftovers of war. Some car carcasses remained there until much later in the 70s. We moved to Enugu from Lagos soon after the end of hostilities. I was six years by this time, and it was 1971. I remember seeing amputees on Okpara Avenue in Enugu, begging passersby for alms. I discovered they were Biafran soldiers and civilians who had lost limbs during the war years. There were some others who wore dirty bandages ostensibly to cover head wounds received during the war. Even as a child, I wondered how the blood on their bandages stayed red. Those ones must have been scammers capitalizing on the fallout of war. Then there were the half-crazy victims of war who were said to be suffering from "Artillery." I now know they had PTSD, but who knew about such things in those early days after the civil war?

We moved into the living area above my father's pharmacy at No. 1 Okpara Avenue, Enugu, a massive colonial warehouse belonging to the UAC, barely a year after the end of the civil war. UAC had leased the building to my father. At the time we came to occupy this structure, it was already one hundred years old.

It was a decaying timber-built house with an extensive compound fenced by chicken wire and dotted with large trees. I remember huge rats racing around the compound even in the daytime. It would be over forty years before I understood why those rats were so massive and so rampant. (They could have gone toe to toe with the average cat). Researching the war years in 2020, someone informed me that after Enugu fell to the Nigerian forces, it became a ghost town with towering grass covering most of the city. Returnees when the war ended had to hack through these stands of elephant grass. In the desolation that the capital city became, rats bred, feeding on abandoned corpses. By the time life returned to Enugu in 1970 - 71, the rats had lost all inhibitions. Their natural fear of man was gone. We would wake up most mornings with bloody maps drawn on our feet in the night by the giant rodents. For me, with that bit of information, a puzzle piece finally fell into place.

By 1972, my mother was pregnant with our last born, and one day, a beggar, a survivor of the war, who usually wandered around Okpara Avenue became the strange final chapter in our family's experience of the Nigerian-Biafran Civil War. This man's features as my mother described him, had been destroyed by fire. The sight of him sent most pedestrians the other way, but my mother always gave him alms. One day, she gave him a bigger amount than usual, and that was the last day she ever saw him. But first, he prayed for her, and told her she would deliver her child safely. When the infant came, he had three healing bullet wounds in his left shoulder and what looked like burn marks in almost the same pattern as the beggar from the Biafran War. If you said "salute!" He would snap off a sharp one at the age of just about two. He had never seen a soldier before. People whispered, "He is a returnee Biafran soldier." Of course he was nothing of the sort, but such are the deep etchings of war - an enduring mystery.

About the Author

Amaka Oguejiofo née Efobi is an award winning writer, publisher and poet who lives in Abuja, the Federal Capital Territory of Nigeria.

Lightning Source UK Ltd.
Milton Keynes UK
UKHW012205110621
385361UK00003B/70/J